# Wedding Song

Marjorie Agosín, *Uncertain Travelers: Conversations with Jewish Women Immigrants to America*, 1999

Rahel R. Wasserfall, *Women and Water: Menstruation in Jewish Life and Law*, 1999

Susan Starr Sered, *What Makes Women Sick: Militarism, Maternity, and Modesty in Israeli Society*, 2000

Pamela S. Nadell and Jonathan D. Sarna, editors, *Women and American Judaism: Historical Perspectives*, 2001

Ludmila Shtern, *Leaving Leningrad: The True Adventures of a Soviet Émigré*, 2001

Jael Silliman, *Jewish Portraits, Indian Frames: Women's Narratives from a Diaspora of Hope*, 2001

Judith R. Baskin, *Midrashic Women*, 2002
ChaeRan Y. Freeze, *Jewish Marriage and Divorce in Imperial Russia*, 2002

Mark A. Raider and Miriam B. Raider-Roth, *The Plough Woman: Records of the Pioneer Women of Palestine*, 2002

Elizabeth Wyner Mark, editor, *The Covenant of Circumcision: New Perspectives on an Ancient Jewish Rite*, 2003

Kalpana Misra and Melanie S. Rich, *Jewish Feminism in Israel: Some Contemporary Perspectives*, 2003

Farideh Goldin, *Wedding Song: Memoirs of an Iranian Jewish Woman*, 2003

Rochelle L. Millen, *Women, Birth, and Death in Jewish Law and Practice*, 2003

# Wedding Song

MEMOIRS OF AN IRANIAN

JEWISH WOMAN

Farideh Goldin

*Brandeis University Press*

*Published by University Press of New England*

*Hanover and London*

Brandeis University Press
Published by University Press of New England, 37 Lafayette Street, Lebanon, NH 03766
© 2003 by Farideh Dayanim Goldin
All rights reserved
Printed in the United States of America
5   4   3   2   1

Library of Congress Cataloging-in-Publication Data
Goldin, Farideh, 1953–
Wedding song : memoirs of an Iranian Jewish woman / Farideh Goldin.
p.   cm. — (Brandeis series on Jewish women)
ISBN 1–58465–344–2 (cloth)
1. Goldin, Farideh, 1953—Childhood and youth. 2. Jews—Iran—Shiraz—Biography.
3. Shiraz (Iran)—Biography. I. Title. II. Series.
DS135.I653G654 2003
955'.72—dc21     2003008352

Cover photo © 2002 Steve McCurry, from Portraits. Used by permission of the photographer and Magnum Photos Inc. McCurry has covered many areas of international and civil conflict, including the Iran-Iraq war, Beruit, Cambodia, the Philippines, the Gulf War, and the disintegration of the former Yugoslavia and Afghanistan. His focus is on the human consequences of war. McCurry's work frequently appears in National Geographic Magazine with recent articles on Yemen and the temples of Angkor Wat, Cambodia. He writes, "Most of my images are grounded in people, and I try to convey what it is like to be that person, a person caught in a broader landscape, that I guess you'll call the human condition." A poster of Mr. McCurry's now iconic "Afghan Girl" is available on his website: www.stevemccurry.com. A portion of the proceeds from the sale of that poster will go towards helping the children of Afganistan.

# CONTENTS

CONTENTS

*This book is dedicated to my family:*

*My husband Norman always believed in me and gave me "a room of my own."*

*My daughters Lena, Yael, and Rachel were the first to pull the stories out of the family well, rich with tradition, life-giving, yet dark and hidden. Along with my siblings and their spouses, they were my first readers. They laughed and cried with me across all these years as I tried to transform my spoken stories into written words.*

*My mother Rouhi, whose* rouh, *her soul, will forever be intertwined with mine. Maman, how could I ever try to forget you?*

*My father Esghel, who gave to our extended family and the Jewish community until there wasn't anything left to give. Baba,* mehila, *please forgive me. I love you.*

*The gate to the city of Shiraz.*

# IRANIAN MEMOIRS

If I had to pick one defining moment in my Iranian life, it would be 5:00 A.M. one Friday in the fall of 1968. I was fifteen. Normally I woke to the sounds of a peddler selling green almonds and fava beans from the sacks hanging on each side of his donkey, the radio screeching the latest news, our only toilet in the hallway flushing, the hustle and bustle of my mother scurrying around to prepare breakfast, to get ready for Shabbat, my grandmother asking me to get to the bakery. But that morning, a scorching odor jolted me out of a deep sleep. At first I thought someone was incinerating the trash outside; I thought my mother had burned the omelet; no, the house must be on fire. Smoke filled my room. I threw off the covers and rushed through the hazy hallway to the kitchen. The entire family was there—my mother, my grandmother, my married uncle, his wife and children, my single uncle, my single aunt, my sister and two brothers—trying to get their breakfast, coughing, their eyes irritated.

My father stood near the mud stove, still in his pajama bottoms and a V-neck undershirt. He was chewing his mustache, so I knew he was angry, but at what? Then I saw it. He was throwing books in the fire, my books, the books I had hidden underneath the bed, behind my clothes in the armoire, in the pocket of my winter coat.

It wasn't as if he hadn't warned me about reading. He had heard from cousins at my school; he had caught me reading with a flashlight in bed; he had seen me walk to school with my head in a book. He had warned me just the previous week after an aunt erupted, "Everyone in the community knows that your daughter reads nonstop, corrupting herself, giving us all a bad name."

Instead of obeying, I became more cunning at finding places to hide my books. I couldn't give them up; they were my escape, the keepers of my sanity. I was reading mostly French and Russian classics in translation. I didn't quite understand them because the stories were so absolutely alien to my reality. Nevertheless, they fascinated me, introduced me to unknown cultures and captivating characters. Now curling at the edges, crumbling, the black of the words disappeared into the red of the flames and the gray of the ashes—exorcised worlds flew in tiny particles from the pyre and swirled in the air. Breathing them, I wondered where I could take my mind now that their magic had fled through the chimney. Perhaps it was time to take my physical self away to the places the books had painted for me.

Although the idea of burning books may jolt many Western readers, I don't want my father to be judged harshly. He wasn't trying to destroy me, but just the opposite. He thought he was saving me by indoctrinating me with the community standards. He didn't know of another person who was addicted to books; neither did I. He told me that I was of marriagable age, that I needed to stay at home to learn to cook and clean since I couldn't resist the corruption of the outside world.

His words weren't new. Most of my male teachers had reiterated the same sentiments in the classroom, telling the few of us who dared to choose mathematics as our major to prepare for marriage instead of wasting educational resources that rightfully belonged to men—men who as the heads of households would have to support their families. Hearing the same philosophy from my father, however, was much more frightening.

I don't think my father meant those words; I think he wanted to keep me in line by instilling fear of a different fate. Traditionally, a desirable candidate for marriage was a naïve girl with "closed eyes and ears," not one who knew of the world. He didn't want me to ruin my chances for finding the best possible husband. And in the end, my father was the force behind my higher education, insisting that I had to have a college degree to find a better husband, emphasizing that I had to be bilingual since English was the language of progress, the promise of a better future.

Later in the week, when no one was around, I uncovered my last hiding spot in the floor of an armoire, pulled out my journal, and burned the pages in the same stove. Now I was truly alone.

Since Iranian schools didn't promote reading, I didn't have so much as a storybook to read for three years. Then, in 1971, as a first-year student, I stepped inside the Pahlavi University library and scanned with amazement the large collection of books in translation. I promised myself I would finish reading all of them before graduating. Read, I did, but I didn't write again until I had immigrated to the United States, married an American, and had children of my own, children who wanted to hear about my Iranian life. And I, who once had tried so hard to forget my past, went searching for our life stories to record them for my daughters, for the next generation who feared visiting the country of my birth. By then, the 1979 Islamic Revolution had forced a mass exodus of Iranian Jews, leaving nothing but the rubble of Jewish life in Iran. I could extract only fragments of recollection, both what I could recall and memories told to me by family and friends in exile, numb, lost, almost as if still wandering through the desert in a weary exodus from Egypt.

For the last seven years, I have scavenged among the "whys and whens" of our lives only to concede that I cannot fully reconstruct our past. Some of my stories are repeated with the obsession of one who cannot let go of an event, a contemplation. Others are just forgotten, disposed of, or too hurtful to retell, leaving holes in the continuum of our life narratives. These memoirs weave my recollections together with those of my parents and their families, often incomplete and sometimes contradictory.

The tales I have gathered are like the picture frame my father gave me before I left Iran. The frame is made of the intricate designs of Shiraz *khatam*, decorated with delicate inlaid pieces of wood and ivory arranged painstakingly to create geometric patterns as if each one were a secret map. I wrapped his present well and hid it securely under my garments on the long flight from Iran. I didn't open the package for years. My father's gift didn't fit the décor of any of the apartments I lived in; it was too gaudy, too elaborate, too foreign, too difficult to open and repack as I moved from city to city. When I finally unwrapped it many years later, bits and pieces of ivory and wood were missing, ruining the congruity of its design if looked at closely. I put my wedding picture in it and hung it on our bedroom wall. I can't see the imperfections any longer. When looked at from afar, the designs still make sense; there is a harmonious pattern to their delicate, crushed layout.

This book chronicles my childhood, my family's lives, and the lives of women who went unnoticed in the southern Iranian city of Shiraz. I yearn to acquaint my Western readers with the essence of Jewish life in the shadow of Islam, the magnetism of Western freedoms, culture, and technology against the lulling effect of Persian thoughts, customs, and ethics.

This is my story.

*Chapter One*

# BLOOD LINES

When I told my mother of my first period, she folded her fingers into a fist and hit herself on the chest, *"Vay behalet!"* She used the Farsi words as if I had angered her. "You'll suffer," she said.

The sun painted the walls of the bedroom I shared with her, etching shadows of the cast iron grillwork on the windows. Two cats fought outside. The water in the shallow, keyhole-shaped pool was green with pollen. I leaned against the wall by the closet, my hair still wild from storybook dreams against a soft pillow, my panties wet, my thighs sticky. My mother stood in front of me but wouldn't look into my eyes. She looked at my left shoulder or maybe the wall.

"Misery will be your share in life, for you have become a woman with all its inheritance of pain," she said. "This is the beginning of your sufferings. Be prepared!"

My mother's eyes were the shade of young dates on a palm tree, hazel with striations of gold. Her curls were unruly, her palms the surface of the desert.

I bit the inner flesh of my lips. There was blood in my mouth. I wondered about this mysterious prophecy of catastrophe. Could I find an antidote to the poison my mother believed would ruin me? A sparrow skidded on the murky water in the pond. Did it think the surface was solid? It flapped its wings in a panic and landed on a water fountain in the middle.

A bundle of rags lay on the closet floor like a sleeping cat. My mother crouched, grabbed an old sheet, put it between her teeth, and tore it with her claws. "There!" With her shoulders stooped, she turned her back and closed the door behind her.

When I entered the passage to womanhood in spring of 1966, I was thirteen years old. In our Jewish home in Shiraz, the monthly occurrence was both intensely private and offensively public. Men never mentioned it. Women spoke about it in hushed voices while shelling fava beans, when rolling mung beans on a round brass platter to separate them from pebbles.

Someone's daughter had started her first period; she was ripe to get married. Disregarding the Jewish laws of family purity, a neighbor's lustful husband wouldn't leave her alone, so she took her rag to the community leader to prove that she was still bleeding, to seek his protection. Speaking of blood, the women covered their mouths with the palms of their hands as if trying to shove the words back, as if the language itself could pollute the air.

During my childhood, I often answered the dreadful call from various women in the family, "Farideh, come. Come to the bathroom and pour water over my hands." Pouring water was the euphemism for helping them wash their rags and bloody underwear. With an *aftabeh*, a copper water jug used for washing our bottoms, I bent over my mother. She wrapped her skirt tightly around herself and squatted by the hole in the ground that was our toilet. In a slow constant flow, I poured water over her hands as she rubbed the leftover soap into the unclean clothes. She didn't use the sink or the wash tub or else they would be contaminated with her *gha'edeh,* her monthly "mandate." She wrapped the clean *tamei* clothes in newspapers, took them outside, and hung them on shrubs in the backyard. When she came back, I helped her wash her hands again over the toilet before she dared to wash them once more in the sink.

Passover was the most difficult time for menstruating women. My mother always mumbled curses underneath her breath, made faces drinking the bitter spinach juice to delay her period. Otherwise, she could not hold the Seder plate as adults did, reciting "*Ha-lakhma* . . . This is the bread of affliction . . . Now we are slaves; next year may we be free." Otherwise, she could not dip her bitter herb in the same bowl of salt water, the tears of our ancestors, like everyone else.

"Damned be the day I was born a woman!" My mother hit her chest whenever she had her period during Passover. "There is nothing for a woman but sorrow and pain!"

As the customs dictated, when menstruating my mother had to drag the *tamei* mattress, pillow, and quilt out of the special closet and spread them in a corner of the bedroom, away from the traffic. I wondered whether she minded that part of the custom. Her impure corner gave her a little space of her own that no one approached for fear of becoming unclean. My grandmother didn't ask her to rise from her warm bed to make her tea. My father didn't tell her to prepare his breakfast at five in the morning before he went to work.

Left alone, sometimes she wrote a letter to her parents. Sometimes she read. Sometimes she sang a song to herself.

My father took the bed at these times. My siblings and I huddled under the blankets in another corner of the bedroom floor. There was a taboo space around our mother where no one dared to intrude. Somehow even the air touching her body contracted the same invisible filth. She ate from plates that had to be washed separately and stored in a hidden space, where no one could touch them by mistake.

I knew all the rules of the monthly curse, the separation, the untouchability, the fatigue, and the blood. They should all have been frightening. Yet when my turn came, something was different. That early morning, when I withdrew my hands from the wetness between my legs, I was not terrified of the blood. I was euphoric. I felt grown up. Now my grandmother wouldn't allow me to bend over with the low broom sweeping the carpets. I counted on her repeating to *me* what she used to tell my single aunt Fereshteh, "Go lie down. Your back must be hurting from the flow. Go rest."

Now someone had to bend over the toilet pouring water over *my* hands to wash *my* soiled underwear. Now I would not be sent out of the room when women gathered to gossip. I was going to be a part of the sisterhood of women. Even with all my mother's warnings, I could not help the ebullience that surged in me.

I knew the secret was out when I went into the kitchen that morning. The men, my father and two uncles, were at work. The women sat on low wooden stools, their skirts tightly wrapped around their legs. My mother mixed grated cooked potatoes, ground beef, and eggs. She took small portions out of the mixture, flattened them between the palms of her hands, and put them in the frying pan on top of a kerosene stove with sesame oil and turmeric to make *shamee*. I loved to hang around for the broken pieces. My mouth watered. Geeta, Uncle Morad's wife, and the bane of my mother's life, chopped tomatoes, cucumbers, parsley, and onions to make a Shirazi salad. That was my job. She had a meaningful smile on her face. She knew.

Picking through the vegetables for a stew, my grandmother looked like a flower amidst a garden of herbs. "Don't touch, don't touch," she said.

I hadn't tried to handle anything. Her calico kerchief slipped off her hair at the sudden gesture, revealing two henna-covered braids. She didn't have her teeth in her mouth. Her words slurred and came at me in slow-moving waves.

It was Friday, my only day off from school, the busiest day in the kitchen before the start of Shabbat. Any other week, my help would have been welcomed, orders given rapidly to wash and clean, to chop and mix. Now I was a nuisance.

Knowing of this reaction, I wondered if my mother had betrayed me by not warning me to hide the secret of my blood; if she had abandoned me by exposing my secret herself. How I had convinced myself that I would be different! I couldn't look at her.

Khanom-bozorg, my grandmother, tried to find a job away from the food area for me. "You can sweep the backyard."

I grabbed a low broom, but lingered by the door. The pots clanked, the water gurgled down the sink, the oil sizzled, the charcoal popped in the mud stove, and sparks flew around a large pot of water. My mother poured the rice in, counting aloud five cups. In comparison, the backyard felt like such a lonely place. Khanom-bozorg must have noticed the sadness and hurt on my face. "Go stand in front of an orange tree and tell it, 'Your greenness shall be mine, my yellowness yours,'" she said. "That should bring you luck, a good husband."

Geeta covered her mouth with her parsley-stained hand and snickered. She spurned me as an extension of her dislike for her sister-in-law. I wished I could free myself from the blood that linked me to my mother, for she was the carrier of my oppression.

In our large garden, I looked at the long rows of orange, tangerine, sweet lemon, pomelo, and sour orange trees lined up against the two walls. Sweet lemons were precious for their medicinal magic. They had to be wrapped each winter to save their delicate limbs from frostbite. Pomelos were reserved for special guests only since they were so rare, large and beautiful. Sour oranges were used for flavoring the food. Their fruits were too tart to eat but every Iranian dish tasted better, more complete with them.

I recalled watching my father cut a sour-orange tree halfway down the trunk, gently make an incision to place a cutting from a tangerine tree. All our trees originated from their species that were hardy and immune to drought and disease. A delicate wind swirled around the tree-lined courtyard, mixing the fragrances of orange blossoms and roses. I chose the tallest sour orange tree, stood in front of it, and wished to be as strong as it was, to stand erect as it did, not bending to the whim of others. I wished to be like its fruit, adding flavor to life, yet tasting so pungent that no one would dare to bite into me.

I went back to the house to face the other women. I took the kettle and made myself tea with the orange blossoms I had snipped from my tree. As I reached for a regular cup, the women stopped their work and stared at me. My grandmother rose half way, but sat down again. She looked at my mother and shook her head. "Rouhi, you didn't show your child where the *tamei* dishes are!"

I had failed my first lesson in womanhood.

My mother grabbed my arm. "Why are you making trouble for me?" she asked. "Don't I already have enough to put up with?"

I didn't care. Since they had made me an outsider, I detached myself from their rules. After the initial hurt, I was content, determined to be different, to look inside myself rather than to their world for answers. I would use another dish the next time and another the time after that. I would wash my underwear in the bathroom sink with good soap and sleep on my own mattress. Let them all be *tamei,* impure, every day and forever.

That night I unrolled my own mattress on the carpet in my usual spot. I fell asleep in the cool breeze from the open window. My parents' whispering woke me up. In the pitch-darkness, phosphate dots shone on a round alarm clock by their bed. "Your daughter's misery has started," my mother said. "Pity on her who will soon know the cruelty of life."

I listened for my father's response, but it never came. I buried my face in the pillow and cried silently. It was all too much—the humiliation of something so private being discussed with my father, the loneliness of being separated from the women whose company I desired. My younger sister, Nahid, rolled to her side and faced me. Her big eyes looked darker than the night. She moved closer to cuddle. I caressed her sweaty hair. We were on a long voyage against the strong tides of superstition and female inferiority, lonely, without our mother.

### Maman: My Mother

My mother was born two years old. My grandparents' first child was a daughter, named Rouhi. When she died a toddler, they kept her birth certificate and gave it to their next child. Therefore, when my father and his brother-in-law, Masood, knocked at their door thirteen years later to ask for Rouhi's hand in marriage, she was legally of marriageable age.

If my mother didn't have her deceased sister's birth certificate, I am sure my maternal grandmother would have found a way to circumvent the law. Girls were married young. Most officials helped families get around the law that forbade child-marriages. My great uncle, Agha-jaan, crossed his hands over his chest and laughed when he recollected his own story of changing his bride's birth certificate. He approached an official to whom he sold fabric at discounted prices. This man told my great uncle to dress his twelve-year-old fiancée in a mature outfit: long skirt, jacket, hat, and high heels. They appeared at the official's door with the young girl made up, kohl around her eyes, and red lipstick smeared on her mouth, slipping and losing control while walking in the unfamiliar spiked shoes two sizes larger than her feet. She refused to hold hands with Agha-jaan, but when asked if she was willing to marry this man, she said yes obediently. She was then pronounced to be legally fifteen and her birth certificate was changed.

Although my great uncle's bride was a child, she had her family close by to check on her. Her parents' home was a refuge even if for short periods of time. My mother was alone. She was given away as a young bride to a man from a far-away city. My parents' official date and place of marriage is 17 October 1951 in Shiraz, but that was a formality they went through when in my father's hometown. The religious ceremony was performed earlier in Hamedan. She was thirteen, he twenty-three.

All my life, I have struggled to understand and accept this implausible union. Many times I have imagined standing outside my parents' bedroom

*Maman in Shiraz after her wedding. My mother wears jewelry given to her as a wedding gift. My father made the gold pin in the shape of two roses, studded with fresh water pearls.*

on the night of their wedding in Hamedan, never daring to turn the knob. I couldn't. I didn't want to see beyond the doors where a young man lay with a child-woman for the first time. I never asked my father or mother about their first night together. My mother would have shared the events, but I didn't want to know.

I do, however, know what my great uncle Agha-jaan once said of his child-bride. She wouldn't let him touch her. Although she had obediently agreed to the marriage, she screamed and wept on their wedding night, wanting to go home, to sleep in her own bed. Even when an older sister went in to sleep between them, the bride was restless and crying. My great uncle remembered his own outrage. He was young; his body burned. This was, after all, his right. She was his wife!

He beat her up. She still resisted him. He forced himself on her. "She eventually came to understand my needs. She became a good wife," he said.

My mother had her first period away from her mother, far away from home at my father's house. She had been married to him for almost a year. Maman approached her mother-in-law with the news, her head bowed low in embarrassment. Khanom-bozorg told her not to touch the food, or wash the dishes, or sleep in the same bed with my father. She showed my mother the closet where the *tamei* mattress was stored, stinking of old blood and sweat. Maman wrapped herself in her winter coat and slept on the floor. I wonder what my grandmother's reaction was to her daughter-in-law's news. For a few days each month, she would miss a pair of hands to help with the women's daily work. It also meant that my mother could get pregnant and produce grandchildren, preferably sons. Instead, a year later, I was her firstborn, a girl.

### Baba: My Father

Like my mother, my father is also the oldest child from a second marriage. My paternal grandfather's first wife had the familiar fate of so many women of the era who died in childbirth. He had to find a wife quickly to take care of the newborn and two older children. He chose Tavous, who was fifteen years old at the time and a divorcée. She was young with strong legs and arms for hard work and wide hips perfect for giving birth to eight children.

Then, when my father was eighteen, his father died of a simple infection and left him with the responsibility of his mother and seven siblings. As the great rabbi and the communal judge for the Jews of Shiraz, my grandfather had earned the unquestioned respect of both Jews and Moslems. He forgave his fees for weddings and circumcisions if the families were poor. Slaughtering the cows as the community *shokhet,* he let go of his earnings if the animal proved to be unkosher due to lesions in its lungs, recognizing the loss of the poor butcher who unknowingly had bought the unusable animal. My paternal grandfather felt honored that, like his father and grandfathers before him, he had been chosen to serve and guide

*Baba at the time of his marriage.*

the Jewish community. Therefore, after an emotional day during which the community closed down to take turns carrying his coffin from the ghetto to the cemetery, after the boys from the Jewish school walked in front of his coffin with lit candles singing *Tehilim,* after the seven days of *shiva,* when everyone brought food and comforted the young widow and her children, all that was left to my grandfather's family was the respect, love, and the devotion of those who had known him.

Members of the Jewish community kept reminding my father that he was a grown man with great responsibilities, that he had to sacrifice his needs to safeguard his mother and seven siblings. Once, as he ate an ice cream sandwich by a kiosk, a distant relative spotted Baba and hit him on the head, saying that my father was stealing food from his own sisters and brothers. Leaving a movie theatre, he was admonished by a community elder for his selfishness. Baba learned to let go of his individualism and to see himself as the core of the family unit, whose sole job was to keep them together, and to help them succeed where he could not himself. Later my father expected his own children and wife to live by the same principles of selflessness. We had to exemplify community standards and meet the expectations of the extended family.

My father's problems were exacerbated when his mother Tavous started showing signs of emotional breakdown after her husband's death. Periodically she struggled to catch her breath, fainted, and had to stay in bed for days. There was no one to run the household. The attacks, many of which I witnessed myself, continued throughout my grandmother's life. I think a modern term for them would be anxiety or panic attacks. She was left a pauper in her mid-thirties with a huge debt accumulated by my grandfather's lengthy illness. With eight hungry children, the youngest only a toddler, Tavous had every reason to be panic-stricken.

Baba approached a few friends and relatives for financial help, but they rejected him. Instead, they suggested that he should apprentice the young boys to shopkeepers and peddlers. Baba refused. Two of his sisters were married very young, partly to alleviate the back-breaking expenses. My father himself had given up his dream of becoming a physician. He decided the younger brothers would fulfill his dreams for him, and no sacrifice to accomplish this would be too great.

My father told me of his struggles to find a job to pay off the debts and feed the younger children. His eyes teared when he remembered betrayals by family members and kindness from strangers. A Moslem man trusted my father with a bag of gold, his first real assignment as a goldsmith. Knowing that this job would determine his reputation as an artisan and an honest man, Baba slept in his workshop to protect the gold. His diligence paid off, and five years after my grandfather's death, my father had an established business making gold jewelry. He told his brother Morad that he must join him in providing for the family. The two worked at a small shop two blocks from the *mahaleh,* the Jewish ghetto, where they lived in my grandfather's house with all but two sisters who married around puberty.

Finally there was food on the table, but my grandmother suffered with the burden of housework. When her "asthma" attacks increased, her married daughters had to leave their own families and rush to the house to nurse her, causing tension with their husbands' families. My father knew it was time for him to get married, to start a family, and at the same time, to relieve his mother of the grueling daily work of cooking and cleaning.

Baba did try to find a wife with a good social standing in Shiraz. Although the community admired my father's devotion to his family, they wouldn't give him one of their daughters in matrimony, dreading the life of poverty and servitude that my father's bride would endure. My aunts and uncles understood the importance of this decision as well and worried for their own welfare. Soon Baba realized that he must find a wife whose family could not question his larger commitments.

Less than a decade after the devastation of World War II, Iran was an impoverished country in shambles. Being financial burdens, Jewish girls were married off to any men within the religion who could feed them. A bride for my father, the family elders suggested, should come from outside the Shirazi community to ensure unobtrusive in-laws. Someone in Shiraz knew someone in Tehran who knew of a family in the Jewish ghetto willing to send their daughter away. My father's brother-in-law, his sister's husband Masood, volunteered to take him to Tehran. The one-day trip by bus took them through narrow passes wrapped around mountains, a most adventurous endeavor for both of them.

In Tehran, they found the house and introduced themselves as *khaste-gars*, seekers of a bride. The family welcomed them, and asked them to take their shoes off and rest against the pillows on the floor. Someone brought them tea, flower-essence drinks, and chickpea cookies. Soon family and friends gathered in the house, filling it with their sounds of joy, ululating, clapping, and singing wedding songs. My father heard someone being sent to get the rabbi to perform the wedding, and he realized that he was going to be married to a woman he hadn't met.

Masood told me years later, "We had two feet, borrowed another two, put our tails on our backs and ran out of the house with our shoes underneath our arms."

When recounting the incident, my father couldn't stop laughing. "I don't know what kind of a girl they were going to glue on me," he said. "I didn't know if she was blind, bald, disabled, or old, but I wasn't going to wait around to find out."

The residents of the *mahaleh* must have been bewildered by the sight of two strangers running in the narrow alleyways with their shoes under their armpits and little travel bundles over their shoulders. But that day, being young, inexperienced, and having never left their city before, my father and Masood panicked. They worried that as revenge someone would report them to the authorities, falsely claiming that they had stolen from the Tehrani family's house.

Fearing the family's wrath, they decided to leave Tehran. Masood suggested a pilgrimage to the tombs of the Jewish heroes Esther and Mordekhai in the mountainous city of Hamedan. He also suggested that they find the Jewish school and wait outside to see if any of the girls looked suitable. When the school let out, the two men followed one of the girls home. In Masood's version of the story, he pointed to a bouncy girl. "That's a girl for you," he told my father.

In my father's version, they followed the girl home, and when they were sitting in her house having chai and rice cookies, my father spotted a girl playing with the prospective bride. She had fair skin and wild black curls. "That one," he whispered to Masood. "That girl is the one I want."

The day after, they went to this girl's house with flowers and a box of Gaz, Isfahan's famous sweet confectionery. My maternal grandmother Touran wouldn't let them in, fearing they could be thieves, staking the house to steal her belongings. They finally convinced her to take the gifts and to check with a certain person who had given his daughter to a Shirazi and knew my father's family.

When they came back the day after, not only had Touran checked their credentials, she had also visited her uncle, Dr. Sayed, asking for his advice.

"Give her to them," he had said.

### Maman's Story

When I was thirteen, the same age as my mother at the time of her marriage, Maman sat down next to me. Her fingers traced circles around the peacocks and pomegranates on the Persian carpet as her eyes watched me. I was stretched out on my stomach, legs crossed and raised behind my back, one arm under my chin, doing my homework, reading the false history of Iranian kings and their conquests. I wished she would go away.

She picked up a book, turned it around, and leafed noisily through the pages. I wanted to tell her that I had an exam the following day, that I didn't have time to give her attention, that she needed to leave me alone. Instead, I stabbed the words on the paper in an attempt to lodge them in my brain, already too preoccupied to absorb the information. I reached to grab the book. "Maman!" I started to tell her to leave, but it was too late. She was reading a poem in a sing-song way. When she finished, she giggled, a child in front of the class expecting applause.

"I was a good student," she said.

"Okay." I rolled over, sat up, and collected my books to leave.

"I was good at everything but math." A muffled laugh escaped her cracked lips; her irises glimmered with green dots I had never noticed before.

I didn't respond. I wondered if I should go to a friend's house to study.

Then my mother told me her wedding story for the first time. "I'd just come back from school," she said, "sitting down just like you to do my homework."

My mother's voice was flat. Her eyes lost their green speckles, their light. She took my pen when she explained how her mother had taken hers and told her not to bother; they had to prepare for her wedding, pack her bag to leave for a new city.

I imagined my maternal grandmother rushing about the house. I remembered her unsmiling face, her rough hands, her hair parted in the middle and severely pulled back. I had seen her two or three times, once during her visit when my brother was born. She and her youngest son, my five-year-old uncle, shared the bedroom with us. My father moved to his mother's room for a few days. Grandmother Touran avoided the members of our large household and constantly snapped at me and my uncle. She kept away from my paternal grandmother, but when in her presence, called her Khanom-bozorg, great lady. Giving respect and honor to her daughter's mother-in-law, she hoped to soften her heart toward my mother. The children, even my cousins, adopted the title to address my paternal grandmother.

During her visit, my mother's mother used the space heater in the room to cook simple meals because she didn't want to eat with the rest; she didn't want to be in the way; she didn't want to impose. Intensely uncomfortable under somebody else's roof, she couldn't wait to get back home. She shunned intimacy; there were no hugs and kisses.

On the day of her departure, grandmother Touran shook her index finger at me. "You take care of your mother now."

I didn't know why my mother was teary. Touran had sent her only daughter away, telling her abruptly that she would go to a far-away city as the wife of a stranger. My reaction was hardly sympathetic. Maman should have felt lucky for marrying into my father's family, leaving her own house crowded with little brothers and an angry mother. Baba always told me that my mother had married above her class.

My mother reported her wedding story in a clear and unemotional voice like a documentary video. I wanted it to end so I could get back to my own life. I much preferred tackling the rote memorization of the chapters in my textbook. Nader Shah was a great king. He conquered India, smashed their idols, killed anyone who didn't convert to Islam, established Farsi as the main spoken language. He brought back to Iran diamonds, rubies, strong slaves, beautiful women.

I had never seen my mother's childhood home in the cramped ghettos of Hamedan, yet I could envision that house with no running water, a mud stove, and little bodies sitting on their knees by the walls, their mouths open wide crying in hunger or anticipation of food. I pictured my mother as she had described herself. A bucket filled with spring water clanged against her legs and wet her skirt as she headed home along dirt-covered alleyways. Moslem boys blocked her way and dropped horse dung in the water before she turned the corner to her house. Having cleaned other people's homes all day, her mother stared at the water in disbelief. It was getting dark and there was no water at home to cook for the little ones. Could that have been the point at which my grandmother decided her daughter was useless? Years later, I wondered if my grandmother feared that when she was out, my mother would get raped or kidnapped and converted to Islam. In any case, she was a liability. My maternal grandfather was detached as a husband and a father, so grandmother Touran decided to pass the responsibility of my mother to another man.

My mother approached her father for help. He shook his head but didn't interfere. She ran away to her aunt's house, who took her home and chastised Touran. "Don't do it! Don't do what our mother did to us."

"Too late!" Touran had given her word. The contract was sealed.

Maman lowered her head. Her shoulders drooped; she gazed across time, not space as she recollected the events. If I could go back in time, I would hold her tight, put her head on my shoulder, and caress her hair. But being a child myself, I traced the birds on the carpet with my index finger as I learned of my mother's childhood grief.

"I threw myself on the floor and begged my mother, 'Maman, Maman, please don't send me away, please, please.'"

It troubled me that she was using the same word for her mother that I called her. I couldn't think of her as someone's child. My feet were asleep. I stretched them in front of me and rubbed them. "Maman, *baseh*," I begged her. "Enough!" My legs tingled. I needed to get up and walk, but my mother kept on talking. She had to recreate the event for me. An army of crows covered the backyard, then rose and swirled away. I wished I could fly. Maman wouldn't stop. Her words held me down.

"I kissed her feet. I told her that I would be her maid. 'Please don't send me away. I'll stay home. I'll clean. I'll cook.'"

"*Baseh*," I said as if to myself. What did she want me to do? I put down my pen on the carpet and slumped. No point trying to study. The smell of a quince stew filled the house with its sweetness, and made me hungry. I wanted to remind her to go to the kitchen and check on it, but I stayed silent. She had to finish her story. So I listened.

"I will take care of my brothers," she had pleaded to her mother. "I am your only daughter. I will be your servant. Please don't let them take me."

My mother paused. She stared into empty space. Her words sat like stones on my chest. I couldn't move. I didn't know why she shared her story with me when there was nothing I could do for her. A small crack opened in her chapped lips, but she went on. "Maman peeled me off and turned her back."

Sweat covered my back. Suddenly, I understood her point. She could do the same to me. I closed the book.

My mother's story still burns in my mind. The wound has become more stubborn and painful since I married and became the mother of three daughters myself.

For many years, I was jealous of my friends whose mothers didn't burden them with the weight of the past, who went home from school to share their days with their mothers. What could I tell mine? That my geometry teacher was failing me because I didn't take private lessons with him? That my calligraphy teacher called me a trouble-making Jew? That I argued with a classmate? That I needed winter shoes? I even left out my happier tales of accomplishments and friendships from our brief conversations. Would my mother care to know that I was the best essay writer in my high school? My life was detached from hers. She took no joy in my happiness, and my problems paled in comparison with her trauma. There was nothing to say. I stayed silent in the hope that she would be too.

I learned to become self-sufficient, keeping away from her to save myself. I drowned myself in foreign books whose characters were strange and alien, whose problems were not mine. During the years I lived with her, my mother told her wedding story over and over. With each retelling, I distanced myself further, until I could scarcely bear to be in the same room with her alone. Finally, when I started to cover my ears and run out of the room, yelling, "I know, I know," she gave up retelling her story.

When I was in my twenties, I could still hear her mumbling it to herself as she sat alone on a low stool plucking chickens, or rubbing the soap into the dirty clothes. She became quiet when I was in my thirties. Instead, she would stare at me. I took her to the theater once when she was visiting me in the States. I chose a musical with beautiful costumes so she wouldn't need to understand the words. But I couldn't concentrate on the stage. Her gaze burned my cheeks.

"Stop it," I reprimanded her. "Don't stare at me. Look at the stage."

"What? I wasn't looking at you," she lied.

If my kids hadn't been with me, I would have yelled at her; I would have left the show.

Now I want her to tell me more of her story, but she refuses to talk. For years she feared that I would forget. Now she is afraid that her writer-daughter will record her pain and bring the wrath of the family upon her. And I am torn apart by her words and by her silence.

### Baba's Story

I have always loved my father's words. I could listen forever to his stories, always fascinating, adventurous.

At age seven, mesmerized by the sound of shopkeepers in the busy downtown, I lost my mother among hundreds of other women wrapped in their *chadors*, crowded among men hauling bundles of linen and carpets on their backs, young boys carrying trays of tea for their bosses, and tribal girls trailing their mothers, buying kitchenware for their dowries. Disoriented and timid, I didn't ask for directions, fearing that I would be tricked

*Baba at eighteen, still wearing a beard as a sign of mourning for his
father's death.*

and kidnapped if the strangers around me knew my mother had left me.
A Jewish girl deep in a religious Moslem neighborhood invited misdeeds,
my grandmother had always told me. I tried to reverse my steps. Remembering that we had walked toward the minaret of the mosque, I turned my
back to it. Finally, I reached my father's shop to learn that my mother had
stopped by earlier to report that I was missing. I didn't cry, but I wanted to.
I bit my lower lip and threw myself in a metal chair, too exhausted to
move. My father gave me a cup of tea with a yellow date and then held
my hand and walked me home. On the way, he told me about his trip to
Bab-e Anar, the village of pomegranates.

When he was thirteen years old, Sha'ul the peddler hired him to help with his accounting in the faraway village. My father had never left home before.

Listening to my father's rendition of his childhood story, the melodic intonation of words mixed with poetry and *zarbol-masal,* Persian proverbs, I forgot my own misadventure. I felt as if I were with him on the back of an open truck on the only paved road heading south into the mountains; I imagined the old tires kicking off dust. Together, we savored the memories of the clear blue sky, the mountains richly painted with mineral deposits, the Bedouin campgrounds beside a small spring, the large expanse of brush against the shadow of the mountains.

The bus reached the village at dusk and my father could barely see the outline of the pomegranate gardens. Sha'ul unloaded the merchandise by the side of the dirt road and asked my father to wait for him there and not move. He was going to make sure that the gates were open and that he could secure a few donkeys to help carry the goods inside. Surprised, my father asked, "Why don't we just drive to the gate, *agha* Sha'ul?"

The merchant was exhausted and impatient, his wrinkles deeper now that the sun had darkened his skin further, leaving white lines around his eyes, crinkled from the bright sun. His graying hair was matted with sand and fine dust. "First of all," the peddler snapped, "a truck is too big to go down this road. Most passengers are on their way to Jahrom and it is getting late in this *biaboon,* in this forsaken place. Plus, do you want me to get killed for a few pieces of merchandise if the gates are closed? What if we have to stay outside the walls with all the bandits knowing about the goods? Stay here behind this hill. No one will see you from the road or the village. I will be back soon." He started walking down the narrow dirt road that led to the village and slowly disappeared in the dark that gradually blanketed the landscape.

Baba waited by the road for an hour in the dark before he started to panic. Now he expected to be robbed and murdered by outlaws roaming through the desert. Totally alert, he stared into the dark, looking for a sign of life. Then his mind wandered, imagining ferocious beasts slowly closing on him, and he shivered. He heard wolves crying in the distance and his hair rose on his body; he felt something rubbing against his leg and screamed, thinking that he had been bitten by a deadly snake. Fortunately, it was just the fringes of a carpet touching his skin. After a few hours, he finally gave up on his boss; he must have been murdered by the peasants or the bandits. He shivered as the desert temperature fell rapidly.

Baba was tired and sleepy but afraid to close his eyes. After all, the same murderer could knife him in his sleep. He wrapped a large blanket around himself and paced around the pile in the dark to keep awake. He was suddenly falling. Baba screamed in terror and called for his mother in Judi, "Ahhhhhh! Mava, Mava . . ." He landed at the bottom of a ditch he had not seen in the dark and recited his *shema,* expecting death to take him. Scratched but unharmed, he decided that the fall could be a good omen. No one would look for him in the hole, and, if the robbers came by, they could steal the merchandise and disappear. He wrapped the blanket tighter around himself and surrendered to an uneasy sleep, in which wild beasts roamed the *biaboon;* black scorpions crawled on his blanket with their venomous tails on their backs; and bandits with black headpieces covering their faces galloped on fast horses toward him with shining eyes and drawn curved swords.

In the early hours of dawn, my father awoke sweaty with a jolt, screaming, thinking that an animal was pulling on him. But it was only his boss shaking him.

"Wake up, wake up, Esghel. We have to load the donkeys."

"I thought you had been killed," my father said, confused, but elated. "What happened? Why didn't you come back for me?"

The man had rushed to the gate of the village to convince the gatekeeper to allow him extra time. But the doors were already locked for the night and the gatekeeper, along with the peasants and their animals, had retreated within the enclosure. It was too dark for him to find his way back. So he had lain by the walls that surrounded the village and had gone to sleep. Baba and his boss threw the goods on the backs of the donkeys, striking their hinds with a stick as they advanced slowly to the open doors.

The following day was Friday and at sunset, Shabbat. As the sun disappeared behind the mountains on that first day in Bab-e Anar, my father along with the merchants prepared themselves to greet the Shabbat Queen. Other peddlers from the nearby villages joined them to make the gathering of ten men necessary for praying. They washed themselves in a stream and changed their dusty clothes. In the absence of women, they poured oil into two homemade clay vessels, put wicks through their narrow openings, lit them, and said the prayers that were women's obligation. Then they sat cross-legged around a *sofreh,* a cloth spread on the ground. One of the men uncovered a bottle of homemade raisin wine from a hiding place. Since alcoholic drinks were forbidden in Islam, the merchants had to be careful not to insult the local villagers. Two long flat breads were set on the table. They stood and softly said the *kiddush,* the prayer over wine in Hebrew, careful that their voices should not reach outside their hut. They washed their hands and said the prayers over bread. For the first time, my father ate a Shabbat meal away from the soothing sound of my grandfather's prayers and the aromatic dishes that were his mother's Sabbath specialty, and he used all his energy not to break down and cry.

After two months, Baba grew terribly homesick. Other travelers brought new merchandise and told him how his mother cried for him as well and called his name. Finally, he started running a fever and was too restless to help in the shop. The peddler gave him a few rials and sent him alone to find a bus on the side of the road. After hours of waiting, a ball of dust appeared in the horizon. A large Mercedes truck wobbled its way down the uneven rocky road to where my father was standing and stopped. Baba paid, climbed the side of the tall truck, and found a seat on the floor with other passengers, crates of watermelon, chickens, a small sheep, and strewn bundles of clothing.

At noon, the bus stopped by a caravansary, a weathered tent and a few stools in the middle of the desert. My father didn't have any food with him, but was too shy and too afraid to go inside to ask for a drink or a piece of bread. There was a barrel of water on the side of the teahouse, but Baba feared that it was for Moslems only.

Under the scorching sun, my father's mouth felt like the sand underneath his feet. He saw Bedouin women going down a steep slope and reappearing with jugs of water on their shoulders. The descent to the spring at the bottom of the hill was not as easy as he had thought. Although the nomads had climbed in and out of the hole with ease and grace, my father slipped and stumbled his way down. He was excited at the sight of the turquoise fluid oozing out of the floor of a cave by the side of the mountain, surrounded by greenery and reeds. Sweaty and dusty, he knelt in the muddy ground by the pool and cupped his hands to scoop the clear water to his mouth. It was deliciously sweet. He hurriedly reached with his open palms for more, but as he lifted his head this time to sip the water, he came eye to eye with a black snake, its white mouth wide open as though it were aiming for him.

My father forgot his thirst. He rushed back up the slippery slope, hanging onto the thorny bushes to pull himself up. Now he was even thirstier, exhausted, and bruised. His pants were torn at the knees. He sat in the shade of a bus, leaning against it for support, feeling defeated and homesick. When the truck reached Shiraz late on a Friday afternoon, my father was delirious from the long, dry journey.

A neighborhood boy saw him and ran ahead to the house, "Mola's wife, Rabbi's wife, Esgheli is here!"

My grandmother rushed to him at the door and grabbed him to break his fall. "Esgheli, what have they done to you?" she cried. My grandmother helped Baba through the orange groves in the backyard to the cool basement. She washed the dirt and the grime of the long journey from his face and hands and knees. She held his head up and helped him drink, brought him clean clothes and changed him like a child. She had made beef stew with zucchini and tomatoes and served it over fluffy rice.

Baba ate as if he had not seen food for months and always remembered the food as the most wonderful meal of his life.

My grandmother helped Baba lie down and tucked him in with a light blanket smelling of jasmine. Baba drifted to a deep sleep for the first time in months. As he slept, he could still taste the delicate flavors of fresh tomatoes, coriander, basil, and mint. He could smell the scent of his mother next to him gently caressing his head. Unlike the nights in the village, he slept without beasts or bandits in his dream. He was home.

That day, after having been lost among strangers, my father's childhood story comforted me and made me laugh. As his sandpaper hand held mine, I felt at home. I had found my way back to him the way he had returned to his mother.

The consequent retelling of the adventure when I was much older, however, lost its magic. I couldn't reconcile the two opposing feelings— my growing wanderlust and his homesickness. Although the taste of my grandmother's food, her touch, her love, was enticing, I didn't want my father to go back. With later retellings, I could not follow him all the way, and I let him return to his mother alone. I thought that if that was my story, I would have gone further away, never to return.

My mother's words, much stronger than my father's, echoed in the back of my head. "You have to find a way to leave this hellhole," she always told me. "Find someone to take you away. Don't allow yourself to get trapped here like me."

I never stopped to think why my mother wanted me to go away. Did Maman realize that she was pushing me to leave my family, even my mother?

As a young girl, my parents' stories of their teenage trials in faraway places and among strangers jarred me. As a teenager, I didn't understand how Baba couldn't identify with my mother's shock of being physically and emotionally violated. Remembering his own cries for his mother at the same age, he must have known that a thirteen-year-old girl would wither away from her family. Having so much love from his own mother, he should have not dismissed the impact on my mother of this rejection by her family. I knew that it was the custom of the times. Had it not been my father, someone else would have married my mother at a young age. Then I wouldn't exist.

I also wondered if the Persian word for bride, *aroosak,* a little doll, meant just that, a doll for men, a body without emotions.

## A New Life in Shiraz

On their all-day bus ride to Shiraz after the wedding, Maman sat quietly, trying to concentrate on the rugged scenery, the bare mountains streaked with blue and purple mineral deposits, the desert covered with thorny bushes, and Bedouins on camels. This was her first trip outside the chilly climate of Hamedan, her first glance of a desolate landscape.

My father's thirteen-year-old brother Jahangeer, who had accompanied him to the wedding, was elated and chatty at the prospect of reaching home. Homesick, he had cried for his mother every night, begging my father to take him home.

This is the scene that pains me the most. Being the same age, my mother and uncle should have been playing marbles on the floor of that bus, chatting about their schools and friends. Instead, the wedding party dismissed Maman's anxiety and sympathized with her brother-in-law's tears for being away for just a short time.

My father's family waited at the bus stop in Shiraz to greet them. They threw green cloth and sugar candy over them, and sprayed them with rose water for good luck, a sweet life.

Aunt Maheen giggled when she saw the bride. She whispered loudly in my father's ear, "You're so tall—why such a short wife?"

Such simple words of gentle criticism Baba never ignored. My mother

*Maman, two years before her marriage, with grandmother Touran and three of her brothers in Hamedan. My maternal grandfather was often absent from home, trying to sell merchandise in faraway villages until Touran demanded that he should return home. His assets confiscated during Reza Shah's reign to help with the war expenses, twice he opened bookstores. Twice they were burned down. He gave up and plunged the family into terrible poverty, forcing grandmother Touran to work as a cook and sometimes a maid in local hotels.* Picture courtesy of Nahid Gerstein.

told me that my father's behavior changed immediately. He became quiet, sad, and kept his distance from her. After the departure of my maternal grandmother, when my mother needed her husband's emotional support the most, he had none to give. Distraught, Baba himself had no one to support or to reassure him.

On my mother's first week in Shiraz, guests came to bring gifts and to see the new bride. Bent over with a low broom, my mother was sweeping the yard on her honeymoon. "Is that your new maid?" a neighbor asked my grandmother.

That embarrassed Khanom-bozorg, my mother told me. She was mad at Maman for allowing the company to see her at work in tattered clothes. She worried that they might become the subject of gossip and criticism.

Worse yet, a distant relative came unannounced to see this new addition to the family. She and my grandmother had never liked each other. The visitor covered her mouth with the corner of her *chador* and laughed, "Look! They've brought a peasant for a bride!"

*Part of my mother's dowry: gold necklace, earrings, and a Ghajar coin.* Photography by Jon and Jennifer Crockford.

My grandmother stewed over the insult and later complained to my father that the snake's tongue had revealed itself.

My mother didn't lift her teary eyes to see who was making the cruel comments. She felt like a bird that had flown in by mistake, banging herself against every clear window pane to reach the wide skies outside, only to get bloodied.

Insecure, conscious of community standards, devoted to his mother and siblings, and thirsty for approval, my father too felt caged by his own mistake. There was no way out. For decades, he sided with the rest, and looked at my mother as a stranger in order not to become one himself. Instead of defending and protecting his wife, my father became a mirror to the family, magnifying their image of my mother, and reflecting it back on her, and sometimes on us as well.

My father and I traveled to Tehran when I was in high school. I enjoyed staying at a hotel, riding on the top floor of double-decker buses, and eating in the cafeterias for the first time. We went for long walks along fashionable streets, lined with foreign-named boutiques, and looked into the cafés whose windows framed young men and women laughing like actors on a movie screen, without worrying about their modesty, without fear of

*A sample of my father's artistry in designing and crafting jewelry, often made for new brides.*
Picture courtesy of Dr. and Mrs. Dayanim.

the community gossips. I had my arm in his, loving every minute of having him to myself, knowing that he too enjoyed the intimacy.

My father and I didn't visit my mother's family in Tehran. I didn't question the decision, but he explained nevertheless. We stood in front of the glass window of a shop where women's robes wrapped around mannequins gracefully as if they were parading to an evening ball. Maybe he too imagined beautiful women walking luxuriously around clean homes in silk and velvet robes.

He had made the wrong decision, he told me for the first time about his marriage. "I was young," he said. "Someone should have told me your mother wasn't right for me." He was entrusted to an elder with little wisdom. There was no surprise that he was blindfolded with false words and had married a woman of no fortune or class.

I didn't tell him that a wealthy family would not have sent such a young girl away. He knew that.

"I cringe when I'm around her family," he added. "I don't want you to be exposed to them."

I adored our time alone and away from life in our chaotic, multi-family house in Shiraz, so I didn't ask him to define class. The robe he bought me obligated me to listen to his grievances. We ate white rice and yogurt in a non-kosher restaurant, since my father didn't fear the watchful eyes of the community. As I drank my tea, he chewed his mustache and recalled event after event at which my mother's family had acted with callousness and disregard for social graces.

"This is the family I fell into," he sighed. "My fate!" Like my mother, Baba blamed his destiny for his unhappiness.

I tried to think of ways to fight this unpredictable, often adversarial "fate," but I couldn't. I was happy. I was enjoying a sweet cup of tea; I couldn't wait to show my robe to my friends. I never reminded my father that he was denigrating *my* mother.

In our house, my grandmother Khanom-bozorg was the head of the household and received the daily spending money from my father early each morning. Baba worked long hours, sometimes not returning home until midnight, and if he had a light day, he went to the movies secretly and alone. My grandmother was dismayed that her daughter-in-law didn't have the skills to cook; my mother grumbled that she had been washing, cleaning, and ironing all day for my father's siblings. Not being able to juggle the needs of the two wailing women, Baba abided by the cultural rules of respecting and obeying elders.

At the same time, Morad wanted to separate from my father and open his own business. My father refused. They were to work together to support the rest of the family, my father insisted. Frustrated and resentful, Morad targeted my mother, encouraging my grandmother to be more strict with her. When winter came, my grandmother gave Maman Morad's tattered coat to wear at home and told my mother to save the one she had brought with her from Hamedan to wear in public to save face.

Desperate and lonely, Maman stole a pencil and a sheet of paper from her sister-in-law and wrote a letter to her great uncle Dr. Sayed, telling him that since he was responsible for her marriage, he needed to help her out of it.

To her mother she wrote, "Please come and take me away or I will die in this foreign land."

But no response came to these letters or the ones after. Then, one day, many months later, a letter arrived telling her that her husband's house was her home and that she had no other home. She leaned against the door and cried. She put the letter to her nose to see if any scent of her mother remained on it, but it smelled like the ink of a scriber in the bazaar. She folded the paper and put it in the pocket of her dress. She read it again when cooking, and her tears, added to the turmeric and the sesame oil, flavored the chicken. My grandmother noticed the letter and asked Maman to read it aloud. Maybe Khanom-bozorg thought the letter contained some gossip from the Jewish community of Hamedan; maybe she hoped it would have regards for her. When my mother refused, she warned my father. He read the letter, threw it in the fire, and demanded the right to check Maman's mail.

"I submitted to my fate," my mother told me. "What else could have I done?"

My grandmother was alarmed by my mother's open unhappiness and watched her movements, so that the community wouldn't discover the problems in the family. They had to save face. The walls thickened. The doors closed.

### Aziza

My mother's isolation impacted my life in many ways. I grew up not knowing most of my mother's relatives, including my maternal grandparents. I had lived in the United States for over twenty years, when I was introduced to some of the relatives on my mother's side. Once I heard my mother's brother Avi, who is three years younger than me, talk about his sister being "so nice."

"Which sister? You mean Maman?" I said, confused.

"No, my other sister, Aziza."

My mother had a half-sister and no one had ever bothered to tell me. My uncle said that Aziza lived in Los Angeles with her daughter Mohtaram. "Don't you know Mohtaram, Parveez, Eshagh, Jamsheed, Maheen, and Farzaneh, her children, your cousins?" he asked.

I felt empty. During my childhood and teen years, I had felt sorry for myself that I did not have a *khaleh,* a maternal aunt. My friends felt sorry for me as well, a sorrow laced with a touch of grandiosity. "You don't have a *khaleh,* what a pity!" A good friend told me as she slapped her cheeks with both hands. *Khalehs,* she told me, were much better than *amehs,* the paternal aunts, because they loved their sisters' children and spoiled them.

I wanted to be spoiled too, to have someone to run away to from time

*My mother's sister.*

to time. I was angry that my mother had six brothers but no sisters. Now, after so many years, Avi informed me that I had a large family that no one had bothered to tell me about. I had been to Los Angeles the month before and, as I found out later, just ten minutes away, not knowing about their existence.

When I made arrangements for my next trip to Los Angeles, visiting my *khaleh* was my top priority. I called her from Norfolk to introduce myself and to tell her that I would like to visit. Her daughter Mohtaram picked up the phone. Their phones, I learned later, were connected so she could monitor her mother's calls. She was delighted and gave me directions to her apartment and the promise to take me over to my aunt's.

I couldn't find the steps to her second-floor apartment and instead rode the dilapidated elevator, trying not to panic in the enclosed cubicle. The walls closed in on me, and I felt my breakfast of soft cheese and walnuts coming up in my throat as I smelled foreign spices aged to a noxious odor that clung to the walls and the tattered carpeting. I leaned against the metal structure and tried to control my breathing. I have never liked confined spaces; they rot the living.

The elevator stopped with a jolt. The doors opened, and the smell of Iranian, Indian, Afghani, and Israeli foods floated freely in the breeze down the corridors, aromatic, pungent, mouth-watering.

Wearing a long dress and carefully applied makeup, I hesitated for a minute outside Mohtaram's apartment before I knocked. The door opened a crack, and a woman in her sixties with short, teased hair dyed a reddish-yellow took a peek through the opening. She looked at me with surprised and questioning eyes. I wondered if I was in the wrong place.

"Farideh," I introduced myself. "Mohtaram *khanom?*"

Her eyes lit up; her body relaxed. "O, my God! I can't believe Rouhi's daughter is here. I can't believe it." She kissed me on both cheeks. "May I be sacrificed for you. Your steps should be on my eyes. You don't know how happy I am to see you."

She asked me to sit in an ornate, imitation French-antique armchair with a matching sofa and dining room chairs covered with heavy plastic. The oversized furniture overwhelmed the tiny apartment. She asked me what I would prefer to drink, sour cherry or quince drink.

"Just water, please." My tongue felt woolly.

She brought me all of them and trays of fruit too. I chewed a piece of watermelon and let it sit on my tongue for a few seconds before swallowing it as I scanned the walls covered with family pictures like so many other Iranian homes I had visited. In Iran, her family would have lived with Mohtaram or nearby. Now in Los Angeles she could keep her children and grandchildren with her as photographs hung on every centimeter of the walls. Mohtaram explained that the separation was because of all the traffic, because of the long distances across the highways, and because of their busy schedules that kept them away.

The clocks run faster in America, I knew.

I pulled out pictures of my children and husband for Mohtaram to see.

"*Mashalah,* what wonders God has fashioned. What beautiful girls!" Her eyes opened wide as she covered her mouth with delight.

I showed her pictures of my brothers' weddings in Philadelphia, my sister's family in Washington, my youngest sister in Israel. I was trying to make up for lost time. I handed her a picture of my mother, taken two years earlier in Israel.

"Is this Rouhi *khanom?*" She stared at my mother's picture.

Maman was in her house dress, her hair matted, a big smile on her face.

"Her beauty is gone," she said, "such a pity."

I resented that she noticed the aging, the burden of life on my mother.

"Your mother was the most stunningly gorgeous girl. She was taken to the hairdresser before her wedding to curl her hair, which framed her face and hung around her shoulders and back in long tubes. She was so beautiful!" Mohtaram said enviously.

My mother had natural curls. Imagining her with a Shirley Temple hairdo, I wondered why they gave her a perm. I remembered the burn on the right side of my mother's head, next to her ear, where the hair stylist had left the hot iron for too long.

"She was a child," I mumbled, not knowing why. Mohtaram knew how young my mother was married off. I didn't need to remind her.

"You know your aunt Aziza wouldn't speak with her father Agha for the longest time?"

"No. Did they have a fight?"

"Aziza was angry at her father for marrying such a young girl after her mother passed away. People think she was mad at Touran *khanom,* your grandmother. That's not true. She would yell at Agha, "Why did you have to ruin the life of such a young girl?""

I was surprised. My grandfather needed company. It wasn't so unusual for a man to remarry after his wife died. Mohtaram seemed to read my thoughts.

"You know, my dear, he had no money. Why did he marry a fifteen-year-old, then give her seven kids he could not feed? Your grandmother had to work every day to provide for the family. See what happened? She had to give your mother away as a child because she was overwhelmed. Your grandmother—may God remember her in favor—was a good, hard-working woman."

Mohtaram's saliva gathered around her mouth and sprayed in an almost invisible mist seen only through the sunlight coming from the patio door. I wanted to know more about my mother.

"Mohtaram *khanom,* do you remember my mom in Iran? Do you know how her life was?"

"Some things are better not known." She shook her head.

I didn't insist.

Mohtaram brought out her photo albums decorated with Iranian scenery, the open spaces around Band-e Amir, an ancient dam over River Kor, in gold and enamel. The pages were stuck together, the pictures yellow, their borders crumbled from absorbing the glue that kept them in place. She showed me pictures of cousins, aunts, and uncles whom I didn't know. I touched their faces, trying to recapture the weddings and family gatherings that I had missed. I felt like a stranger.

"Can we go see my aunt now?" I hoped for a connection there; maybe if we touched, our bond would reveal itself through the shared blood.

I was anxious on the short walk to my aunt's house. Her door was ajar and a long security chain held it together, which Mohtaram reached to unlock. The chain didn't provide security. My cousin noticed my perplexity.

"I have no choice but to lock her in. She walks out, gets confused, and goes to other people's apartments. I come and check on her every day. I bring her food. Sometimes I take her to my place for lunch. Two nights a week, I sleep here. The others come and visit every Wednesday. She is lonely, I know, but what can I do? In Iran, family was always around. Here, we struggle. Who knew this would be our fate, living in *ghorbat,* away from home in our old age."

Frustrated with the chain, I helped her open the door. An old woman stood bent over next to a sofa covered with a beige fabric to keep it clean.

"It's burning." She pushed on her lower abdomen. "It hurts."

"It's okay," Mohtaram reassured her. "Your acid is high. I have been trying to get hold of your doctor. This is Rouhi's daughter. She has come a long way to see you."

Aziza looked at me from underneath her thick glasses, and I didn't know how to react. Then she burst out into a deep cry, reaching with both hands for me. I took a big step and held her tight, crying myself. She smelled old and medicinal. Her grasp was tight and her bony hands didn't let go of me for a long time. Her shriveled frame was hidden in my embrace, her head rested on my chest, and I felt the wetness of her tears through my dress mixing with my own perspiration in the hot room. I caressed her disheveled hair, white and coarse, sweaty from the exertion of her slightest moves. My tears fell on her scalp, which showed through the thin silver fuzz. I bent over and kissed her on both cheeks, and she kissed me back. Her face rubbed against mine, wet and soft, and tickled me with a few old-age hairs growing on her chin.

Between the sobs she repeated, "I can't believe I am seeing Rouhi's daughter. I can't believe." Her accent was unfamiliar.

"Sit down Aziza *khanom*," I told her, not sure of what to call her, not daring to call her *khaleh*. An aunt is more than a physical being; she is a re-lationship, but I was seeing mine for the very first time at age forty-five, when she was ninety years old and forgetful. She sat on the edge of the sofa with her hands folded on her lap. Her bare feet on the carpet, the toe-nails thick, yellow, and cracked, piggybacked on each other like a row of fallen dominos.

"I have some pictures for you," I told Aziza as I sat next to her. I showed her my daughters' pictures, and she sobbed some more. I gave her pictures of my mother, grandmother, and grandfather. She was confused.

Mohtaram explained it to her again. "This is a picture of Touran, Rouhi's mother."

"Is Touran here?"

"No," I said, "in the picture." I didn't tell her that my grandmother had been dead for a long time. I pulled out old pictures of my maternal grand-mother holding my youngest uncle at the time, with my twelve-year-old mother standing next to her. As I expected, she recognized them; they were frozen in time, as she had last seen them. Then I showed her a recent picture and told her that this was my mother today. The light came back in Aziza's eyes.

"This is Rouhi? O my God, Rouhi." She sobbed again, touching my mother's face in the picture. I showed her my grandfather's picture.

"Agha has not changed at all! I dreamed of him last night. He was here visiting me. I have not seen him in a long time."

I didn't know how to handle the situation.

"Agha is dead," Mohtaram said. She was used to reminding her mother of the past events that Aziza forgot constantly.

Maybe she should let it be, I thought, as I saw Aziza mourning her fa-ther again, her chest heaving.

"Mother, don't cry. Remember, this world is for nothing," Mohtaram said. "It isn't worth upsetting yourself so much."

It was time to leave. Both Aziza and I were emotionally drained. "Good-bye Aziza *khanom*." I hugged my aunt again and kissed her on both cheeks. I felt guilty for not taking her out for fresh air, for a walk around the block. I was an outsider, I thought. I couldn't change their lives. I felt a sudden need to leave the stuffy room. "I will come back to see you again before I leave," I promised my aunt. Aziza stared at me.

"Who is that woman?" She whispered loudly to her daughter.

"That's Rouhi's daughter."

"Is Agha here?" Aziza asked in her shaking voice.

"He is dead. He died years ago."

My aunt sobbed again. Aziza mourned the same deaths every day. Every time she was reminded, she mourned them anew.

On the way out, Mohtaram locked the door behind her.

"I am very sad we never met when I could have talked to her, when she could have told me about her life," I told Mohtaram. "Why we didn't ever come to visit her, I don't know." I paused. Then I asked Mohtaram. "Why didn't Aziza *khanom* come to visit us in Shiraz? My mom was so lonely, so far away from home."

Mohtaram looked at me and bit her lower lip. "You know we have other family in Shiraz," she said abruptly, as if she was afraid she might change her mind if she hesitated.

"No, I didn't know." I turned to face her.

"One of my cousins married a Shirazi man." Mohtaram continued without looking at me. "When Aziza went for the wedding, she and a few cousins stopped by to see your mother. A woman opened the door just a crack and told them she was not at home. They asked, 'Who are you?' Where would a young girl go? How far had she gone? When was she going to be back? Without identifying herself, the woman repeated 'Rouhi is not at home.' They persisted. 'When can we come back then to see her?' Again the reply was, 'She isn't here.'"

And the door closed.

*Chapter Two*

# MY GRANDMOTHER'S HOUSE

On a cold day in January of 1953, two years after my parents' wedding, my mother, age fifteen, gave birth to me at Morsalin Hospital, a missionary facility. My birth sealed her place in my father's family, the family she had contemplated leaving every day. Learning that other imported brides had simply taken the bus back home, she had begged my father for a divorce. He refused. She didn't have money for a bus ticket anyway; and having spent most of her time at home, she didn't know the city well enough to find the station. And even if she could, where was home and who wanted her? With my birth, her hope of running away and escaping her life in Shiraz ended.

At the same time, she felt that maybe she finally had something of her own—a little girl who would alleviate her deep loneliness among strangers, a daughter to listen to her story, to sympathize with her saga of pain, abandonment, and abuse.

Instead, I distanced myself from her constant retelling of the same tale. What did she expect of me? That I would be the historian of her life, conspiring against my father, grandmother, aunts, and uncles? Impossible!

Giving birth in Iran was often a family affair. Women of the family came as they heard the news of a family member or a neighbor in labor. They used pillows to support the pregnant woman's back, spread fresh ashes underneath her thighs, and rested her legs on top of bricks. They brought in chai and aromatic drinks, sweets and nuts, a freshly prepared waterpipe, and all their gossip. They sat around the room talking and laughing to distract the woman in labor from her pain. They ate, sang, and exchanged gossip while the mother-to-be screamed and cursed.

Once in a while, a guest would tell the screaming mother, "Calm down, you think you are the only woman who's ever been in labor?"

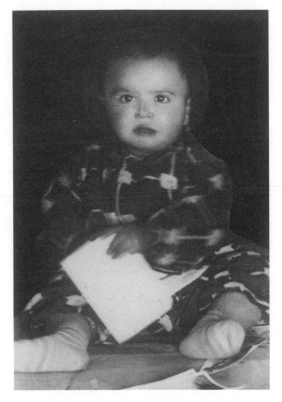

*On the back of my baby picture, my father wrote, "Farideh is actually a pretty child but she wouldn't sit still for a picture."*

If they felt the labor had lasted a long time and the mother and child were in danger, they prayed, "O, God! Let one body emerge from the other. Let one life separate from another."

My mother had witnessed this ritual a few times, once walking out in disgust as women tried to drown the screams in their own laughter. She made my father promise that she would give birth in a hospital. She didn't tell him that she didn't want the women to stare down her open legs as they cracked watermelon seeds. Instead, she convinced my father that the midwife's dirty hands and unsanitary conditions at home could infect both her and their child. To the family's chagrin, my father sided with her.

Even in hospitals, it was essential for women to help one another in childbirth. Mothers followed their daughters through the pregnancy, labor, and birth, and were often present in the birthing room. My aunt Shams once helped her daughter give birth when the doctors at Namazi Hospital, a newly built modern facility, were busy and didn't believe that my pregnant cousin knew that her baby was ready to see the world.

Years later, when I was visiting one of my aunts at the same hospital where I was born, I witnessed the birthing of a baby. The dark waiting room was filled with women from the surrounding villages. It smelled of the fresh soil of wheat farms, the pungent sweat of horses and sheep, the greens of fava bean pods. As the head nun screamed at a Ghashghai woman from a nomadic tribe outside Shiraz that it was not yet her time, the women of her family surrounded her in their multi-skirt costumes and long colorful head covers, reached under the layers of red, green, and gold fabric around her waist, and pulled out a screaming, slippery baby, right there, squatting over the dirty floor. The nun ran to them in her long dark robe, her hair covered in white fabric, her face tired and weary from long hours on her feet, and pushed them away as if they were primitives who had rushed God's work.

Since my maternal grandmother lived far away and was herself pregnant with her sixth child, she wasn't there to help my mother with my birth. My father's aunt Khatoon-jaan, with henna-covered hair and multiple braids hidden underneath a long kerchief, kept my mother company at the hospital. She hung onion bulbs and salt crystals on the door post to keep away the evil eye. From her bed, my mother watched her. Just outside, she could see Moslem visitors getting ready for morning prayers. They washed their arms and legs in the freezing water of a pool, spread their prayer rugs under the leafless orange trees, and barefooted they bowed in the direction of Mecca. A blind priest stopped by to convince my mother to seek comfort in Christ.

One damp rainy day, when my cloth diapers wouldn't dry, Khatoon-jaan sat cross-legged on the cement floor of the hospital room, spread her long skirt about her, and held a diaper over a brazier filled with hot charcoals. When the fabric caught on fire, she threw it on the floor and stomped on it, coughing from the smoke. It was Shabbat and touching fire was forbidden. She fasted every day for a week for the sin of disobeying the commandments and gave her meager earnings as *tsedakah* to the poor. Khatoon-jaan never forgot the incident. Ten years later, when I visited her to say goodbye before she left for Palestine, she cried and hugged me tightly, while reminding me of her love toward me and of the sin she had committed for me. She asked me not to forget her.

The year I was born, 1953, was to be remembered by the historians of Iran. Electrical lines were finally stretched on the tall walls of the *mahaleh*. Little bulbs, with their dim yellow light, changed the shape of shadows in the alleyways. Baba bought a radio, a large square box that sat on the mantel in the common room like a special guest, covered with a pretty doily. It was an amazing change for my family. During World War II, my father had run to the British embassy every day to listen to the news and report back home. Now he could listen to the happenings in the country while he sipped tea with a sugar lump between his back teeth; my grandmother puffed at her waterpipe; my mother nursed me; my two aunts and three uncles living with us warmed their hands over the embers in the brazier and cracked watermelon seeds between their back molars; and the younger ones tried to do their homework in the dim light of a newly installed light bulb despite my grandmother's protests that they were going to ruin their eyes.

An invisible ray of hope penetrated into the heart of every Jew who could now hear the reports of the State of Israel, established just five years earlier. The sick, the hopeless, the truly downtrodden inhabitants of the ghetto left for Israel first. As the Israeli economy improved, other waves of Jews who were tired of living in the ghetto, who found the anti-Semitism intolerable, immigrated to Israel as well. Those who stayed behind knew that an escape was available if they needed it. If the Iranian economy and the condition of Jews had not improved so rapidly during the reign of Mohammed Reza Shah, they would have left in masses as well.

Around the time of my birth, Dr. Mosadegh, a European-educated lawyer and the head of the Communist Party, was elected as the new prime minister in Iran. In that position, he started a showdown with the British government, which wanted to continue its control over the Iranian oil fields. In response, the British administration persuaded Eisenhower to overthrow him. Americans, who were fervently anti-communist, pressured the king as well. Manipulated by the two countries, the Shah dismissed the prime minister in August of 1953. However, Mosadegh's message was popular in Iran, because he was a nationalist and an anti-imperialist. Thousands of Mosadegh followers demonstrated on the streets of the capital. Fearing a violent coup, the Shah fled the country.

On August 19, American agents in Iran incited the crowds to set fire to the offices of Dr. Mosadegh's newspaper. They also distributed pro-Shah flyers and articles in Iranian papers and paid off enough people to rally for the Shah on the streets. The tide quickly turned against Mosadegh. The American government begged, cajoled, and mediated the Shah's return. Financed, armed, and supported by the United States, the Iranian military gunned down hundreds of civilians in Tehran, and organized a house-to-house search to arrest communist sympathizers.

Uncle Beejan, a student at Tehran University, had come home and taken to the streets with the rioters, making speeches, writing and distributing anti-Shah flyers. Being his guardian, Baba feared for my uncle's safety and our family's as well. As the police neared our home, my father tore through my uncle's room, searched in the Passover dishes in the attic, and dug among the onions and spices in the pantry, looking for illegal documents. He found armloads of anti-Shah literature and tossed them in a bonfire. In his haste, he also burned my uncle's collection of poetry, short stories, and paintings, along with carefully stored bags of dried herbs and spices. By the time the American-supported agents reached our home, the only traces of the passionate arguments against the king were deliciously spiced ashes flying in the wind.

No one knew then how the 1953 crowning of the Shah by the West would come to haunt us all. Although not witness to this history, my generation experienced this humiliating loss of self-determination through our parents' memories. Despite the presence of the Shah's "ears" everywhere, there were those who whispered about our puppet king in the hands of the British and Americans, who had conspired to take over our lives, to make us into a shadow of themselves, to control us. The voice became stronger as I grew older.

During my years in elementary and high school, our teachers told us to dress neatly and bring flowers to school the day before the Shah visited Shiraz. The school administration threatened us by saying that only traitors to the country would not show up. We lined up by the streets from the airport to the Shah's castle. Our teachers prompted us to shout pro-Shah slogans as we awaited the procession for hours. They didn't allow us to sit, eat, or drink. There were no bathrooms available. And when the king and queen passed us in black limousines, we threw the flowers, scrambled to see their faces from behind the smoky glass, and screamed: *"Javeed shah,* long live the king." Then, our teachers tried to form us into lines to march back to school.

When I was a teenager, a new complication arose from the dreaded days when the Shah visited Shiraz. Students from the men's school took advantage of the momentary chaos as we regrouped to pinch our buttocks and touch our breasts.

Although none of us minded a day off from school, many wondered if the king was so naïve as to think that he was loved; and some asked sincerely if their majesties had to use the bathroom like the rest of us, since they claimed to be appointed by God. In high school, I started noticing people who sat during the rendition of the national anthem in the movie theaters, who refused to clap at the end. Most of us were too afraid to contemplate such disobedience. And in college, a classmate who assured me that Marxism and Islam were compatible, tried to pass me Marx's *The Communist Manifesto*, knowing that its possession warranted a death sentence. Others started to wear Islamic garbs and openly shunned me for my religion.

And then there were those who embraced the West, wanting to make it theirs. They packed the movie theaters with images of American, French, and Italian icons. Men, lusty after watching naked bodies, poured out of the theaters, molesting women in their way. They danced to the beat of the Beatles and the Rolling Stones in fashionable dark discotheques, colored lights pulsating on the floors and the walls. They learned English and fashionably mixed it into their discourse. They dreamed of America.

I grew up in the pull between these two ideologies that paralleled my parents' opposite plans for me. I struggled to balance my cultural heritage against the enticing Western life style that I secretly read about in my books. I yearned for a home that differed from my father's, in which multiple families lived together. Yet my mother's plans for my escape into the unknown, to any place away from the family she had married into, both intrigued and frightened me.

## My Childhood Home

The house in which I spent my early years originally had been a part of a much larger building and gardens owned by my great-grandfather, the chief rabbi and judge of the community. The position, through the first-born sons, was passed down from generation to generation. When he died, the house was divided. My grandfather, who had inherited the position of *dayan*, the judge and spiritual leader of the community, built a small house on one side with two rooms upstairs, two basement rooms downstairs, and a kitchen and a bathroom at the far end of the garden. The larger side, including the existing house, was given to his father's second wife, Mori-jaan, and her three sons and extended families. The new front door of each house opened to a shared space that was the entrance to the original house, with its large wooden doors still in place.

In this cool common hallway between the two houses, Mori-jaan held her own court on summer days. Her grandchildren put a colorful *kilim* on the freshly swept clay floor in the corner between the door to her house and the hallway wall. She sat in her usual place by the door every morning, leaning against a mountain of pillows. Her dog, named Hitler by the neighborhood kids, lay by her left side. To me, she looked like a queen who had tamed a monstrous lion. The dog, with its light brown hair and thick mane, almost resembled a huge kitten. She was cuddly and sweet when her tamer caressed her back, but the beast horrified everyone, including my parents, when they encountered her away from her owner.

Mori-jaan's powerful presence, her confidence, and her show of authority intrigued me; she was an ancient maternal symbol. To preserve her dignity and modesty, she pulled a large kerchief over her hair whenever she heard footsteps. But minutes later, it slipped down to her shoulders, leaving her hair disheveled. Strands of silvery hair escaped her tight braid, pulled away from her head in a halo, and made her look like an electrified female Einstein.

A narrow wooden bench obscured Mori-jaan from the stares of passersby. From this hideaway, she enjoyed the cross breeze. Her floral *chador* covered her shoulders and draped most of her body as she puffed at her waterpipe. I wondered what gave her eyes the power to humble everyone around her, the strength to quiet anyone she did not want to hear, the ability to pull words out of women who were too hesitant to speak.

Her daughter-in-law, a new bride, periodically refreshed the tobacco in Mori-jaan's *ghalyan* with a new batch, replaced the charcoal with hotter pieces, and exchanged the warm, tainted liquid at the base with cold fresh water. She drew a puff to make sure the tobacco was burning with a perfect aroma before handing it back to her mother-in-law.

Watching Mori-jaan's bride with envy, my grandmother praised the woman's obedience and devotion, saying, "Look, she walks backward when in the presence of her mother-in-law." She sighed as she looked at my mother.

Mori-jaan smoked first and then honored the rest of the women. The gurgling of the water at the *ghalyan*'s base was mesmerizing, a soothing sound that rarely stopped. The genteel *taarof* and niceties were the only sign that the instrument was changing hands.

"Hope your hands are not aching," said my grandmother before taking a puff.

"I'm not worthy of your kindness." Our next-door neighbor reached out to touch Mori-jaan's hand and then kissed her own fingers as if the old lady's grace had been attached to hers now.

"Your shadow should not decrease over us," added another woman as she raised herself slightly and bent forward in a bow.

Although my grandmother Tavous was the head of our household and received much respect as the widow of the last great rabbi of the community, she did not have as much clout as Mori-jaan. Wisdom and respect, in those days and in that part of the world, came mostly with age.

Women dropped by to pay their homage on the way to the vegetable stand or the bakery. There was always good chit-chat and sharing of gossip. The women sat there attentively. In the hallway, they could learn who would be marrying whom, how much dowry a daughter had taken to her husband's home, or how a new bride was pleasing her mother-in-law. It was also a fine place to try to match young men and women.

One woman said, "You know, Nasreen, the daughter of Mashallah, would be a good match for Saeed, Rahman's son. Both fathers are jewelers."

The other added, "They say he wears glasses; his eyes are no good. Who would want their daughter to marry a man who is disabled?"

A third joined the conversation, "Well, that's not right. His mother, Bagom-jaan, was here yesterday, and she said that he is *gherti*, wears glasses to show off. They are supposed to make him look *farangee*. The young kids nowadays think anything American is the best. It is a different world. Who knows, maybe Nasreen would like it too."

Yet another woman said, "And since when are girls supposed to like or dislike their suitors? Look at the Moslems—the first time a woman sees her husband's face is when he lifts up her veil in front of the *mola* who is marrying them; and I say that's the way it should be, or otherwise there would be chaos. It has always been the job of the fathers to evaluate the boy and the girl to see if they are good for each other, to negotiate the terms of marriage and God forbid a divorce."

Women came to talk about what made them happy, but mostly of their hardships. Looking back, the idea was quite modern, a natural support group down the street on the way to the market place, where women could *dard-e-del,* speak of the ache in their hearts, where they could share their miseries and be comforted by the knowledge of the other women's hardships.

At these gatherings, I ran errands for my grandmother, bringing refreshments and cleaning the dishes filled with the shells of watermelon seeds. If my mother was not at home cooking and cleaning, she sat there invisible, silent. She was an outsider, and by extension I feared that I could be one as well. For my mother to share her secrets, to tell of the ache in her heart, she would have to talk about the people present, my grandmother and the rest of my father's family. Complaints about one's in-laws were the most basic *dard-e-del,* the essence of mental health, the one most expected to be discussed with one's family and friends. My mother had no family around and was not allowed to establish close friendships. Since we were well known and respected in the community, any complaints from my mother would spoil the aura of stability, integrity, and if not happiness, at least harmony of the family.

For generations, our ancestors had been given the honor of serving as community judges, bringing the community together and solving problems in order to keep away from the Moslem courts. But that umbrella of justice did not protect my mother. She lived in silence for much of my childhood, lost in her unspoken thoughts.

### A Day at the Hamam

Silently, my mother gave me baths in our backyard on summer days. When the heat rose off the bricks in shimmering waves, when my feet burned even through my shoes, she dumped well-water in a large basin and left it in the yard to warm in the desert sun. I sat naked on a low wooden stool, letting her scrub me with the rough cloth of a *kiseh,* a square glove used as a wash cloth. Dead skin peeled in black rolls. Her touch was the measurement of her inner turmoil. If I was being skinned, I sat quietly, knowing that she was going to be silent as the volcano inside her heated. If she was gentle, I asked her to sing me a song.

"*Arousaké khoshgele man,*" she sang. "My beautiful doll wears a red dress/ She sleeps on a blue velvet bed." She folded the soaked, pulverized leaves of *konar* in my hair, massaging my scalp. "My doll, wake up, wake up/ Go to sleep at twilight/ Now it's time to have fun, jump rope and run."

Sometimes when she washed herself in the yard, scrubbing her rough heels with the pumice stone, I could hear her singing it to herself.

When the weather turned cool, she washed me in the kitchen. The garden filled with orange and tangerine trees separated the kitchen from the main building. Maman pulled the water out of the well in the kitchen and warmed it in cooking pots on top of mud stoves. Her cheeks puffed as her mouth sucked the air in to blow on the glowing charcoal. Her eyes turned red and watered. A thick smoke swirled around the dark kitchen and found its way out of the paneless windows. The log burned bright orange.

I sat on a stool shivering instead of rubbing the pumice stone on my heels.

"What's with you?" Maman screamed. "You'll catch pneumonia if you don't hurry up." She put a pot of warm water next to me. I poured it over my head and felt the *konar* slide down my back, cold and slimy where the pulverized leaves were fine, and the rest remained in my hair, coarse and grainy. I hugged my knees for warmth and watched the water find its way to a shallow drain that carried it to the yard.

"You wasted all that water." She sighed as she poured a cup of water on my hair. "Hurry up. Rub it out."

"It's gone," I lied. My teeth chattered. I grabbed the towel, dried myself and pulled a dress over my head. It stuck to my damp body. The water dripped from my hair, found its way through my collar, and slipped all the way to my legs. The orange trees had no leaves. My nails were blue.

Maman wrapped a kerchief around my head. "Who's going to take care of you when you get sick? Look at that wet hair! Can't even dry yourself!"

I ran to the house feeling dirtier than before I had the bath, my scalp itching as if I had lice. I wondered why we couldn't go to the public baths like our neighbors. Mahvash, my second cousin who lived on the other side of the wall, always bragged about her visits to the *hamam*. She told me that the all-day affair was so much fun, and she couldn't believe that I had never been there.

In a few weeks I got my wish. I was five. A chill had set into our valley. Flocks of birds still covered the skies on their migration to the Persian Gulf, but the mountains surrounding Shiraz were dusted with an early snow. My mother needed to go to the *mikvah;* my grandmother had heard about a wedding party heading for the bathhouse; and my two single aunts needed to be presented to the public.

We gathered around the samovar for tea and buttered bread one morning when my grandmother announced, "We're going to the *hamam* tomorrow." I wanted to run next door and tell Mahvash, but there was much work to be done. Going to the *hamam* was not a simple task. Like everything else in our lives, it had its own rituals.

That day, the women made lunch and dinner ahead of time and put them on a slab of ice under a big colander. My mother made *koofteh,* giant meat balls with rice, meat, and herbs. My aunts washed and patted dry tarragon, basil, and spring onions. I squeezed fresh lime for a big jug of limeade. My grandmother prepared a waterpipe. She wrapped the *ghalyan* carefully among our clothes, along with the best pieces of charcoal and the tobacco she had prepared herself. I packed pumice stones, *konar, gelezard,* henna, and a few *kisehs.* My grandmother hired the washer-woman to come to the baths around noon with our lunch, fresh bread, and the waterpipe and all its accompaniments. That night I was so excited about my first trip to the *hamam* that I barely slept.

Very early the next day, we left our house in the *mahaleh* and crossed the main street that divided the ghetto. Few cars, but many horse-drawn carriages and donkeys carrying fruit and vegetables to the market crowded the dirt road. We passed bathhouses that served Moslems only during our half-hour walk to the Jewish *hamam,* where we entered through two large doors.

The first thing I saw was the *mikvah.* "What is that?" I wanted to know.

"Nothing," my mother said.

"How deep is it? Can you swim in it?"

"No."

"Maman, are you going to drown in there?"

"No."

"Is it not too cold? Why does it have leaves and stuff floating in it?"

"That's *enough.*"

"Are there any lizards in there?"

Silence.

"Aren't you afraid of getting in it?"

My questions were endless and I was told that if I continued being such a *verag*, I would be sent home. I shut up then and decided not to jeopardize my good fortune. I would watch and listen, and that would be good enough for me.

We stopped by a small room next to the entrance to pick up our utensils from the frowning bath keeper. His hair and even his thin mustache were greasy as if he didn't know about the bathhouse himself. His left ear stayed glued to a radio whose sound was barely audible. A rolled mattress was set against the wall with bubbling plaster, crumbling in the humidity of the bathhouse. He and my grandmother haggled over the price.

"Charging so much for what?" my grandmother said. "Last time you ran out of hot water and we froze." She put a few rials in front of the *hamami* and wrapped her *chador* tighter around herself.

"You use too much water. I can't give you but one pail." The man cracked his knuckles. His thick nails had rough edges. He picked up a small knife and dug underneath them to dislodge the dirt.

My grandmother gave him another few coins for a beaten-up aluminum pan for hot water, another for cold, and a bucket with a rope tied to the handle for pulling the water out of the water hole.

The dampness seeped through my dress as soon as we stepped inside. Wide columns and arches supported the vaulted ceiling of the main building. A few small, fogged-covered windows on top were the only sources of light. When my eyes got used to the darkness, I saw the two water holes at the end of the hall, one for cold and one for hot water. I had pulled water out of our well in the kitchen for cooking many times, and, therefore, I was efficient in retrieving water for bathing. Nonetheless, every time I dropped the bucket in, I worried that its weight might pull me down. I was short and did not have much leverage dangling through the window. I competed with a stream of naked women who lined up by the hole to draw water, and, as I looked around, I appreciated my grandmother's forcefulness in securing a spot away from the busy area for us.

She had eyed a spot close to a pile of burning coals to warm the *hamam* and told us to claim it, and when the others around complained, she used her usual tactic, "Do you know who I am?" She gave them a long stare, and put her henna dish by the column. "I'm the widow of the great rabbi." The other women moved a few steps away.

Like everything else in our lives, social standing in the community determined one's space in the bathhouse. The farther one sat from the door and the traffic, the higher was her position in the society. I didn't question the class difference. I assumed that it was our right. In the same way, most people with lower status in the community succumbed to it and did not try to sit in the higher position. They made themselves comfortable by the drafty door and in the line of the traffic.

We spread our belongings around so other women would not crowd us. My grandmother poured the henna into a small container, mixed it with warm water, and set it on hot coals to activate the color. I soaked the *konar* leaves and the yellow mud in warm water. We wet ourselves and waited for the warmth of the *hamam* to soften the dead outer layer of our skin.

My grandmother took big dollops of henna, isolated a lock of her hair and meticulously ran the henna through it, then did another section and another. Finally, she piled her long hair on top of her head and tied it with an old kerchief. She smeared the rest on her hands and feet and waited for the color to set.

We peeled off the old skin with the wash cloth, and, after many apologies, we each designated someone to whom we would turn our backs for scrubbing. "*Bebakhshid,* please forgive me," everyone *taarof*ed. The polite answer was "A flower doesn't have a front or a back."

We took turns scrubbing my grandmother's body so she wouldn't exert herself. I took the wooden comb and combed her henna-reddened hair and let it cover her back. Since she usually kept her hair in braids and covered under a kerchief, I seldom saw her hair framing her face. I felt proud to be the one chosen to groom it.

The washer-woman stopped by with our lunch, clean clothes, and my grandmother's hookah. We sat cross-legged and naked in a circle and spread the lunch on a plastic cloth. The *koofteh* tasted even better a day old and cold. The strong flavors of tarragon and dill were mixed through the chopped meat and rice. We made sandwiches with flat bread, a piece of the big meatball, fresh green onions, and basil, and squeezed a bit of lime juice on top.

The limeade washed down the food, cooling my insides, and giving me goose bumps. My grandmother took a puff of her *ghalyan* and offered it to my mother and aunts. They were not smokers, but the honor was too great to pass. Each one took a puff, and they even allowed me a turn. I bent over, took the wooden piece in my mouth and drew hard. I gagged and choked on the smoke. Everyone laughed. I caught my breath and asked for another puff, but my grandmother said that was enough.

From another corner of *hamam* now came the loud voices of women singing *vasoonak,* a collection of wedding songs traditionally sung by Jewish women of Shiraz:

> Bath keeper, bath keeper, refresh the water in the *hamam*
> The bride is coming, prepare for her a refreshing *sharbat*

That was the group with a new bride! Many circles of women joined in singing to the bride, and their ululating voices rose and bounced off the high wet ceiling. My grandmother asked me to carry the waterpipe, as all of us went to the bridal group, clapping and singing, offering them our best wishes and a smoke. In return, they offered us *sharbat* made with the essence of fragrant flowers and sugar.

I saw my friend Mahvash. She spotted me and skipped her way toward me, her wet, blond hair shining, a devilish smile parting her lips. "I guess the bride doesn't have to spend an extra hour shampooing and combing her pubic hair any more," she said, chuckling.

I looked at her dumbfounded.

She parted the naked bodies and made room for the two of us in front of the bride. She pointed to the woman's privates and whispered. "Look, now she is all bald! I used to tease her for taking so much time cleaning herself there."

I covered my mouth and joined her in giggling.

I looked at the bride's body. She was soft and beautiful, stomach flat, breasts hard and round, hair shiny and flowing. That was the way all the young women looked. The contours of their bodies differed, but they all looked healthy and radiant. This was the best place for match-making. Mothers and grandmothers with eligible sons and grandsons came to look and choose; mothers and grandmothers with daughters and granddaughters came to show off their merchandise.

But even as a child, I could see how fast new brides lost their vibrancy. The arrival of consecutive children and poor medical care ruined women's bodies, stole the shine from their hair, and sometimes even from their eyes. For every beautiful girl and bride, there were many married women with stomachs bloated and wrinkled like giant prunes, breasts lined with dark vertical lines and drooping as though children had squeezed not only the last drops of milk, but also the substance of the breast itself, the fat, muscle, and tissue.

Years later I would look at my mother's pictures at the time and marvel at her beauty that was so hidden from me. All I saw then were her luster-less eyes and her permanent fatigue, her sacrifice for me.

I didn't want to get married.

A stench came from another corner of the *hamam*. An old, wrinkled and stooped woman with white and disheveled hair stood next to a col-umn, smearing a brown pasty substance on her arms, legs, and private parts. I stared at her, since I had never seen body hair removed chemically.

She cussed at me, screaming, *"Boro gomsho nane jendeh,* go get lost, you daughter of a whore."

I stood there smiling until my mother heard her and dragged me away.

At my mother's request, I threw some dirty clothes on and went out-side to tell the *hamami* to leave. It was time for using the *mikvah*. My mother climbed in and immersed herself completely three times. Her curls disappeared under the murky water and surfaced longer and straight. Each time, I worried that she might slip and drown and I would be help-less to save her. I prayed that she would be okay, and, at the same time, I resented having to watch over her. She finally came out shivering and blue, and we headed back to the baths. It was time for a final soaping and rinse, and then we dried and dressed. My mother braided my hair into two long plaits and covered my head with a flowery kerchief so I wouldn't catch a cold outside with my wet hair exposed.

I walked home in front of everyone. Sunshine felt good on my skin. Rubbing with the rough cloth had given my body a wonderful tingly sen-sation all over. I skipped every few steps, happy with a feeling of belong-ing and a satisfied sense of adventure. My mother, grandmother, and aunts kept reminding me to stop such immodest acts since we were passing Moslem shopkeepers, who were bombarding us with their *matalaks*. I had to be reticent and dignified. But I felt too good to allow the shopkeepers' dirty little phrases to bother me.

I took a long breath, closed my eyes, facing the sun, soaking its warmth. I opened my arms and twirled around, letting my kerchief slide down and my braids fly. When I opened my eyes, I came face to face with my mother. I expected a look of disapproval, but she had a little smile on her face, and there was a brightness in her eyes that I did not know she possessed.

## The Question of Virginity

Winter was finally over. No more snow would fall to bring down the thatched roof on our heads as we slept. My father hired laborers to patch the roof before spring showers poured through the makeshift strips of metal covering the holes. Tiny green leaves waited to push their way through raised spots on the rose tree. White petals burst out, perfuming the air, flavoring our teas. Sparrows sang again among the orange grove.

My mother and I sat across from each other, rubbing the soap into dirty clothes. I took my eyes off Maman's nails, thick and cracked like those on the hoofs of a mule. Instead, I stared at the clear blue sky stretched over the orange trees. I wondered how the birds had sneaked back without me noticing them. The sun made rainbows in the bubbles. I made them bigger and bigger, prettier and prettier, while trapping them between my two thumbs and index fingers like a heart. I blew the rainbow in the air. My mother smacked me with her soapy hand; she had winter in her heart, washing and hanging the clothes in silence.

I didn't want to help her anymore, so I went looking for my grandmother for something more exciting. Like the facets of polished ruby in my father's workshop, the geometric designs of a Bukhari carpet surrounded Khanom-bozorg. Facing the open French doors, my grandmother ran a wooden comb through her henna-colored hair. The morning sun filtered through the large rose tree and brought in warmth mixed with strange shadows. The house was quiet.

My grandmother felt my gaze and turned to find me perched at the door, an invisible shadow with the darkness of the hallway behind. She fanned her right hand fingers toward herself, motioned me to come closer, and gently sat me on her lap. Khanom-bozorg combed my hair, splashing a few drops of water on it to harness the unruly mess. When the black hair hung softly, she cleaned the pulled hair from the comb's teeth, and braided my hair into one single strand. My head hurt but the price of pain was worth the moments of love and intimacy. I took the comb with its missing teeth, two in the middle just like mine, and wove hers into two braids the way I knew my grandmother liked, very close to each other, hanging side by side on her back. When I was finished, Khanom-bozorg covered her hair with a large flowery kerchief and tied it loosely under her chin. She opened her mouth in a toothless smile and made a scary face. I covered my mouth with both hands and giggled. Then I ran to get her false teeth from a chipped water glass on the mantel. She thrust them into her mouth and moved her jaws to adjust the fit, drawing out more giggles.

She examined me critically. The colorless dress hung on me like a wet sheet hung on a tree to dry, the leftover fabric thrown together carelessly, wrinkled after being slept in the night before. I was suddenly ashamed. The dress was big to accommodate a year of growth. My mother had dressed me in mismatched pants and a long-sleeved shirt underneath the dress. As fall led to the colder days of winter, more layers of shabby odds and ends would be added in an effort to keep warm.

"Feri," she addressed me with my nickname, "don't you have anything better to wear?" She made a face.

She knew our financial situation; after all, we lived in the same house as one family. As the eldest, she was in charge of the household allowance. I knew that. I recognized this as an indirect way of criticizing my mother and felt my usual pang of insecurity that came when the two women I loved used me as a tool against one another. I tried to evaluate the situation, averting my eyes. In an Iranian gesture, I threw my head back for a "no."

"Anything cleaner?" She squinted her eyes. When no answer came, she sighed, "Run and ask your mother."

I hesitated, fearing my mother's anger that would undoubtedly come.

"Well, do you want to go out or not? I can stop by your aunt's house and take one of your cousins if you don't."

She knew I was dying to go out, to get out of the lonely house. I tiptoed to my mother, who was still in the same position I had left her, in the back-yard washing the dirty clothes in a large, soapy aluminum wash tub. I could see her back, bent and rounded. Her short curly hair was a mess in need of a haircut. Her hands were rough and raw from the rubbing and contact with cheap soap. Her dirty, deeply cracked heels hung out of a pair of rubber flip-flops. I couldn't bear to watch them. She was sitting there alone, in silence, mumbling stuff to herself, just stuff. I felt sorry for her, for her hard work, for her loneliness. My job was to hang the wash on the clothesline, and part of me felt ashamed for leaving her by herself. At the same time, I hated her for creating such emotions in me.

I swallowed hard and asked, "Maman, is there anything clean for me to wear?" She turned, obviously embarrassed to have been caught complaining to herself, and looked at me with a child's eyes, vulnerable, hurt.

"Going out with your grandmother, *haa?*" she mumbled.

I stood there, not knowing what to say, hating her and pitying her. She pointed to another dress hanging on a tree without looking at me and disappeared again into her own world. I grabbed the dress, changed quickly, threw the dirty one on the pile next to her, and happily ran back to my grandmother.

Khanom-bozorg pointed to a large sugar cone sitting on the mantel to be brought to her. I pressed the heavy piece against my stomach as I carried it and laid it down on a large flowery napkin. She tied two opposite corners on top of the cone and then the other two. It was a pretty package. I was curious to know what it was for, but knew not to ask any questions. I didn't want to be called a *verag*. The despicable adjective was attached to me, and I couldn't cleanse myself of its negative connotation. Adults didn't appreciate too many questions from children; I had learned to draw information by deciphering the circumstances and by listening and watching. I knew we had to be heading to a *simkha,* a happy event, since the sugar cone was used as a gift for such occasions.

Khanom-bozorg adjusted a white calico *chador* with tiny black polka dots on her head, making sure the sides were of equal length. I picked up the gift and followed her. We walked down the old stone stairs to the yard and stopped by my mother's station. While my grandmother gave her instructions for the day's chores, I refused to make eye contact with Maman, refused to feel like a traitor. I was heading out for adventure and would not allow anyone to ruin it for me.

My grandmother and I walked down the narrow alleyways of the *mahaleh.* Khanom-bozorg gathered and lifted her *chador* when she reached a small puddle in the middle of the road, and held its top corners with her teeth to keep it from slipping down her head and disgracing her. She cussed from under her breath, "May they meet the washer of the dead!" She stopped, turned sideways, and made herself as small as possible to avoid any contact with a man passing through. "It's hard enough to walk down the alley without touching the walls. It's so narrow. How is one supposed to stay clean in this place?" She bent her head and added her own spit to the dirty water.

We stopped by the Great Synagogue, put our lips on its heavy wooden doors, made a wish, and kissed it. On my grandmother's request, I ran inside to give the old homeless woman living there a few rials. Her fragile, wrinkled frame was bundled up in a black *chador* as she sat in a corner of the yard trying to soak up the warmth of the morning sun. "May God give you a good life for remembering this forgotten old woman," she said.

This was a good beginning. My grandmother's face had a glow now that I loved. We stopped by the public water spouts, where she was greeted by women drawing water. "*Khebeen, khesheen?*" They asked of each other's health in Judi, a language spoken only by Shirazi Jews, which I understood but did not speak.

"*Shalomalekhem, shalomalekhem,*" may God be with you, everyone said, as if the two words were only one—none knew Hebrew and the words had become an extension of Judi. I watched and listened, invisible. They stood in a tight circle, heads together whispering secrets, looking like a pyramid of patchwork quilt.

When the women finally tore apart, we continued the trip to the deeper sections of the *mahaleh*, places I did not recognize. We stopped and asked for directions many times. I started to wonder if we would ever find the place or make the event in time. We stopped by a pair of small wooden doors in the mazes of alleyways. "Where's the house of Maryam, daughter of Yehuda, the grocer, the wife of Raheem, the carpet man who has a shop by the Karim-khan Bazaar?" my grandmother asked. We were pointed to the direction of another alleyway but were soon lost again in the crossroads of narrow passes. Khanom-bozorg clutched the brass doorknob to another house, but before she could knock, the door opened. She gossiped with the women inside, then asked for directions. Alluding to the event that we were attending, the woman said, "Always good occasions."

My grandmother responded, "May happiness come your way too."

A little later, Khanom-bozorg stopped by a kiosk crowded with half-filled burlap bags of split yellow beans, short-grain rice, whole turmeric, and odds and ends of the household—charcoal, short home-made brooms, and knick-knacks that were jammed into a small corner of a wall. She asked the shopkeeper where Maryam lived. But she didn't leave without asking for the price of the dried limes and powdered sumac and complaining that they were too expensive. The sugar cone was getting heavier at each stop.

Finally, we were there. The house was like most homes in the *mahaleh*, with a small sturdy door opening to a narrow walkway that ended with another set of heavy doors. We entered the house through its courtyard paved with bricks and the usual little pool in the middle, now temporarily covered with a piece of plywood and a *kilim* on which the musicians were to perform later. Men were busy spreading worn-out Persian carpets on the floor of the yard. I imagined the wedding party, families sitting cross-legged on the carpets, the musicians playing Persian drums and violin, women ululating and singing wedding songs.

Like any traditional Iranian home, the living quarters surrounded the courtyard, each section having a basement, a first-floor living area, and an attic. When male members of the family married and had children, they would be entitled to a section if the house had enough rooms. Otherwise, they had to share the space with their parents and other siblings.

I followed my grandmother up the stairs and into a room crowded with women, and surrendered the sugar cone to a woman who seemed to be the bride's mother. We took off our shoes at the door and lined them up by the wall as the etiquette required. A few pillows were piled up on top of a blanket in the far corner of the room. I wondered if we there to watch someone sleep. Was that possible? I watched the women draped in color-ful *chadors,* covering their mouths with a fabric-wrapped hand when lis-tening and uncovering their lips when pouring out the words.

I stood on a chair by the exit, watching the women's backs. The mother of the bride entered holding her daughter's elbow, and walked through a path that the women opened for them. The bride had light cocoa skin with a nap of soft black hair on her upper lip and full, connected eyebrows; the *bandandaz* would surely take care of the facial hair. She was unadorned and natural in a modest dress. Her black shoulder-length hair barely moved as she walked. Her feet were bare like those of the rest of us. Her eyes, dark and shy, avoided eye-contact with the spectators. Without a covering, her hair and body were there for everyone to judge.

Women unveiled their mouths slightly and murmured to each other. My grandmother whispered to the woman next to her, "She is *najeeb,* chaste-looking."

The woman answered back, "Poor thing. She is so shy."

Khanom-bozorg added, "She is dark, but it's all right. She has 'salt,' she has charm."

The bride's mother helped her lean against the pillows. A person in the back of the room warned, "Cover the windows, cover the windows!"

But someone from the groom's family complained, "There isn't enough light."

A woman wearing a light brown *chador* with pink flowers opened the door a crack and ordered everyone to leave the yard. I couldn't see anything over the head of the women, so I bent down to look through their feet. Two women knelt by the young bride-to-be, took off her panties, spread her legs apart, and leaned down to examine her.

One plain dark-blue figure said, "Look, here it is."

The voices from the groom's side protested, "Where is it, where? We can't see anything."

Finally all the women managed to see whatever there was to see. They dressed the bride, who was shaking too hard to manage the job herself, and began to sing: "Kililili." Their ululating voices signaled the completion of the task. There was going to be a wedding. The courtyard filled again with men hurrying about. Someone walked in with trays of sour cherry *sharbat*. Everyone insisted that the bride should be first to drink.

The bride looked flushed and unsteady on her feet. Her mother consoled her, "Don't worry, dear. It's done!"

The sound of ululation in the small room was deafening. My grandmother pushed me to leave the room, congratulating the two families. "A good fortune," she blessed the bride.

Another woman added, "May she be blessed with wealth and happiness."

My grandmother and I left first since we were in the back, put our shoes on, and headed down the stairs. She asked others to point out the groom.

Covered in sweat, the groom was helping the other men set up the chairs. He looked old to me. Though he had covered the baldness on top of his head with a long strand of hair from the right side, it had moved to his forehead, leaving the bald spot bare. He had a big smile that showed small yellow teeth.

My grandmother blessed the groom, "Don't worry. Everything is fine. May you grow old together."

Another woman chimed in, "*Mazal tov*, congratulations! Next year may you have a son in your arms."

The groom blushed and bowed in a gesture of gratitude. I had never seen a man turn color in shyness. Maybe he was going to be a good husband, I thought. The two of us, short and tall, headed for home. I was content. I felt a deep love for my grandmother, who had shared her outing with me, although at the time I was not quite sure what it all meant. I was also pleased not to have the burden of the sugar cone. As we maneuvered our way through the busy alleyways, I felt tired, and a bit worried. The image of women gathered by the waterspouts and at the ceremony contrasted sharply with the picture of my mother's lonely figure at home—a picture I had successfully managed to forget for a while.

What about my mother? I thought. What about her?

## The Garden Wedding

As my mother despaired and retreated into deeper silences, I became even closer to my grandmother, learning from her, getting to know the world around me, escaping my mother's increasing gloom. That year, Khanombozorg was excited because my aunt Shekoofeh was engaged.

Shekoofeh had qualities that Iranian men favored: black hair that contrasted with her fair, clear skin, and a curvaceous body that was noticeable even underneath her modest clothing. She wore an air of optimism, smiled gently, and practiced lady-like manners. Being a good student, Shekoofeh cried and begged to be allowed to finish her last year of high school, but the decision was made for her.

My grandmother chose me to help her shop for the dowry. In the indoor bazaar, I held tight to a corner of her *chador,* not wanting to lose her among the masses of shoppers. My neck hurt from looking up at the vaulted bazaar, decorated with handmade bricks and colorful mosaics. Light glowed through windows beneath the ceiling. I kept bumping into people as I stretched my neck to see stalls filled with Persian carpets, Indian silk, tribal sheep-skin coats and hats. Burlap bags of spices, turmeric, saffron, cloves, and cardamom lined up beside bags of herbal teas.

On the first shopping day, my grandmother and I found our way to the silversmiths' market, looking for the best quality silver and craftsmanship at the lowest price. She inquired from a shopkeeper, "How much for a bride's package?"

As she bargained, I amused myself watching passersby. I joined a laughing crowd to see what was so funny. A mule had stuck its feet in the dirt floor of the bazaar and refused commands to move forward. The more the owner pulled on the noose, the harder he hit it with a stick, the more stubborn the mule became, leaning backward on his hind legs until its cargo of charcoal slipped and fell behind it. The owner screamed and gave the mule a good beating. The animal let go of its bowels on top of the coal. I was laughing with the rest of crowd when I felt a hand on my back,

*Maman, my sister Nahid, and me at my aunt's garden wedding.*

pulling on my sweater. Then I heard my grandmother, "You want to get lost? You want these men to kidnap you for slavery? Didn't I tell you not to wander off?" I was scared that she would report my behavior to my father, but she was preoccupied with other thoughts, grumbling, "Calling me a cheap Jew! The thief! *Najes* himself, calling *me* impure, he with *goh* on his underwear! He doesn't know how to wipe his own behind and calls *me* dirty."

Watching the stubborn mule, I had missed Khanom-bozorg's interaction with the silversmith. We went from one shop to another until she found a respectful person who offered the right price. I was amazed that my aunt's hairbrush, her wooden comb, and the pumice stone were to be encased in silver; I couldn't imagine such beauty. Perhaps being a bride was not such a bad thing after all.

When we returned home, the engagement was off. Shekoofeh had visited her fiancé's family and refused to marry a man who lived with his parents, brothers, and their families. My grandmother and father agreed with her. They didn't want her to have a situation similar to my mother's, I guess. And who could blame them? The shopping came to halt.

But the shopping and the frustration had taken a toll on my grandmother's health. Sleepless, she moaned and struggled to fill her lungs with air all night. My father took her to Tehran, visiting doctors and touring the city to improve my grandmother's anxiety-related attacks.

At this time, my mother's family had moved to the capital, which was much closer to Shiraz than her hometown of Hamedan. Still, my mother had not seen her family for a long time and would have loved to accompany my father and grandmother to Tehran to visit her parents and brothers. Instead, she stayed behind to take care of me, my infant sister Nahid, and the aunts and uncles who lived with us. She slammed the pots as she washed them; she didn't bother to rinse the clothes well before throwing them on the laundry line; she burned the shirts under the charcoal iron as she sobbed, homesick.

To make matters worse, once in a while she received a letter from my father, who wrote on behalf of my grandmother to remind her of her duties: "Don't forget to take food to Bibi." Over and over, my grandmother ordered Maman to take care of my great-grandmother.

Grumbling, my mother sent me to deliver the bundles of food to my great-grandmother, although I was barely six. I hated passing through the narrow unpaved mazes of alleys lined with small stalls, jostled by shoppers with woven plastic bags filled with vegetables, prostitutes with bright red mouths, villagers, peddlers following watermelon-loaded mules, and rarely a familiar face. The crowd jammed the space between the tall walls and bumped and stared at me as I tried to find a landmark leading to the small door of Bibi's house.

That was a period of hardship and absolute loneliness for my mother. Morad showed his resentment at having to work alone to support the family by giving extra orders to my mother. Overwhelmed with two young children, Maman envied her sisters-in-law who used school work as an excuse not to help her. When my father and grandmother returned with gifts of beautiful dresses for both Shekoofeh and Fereshteh, but nothing for my mother, she despaired.

Upon their return, the elders from the suitor's family, the *khastegars*, came often to talk with them. Each time, they trotted to our common room and sat cross-legged, leaning their backs against large pillows. My mother ran out to the bakery for cookies, and I served them tea and sugar cubes.

As the negotiations continued, Shekoofeh hoped that with the delays she could still graduate from high school, but the principal found out about her engagement and would not allow her back. Once a woman came in close proximity to a man, she already knew too much and could corrupt the innocent virgins. There were rumors that the groom's family had alerted the school when the engagement was broken off in order to press for reconciliation when school was no longer an option.

Finally, both families agreed that although it was impossible for She-koofeh to have a separate house, the groom would create a separate space for his bride by adding a bathroom and a kitchen on the second floor of the house that he shared with his mother and siblings. My grandmother resumed her shopping to assemble a dowry.

The banging of metal against metal could be heard long before we entered the coppersmiths' bazaar. Far from the main market place, this section lacked the protection of a roof and the beauty of handmade tiles and arched doorways. It was the most chaotic section of the bazaar. Donkeys carried loads of metal, fabric, or fruit through the crowd of shoppers and workers, littering the place with their droppings, which accumulated until the city workers cleaned the ground at the end of the day.

I was surprised to see so many teenagers kneeling on the dirt floor hammering at utensils. Apprenticeship was their schooling, and I was frightened by such a fate. I kept away from them, as if their future could rub off on me and leave a residue of misfortune and hopelessness. Khanom-bozorg found the best price for the pots that we had brought from our home and traded them for new ones to go with the bride to her home. Hanging onto the corner of her *chador*, I turned my head and watched the boys hammering as we walked away.

Since we had traded away our nicest pots, we had to use cheaper ones at home ourselves. Years later, when I was browsing in an antique shop in New York City, I would realize what treasures we had given away. That day, however, I was merely enjoying the sights, sounds, and smells of various parts of the market.

Back in the main section, we saw a group of Ghashghai women, a nomadic tribe outside Shiraz. They were known to be tough women, who could move herds of sheep over the mountains on horseback, a rifle on one shoulder and a baby on the other. I had mostly known women who seemed powerless and defeated by life. I looked at these nomadic women in awe. They walked tall and regally, their strong presence claiming the ownership of the space they occupied. Strong, beautiful, and feminine, they wore many layers of long puffy skirts in colors of the desert, of the mineral deposits of the mountains surrounding our city: rust, purple, yellow, maroon. Silk scarves, bordered with gold coins, covered their raven hair and shoulders; peacock-colored sashes wrapped around their foreheads and tied loosely in the back of their necks. The group passed us, creating music with the jingle of their gold bangles and anklets. Their many rustling skirts gently stirred the spiced air of the bazaar.

Finally, the shopping was done. The bride's quilts were specially designed and handmade with beautiful geometric stitching, filled with clean whipped cotton, and covered with blue satin. Pots and pans gleamed; the silver-covered toiletries were delicate and regal; and new clothes, trimmed with ribbons, were ready for everyone, including me.

I watched with excitement as a few strong men stopped by the house, packed and loaded the dowry on top of their heads, and paraded them down the street to the groom's family. In return, many large trays of sweets arrived carefully balanced on the heads of the baker's apprentices. Delicate chickpea cookies shaped like clover leaves, puff pastry bows, raisin cookies, and *bamieh* were all arranged patiently and artistically in gigantic pyramids. The trays were marched through the streets so that everyone could admire the generosity of the groom's family.

Shekoofeh's wedding was the first one in the family since my grandfather had passed away. My grandmother decided that a garden wedding would be best since our house in the ghetto was too modest for such an auspicious ceremony.

My father hired a large truck with a canvas-covered back to take the fruit, vegetables, and meat to a garden outside town. Neighbors helped load Persian carpets and *kilims*, some ours and some borrowed; then they put me in the back to "be a big girl" and watch the food. I sat there in my pretty white dress, my baby sister Nahid on my lap. I arranged her dress around her hip to hide the long incision that had drained an infection after her birth. My mother gave me two bottles and asked me tend to her. I wasn't sure if I was really being a big girl or if they wanted to get rid of me. Partly, I was sad to leave all the excitement at home; yet I was delighted to be the first one at the garden to watch the wedding preparations.

On the dusty, unpaved road, my sister cried nonstop. I fed her one bottle to quiet her despite orders from my mother to save the milk for later. Then the other bottle fell over and the milk splattered all over the place. I didn't know if I needed to be more anxious about losing the baby food or for spilling milk over food designated "meat," which had to be separated from dairy. When my mother finally arrived, I tossed her the baby and the empty bottles and left quickly before she could scold me.

I went snooping around to see what all the excitement was about. There were huge pots set up on top of makeshift charcoal-burning stoves to prepare the rice and stews. The aroma of chopped dill, coriander, and fenugreek mixed with the scent of chickens braised with caramelized onions and turmeric. A cook with stubble and a friendly face was alternating beef and onions on a skewer. Noticing me, he gave me an apple and shooed me away. Fruit trees and grapevines shaded the Persian carpets spread by a stream. The guests leaned against large pillows; a few recited poetry or harmonized with the musicians.

My aunt finally arrived with her future husband, passing between two rows of friends and family. Men clapped. A few women cupped their hands over their mouths, rolled their tongues and ululated, when the others sang wedding songs.

> We have come to take the bride away and isn't she beautiful!
> Are the alleyways narrow? Yes indeed!
> Is the bride beautiful? Yes indeed!
> Don't touch her hair for it is braided with pearls, yes indeed!

Actually, my aunt's hair was decorated not with pearls but with white feathers shaped into a halo. Her white silk bridal gown shimmered in the glow of sun filtering through the trees in the garden. Shekoofeh's eyebrows were tweezed into thin fashionable lines, and she wore makeup for the first time. Her provocative bright red lipstick contrasted with her demure body language—head slightly bowed in shyness, eyes lowered in virginal modesty.

When she reached the carpeted area, her sister Fereshteh helped her to sit on a Persian carpet, and fluffed her skirt around her for a picture. She was a romantic sight, bringing the wedding song to life. She sat there most of the day, looking pretty and finally let me touch her dress and feathers.

At first, she refused every food offering, afraid that even a taste would smudge her lip color. Aunt Fereshteh asked me to help the bride with her meal. Every time Shekoofeh opened her mouth for a spoonful of rice, I giggled, feeling like a mother bird feeding a chick in her nest. When she was finished, I picked at the leftovers and looked for something else to do.

Two belly dancers with colorful dresses entertained the guests. They changed behind a makeshift curtain sheltered between the trees. Fascinated by their costumes, I sneaked behind the curtains to watch them change, and was surprised to find out that I wasn't the only one interested. A dancer pushed me out, along with male guests who had had too much *aragh* with their kabobs.

My mother found me and told me to join a group of women who were eating and smoking a waterpipe. She put a plate of chicken, rice, and fava beans in front of me. As I nibbled, I scanned the area for action.

Someone shouted for towels to be sent to the far side of the gardens. Apparently a few men, including my father, had decided to refresh themselves in a water hole. I jumped up and volunteered. I would have liked the women to have a turn as well, but that wasn't modest. I lingered to watch the men exit the water in their wet underwear. They got out one after another to jump back into the shallow water again. They all looked down at themselves first, then at me with a smile, and I smiled back. My father called my mother, who dragged me away.

Eventually, it was dusk and the party had to end. My father, acting as his sister's guardian, wrapped a piece of silk cloth around her waist, symbolically giving her away. They hugged tearfully. The groom took away my aunt in a black Mercedes decorated with flowers. My grandmother and aunts followed them, singing and clapping, tears streaming down their faces.

The musicians and dancers packed and left. The carpets were rolled and loaded again onto the truck. I climbed in there and fell asleep, dreaming of white satin and feathers, the soft rhythm of Persian music, and my aunts singing *vasoonak*.

My grumbling stomach woke me up from my dreams on the way

home, a reminder that I had been too busy with curiosity to make time for food. The leftovers had been given to the workers. There would be no food at home. After such a bountiful day filled with food, fun, and beauty, I was starving. I looked at my mother sitting across from me with the baby at her breast, a vacant look in her eyes. Her hunger differed from mine.

## A Divorce in the Family

Little pieces of gloom lodged inside my mother like prickly thorns flown in the wind from the desert surrounding our city. The happiness of Shekoofeh's lavish wedding worsened Maman's mental state. She mumbled about her own wedding once in a while when she thought no one was around.

A widowed woman, Anbari, and her daughter came to our house once a week to help with the time-consuming, back-breaking job of washing the clothes. They carried water from the kitchen across the yard to the cooler basement, filled the basins, and soaked the dirtier pieces in the warm, soapy water. They set up laundry lines next to the summer platform by the musk rose tree.

Khanom-bozorg had my mother sit at the basin with the laundry women, and I helped with carrying and hanging the clothes. My grandmother brought in two organza dresses belonging to my aunts Fereshteh and Shekoofeh, the same dresses that were gifts from Tehran. I don't remember why Shekoofeh's dress was at our house since she was already married. Homesick, she visited often, and my grandmother was probably trying to ease her load. She told my mother to wash them first, separately, and with more care.

The washer-woman stared at the dresses and, when my grandmother was gone, asked my mother, "Ma'am, which one is yours?"

"Neither one," Maman sighed. "I don't have any dresses like those. They both belong to my sisters-in-law."

There was a twinkle of understanding in the washer-woman's eyes. A moment of uncomfortable silence marked the unspoken reality that a certain boundary had been crossed. Sharing any grief with these strangers, who went from home to home and gossiped, could taint the family myth of tranquility and shared love. The washer-women, notorious for their gossiping, had a precious piece of information that they could expand and talk about at various homes in the neighborhood. My mother knew that she was responsible for that opening, for showing her hurt, for having to care for clothes that she could not herself afford; and I, even as a child, recognized the problem. All day I thought about what it meant.

That night, the women gathered in a room on the second floor that served as a living room, dining room, and bedroom for my grandmother, aunt, and uncle Morad. Waiting for the men to return from work, Khanom-bozorg put a few little potatoes under the ashes of the coals in the charcoal brazier. My mouth watered. Maybe I thought that I could get one as a reward without begging. Maybe I wanted to get at my mother. I don't know why, but the treacherous words just spilled out of me: "You know what Maman said to the washer-woman today, Khanom-bozorg?"

She smiled at me with both her mouth and eyes. "What? What did she say?"

My mother's face had a frightened look. She stopped chopping the vegetables and pointed the wide knife toward me. "Stop it," she said, "I didn't say anything."

My grandmother interfered. "Let her talk."

"Maman said you buy pretty dresses for my aunts and not for her." My grandmother gave me a potato. I gobbled it up, slightly burned outside, hot and smoky inside, the way I liked it. I couldn't look at my mother.

"Go to bed," Maman ordered.

I refused. I was scared to go across the open hallway to my parents' room to sleep. My baby sister was already asleep there, but she couldn't keep the night demons away from me.

"I want to wait for Baba," I said.

Maman jumped up, waving the knife at me, wanting to hit me with its broad side. I screamed.

"Let her be," my grandmother said, and she told me to sleep in the bed set up for her, my aunt, and my uncle on the floor. I couldn't go to sleep with my mother in the room still using the knife, but I was afraid that if I got up I would anger her further. I finally drifted into a fitful sleep filled with nightmares. My father held my baby sister in my dreams the way he prepared chickens for slaughtering. He jerked Nahid's arms back with one hand, grabbed her hair and pulled her head back, and slashed her throat. I stood there in this hallucination and watched with excitement, not caring about my sister with her big, black eyes.

I woke up tired the next morning, and went looking for my grand-mother to interpret my dream, to tell me that it was nothing. There was no one in the room. I opened the door and went down the stone steps to the backyard. I saw my mother at the platform standing with her head down. My father stood with his hands on his waist, chewing his mustache, his face red from anger. My aunts, grandmother, and uncles were there too. I had completely forgotten about the troubles the night before and in-nocently asked what was going on. My father told me to shut up and sit in the corner because the whole thing was my fault. Morad looked at me and smirked. I obeyed.

Baba shouted for someone to summon his half-brother Mashalah. Be-fore my grandfather died, he divided his community responsibilities among his two older sons from his two marriages. My father was in charge of *shekhitah,* the ritual slaughtering which he hated, and Mashalah inherited the performance of *brit-milah,* the circumcision, as well as the weddings and the divorces. He had been summoned once before to Hamedan, my mother's town, to wed them. This time, he was to perform their divorce ceremony.

My father wore his pajama bottoms, white undershirt, and plastic flip-flops. "I am sending her back to Hemedoon." He used the colloquial word for my mother's city of birth, pacing back and forth, waving his right hand. "I don't want a *zaifeh* who disrespects my mother and sisters."

Although the insult was addressed to my mother, I felt like a *zaifeh,* the weak one, myself. At the same time, I was puzzled that my mother was being sent to Hamedan although her parents had moved to Tehran. Later I understood that calling Hamedan my mother's hometown was another way of putting her down as someone unsophisticated, a villager. To ac-knowledge that her family lived in Tehran, the capital of the country, would have given her an upper hand, in a subtle way only Iranians understand.

I stood in the corner and for the first time really looked at my mother. She almost had a smile on her face. She could finally leave this hellhole that had never become her home. But inside me, a voice called, "What about me?" I would have to take care of my sister, to take over all that was her responsibility. If she left, however, I could understand and even forgive her. And who would forgive me? I was the one to blame, guilty of *veragi,* talk-ing too much with a biting and hurtful tongue.

Maman turned her head slowly toward me and returned my gaze. Her smile disappeared, and for the first time she meekly said something in her defense, trying to call the entire thing a misunderstanding. Her apology diffused the tense skirmish. My father yelled at her a few more times, but the rest of the family calmed him down.

I soon realized that the entire show was meant to humiliate my mother and that my father never seriously planned to divorce her. He wouldn't find another wife willing to take care of his mother and siblings. My father was stuck with my mother. He was stuck with us, our mother's children, and girls for that matter: one obstreperous and the other with a severe limp, both imperfect specimens in Iranian eyes.

*Chapter Three*

# MY EDUCATION

*Private Lessons: Fear*

My daughters have a hard time reading my childhood stories. They are so dark. Something good must have happened, they say. I must have forgotten about the good parts. Life in a Jewish ghetto in a small Iranian town is inconceivable to young American minds.

Dark nights, absolute silence, waiting anxiously for my father to come home dominated my earliest memories. Before dusk, Baba sent home an apprentice to pick up a snack of flat bread, soft cheeses, walnuts, and a pot of tea for him and his brother Morad to eat at their shop. In the Iranian tradition, dinners were always served between nine and ten. The women, my mother, my grandmother, and my aunts, sat by a basket filled with torn socks, mending and patching them, as they waited for the men. On winter nights, the water boiled on top of a samovar, little potatoes roasted under the hot ashes in a *manghal*, a fish stew simmered slowly on top of a space heater in the common room. Only when my father and uncle arrived would my grandmother add the last ingredient, a beaten egg, for our late-night dinner.

In the quiet, without the men, every noise seemed exaggerated. As the wind went through the orange trees, the women sat straight. One invariably screamed *ayy* in fright. Was there anyone in the yard? Did we have an intruder? Were the main doors locked well enough? On these fear-filled nights, I begged my mother not to make me sleep in my parents' room across the open hallway. I wanted to sleep in the common room with my head on my mother's lap, hearing the hum of women's conversations. I usually lost the battle. Many nights, my grandmother lay next to me, and

I held her long braid, caressing it to ensure that she would not go away. If the adults worried even when they had each other for support, I wasn't about to tackle the danger by myself in a separate room. If I woke up alone, I comforted myself by rubbing my own braids, pretending they were my grandmother's. Mostly I screamed until my mother took me back to the common room to sleep on the carpet next to the women.

I lay there half asleep, half awake, since one had to be on guard perpetually. In the blurred zones between dreaming and reality, I heard my grandmother worry about the men. What if someone followed them and stabbed them in the dark alleyway? What if they were robbed and killed at their shop as they worked with the gold? What if the thieves knew there were only women at home and would rob the pots and pans from the kitchen on the other side of the house, close to the front door? What if intruders were more daring and attacked the women? Who would hear us over the tall walls separating us from the neighbors?

My grandmother added to the darkness of the night by telling us horror stories of *jude-koshi,* the killing of the Jews. On winter nights, as she roasted little potatoes under the hot ashes in the brazier, as we all huddled under a blanket, as the other women knitted and mended, my grandmother taught us history.

The ruling power rarely interfered, my grandmother emphasized as she added more charcoal to the samovar. When my father was my age, the plan of an attack on the Jews was drawn by the governor himself. The entire horror was set in motion by an event just like this, "warming the water for a cup of tea," my grandmother whispered. Mr. Ghavam visited a Jewish merchant's home to buy jewelry for his daughter's wedding. The wife of the jeweler showed her appreciation by burning *toman* bills in the samovar to warm up the water for tea. Ghavam's wife was incensed; a Jew had shamed them by her show of wealth. These low-lives thought themselves richer than the governor of the state of Fars. Knowing that religious fanatics believed that the Jews did not have the right to material goods, he sanctioned them to take away what was rightfully theirs. Pretending to protect the Jews, Ghavam's soldiers stood on the connected flat roofs of the ghetto, eliminating the only escape route. As the hordes of people poured through the homes, the first to vandalize and rob were the soldiers. The Jewish community lost everything: jewelry, kitchen utensils, carpets—my grandmother looked at me—and even young girls.

After many of these dark, fear-filled nights, my father and uncle came home one sunny afternoon for lunch with a brown puppy. I put the puppy on my lap and rubbed its back, but my father sternly told me not to touch it. He wanted to raise it as a guard dog, not a pet.

The two men played rough games with the dog and trained him to bark at anyone but them. Before the dog was fully grown, we feared its ferociousness. One of the men stopped by the house and unfastened the dog's leash every day at dusk. We were imprisoned in our living quarters until the next morning, when the men tied him up again before leaving for work. The dog barked at every noise; he bared his teeth, foam covering his mouth, as we passed him during the day. A few times he freed himself and terrorized us to the point that we had to hide in a basement room until my father and uncle came home for lunch. As the problem grew, the women decided that they would rather fear the thieves. The men released the dog in the outskirts of a faraway village.

Even now, if I see a dog blocks away, the palms of my hands sweat.

Fear permeated our lives. I didn't know then that the frequent attacks on the *mahaleh* had not only instilled terror in my grandmother's generation and those before them who had witnessed such rampages, but also on those of us who heard the horror stories connected with the raids.

During the Moslem holy month of Moharam, my family was especially careful. "Don't wear colorful clothes," my grandmother reminded us. It was a month of mourning, of wearing black. None of us wanted to provoke hostility by any implications of happiness. The men came home early every night, bringing their work home if they could, although there was not much business at such times, since most of their customers were Moslems preoccupied with their rituals of grief.

Although fearful, we were also curious, and even entertained by the parade of mourners. "They are coming! They are coming," some neighborhood child would call out, running ahead to inform us of the procession. All activities stopped. The herbs were put under a colander, the meat was thrown on a slab of ice, and the rice was put away hastily. I slipped on my rubber-tire flip-flops like everyone else; my mother, grandmother, and aunts grabbed their *chadors*. I was only six and did not need a full body covering; instead, I wore a kerchief for modesty. We rushed out through the heavy doors to the dirt-covered alleyway, ran under the arched entrance of the *mahaleh,* and out to the large paved sidewalk of Moshir Fatemi Street. Women in black *chadors* and shopkeepers in dark attire lined up solemnly on the sidewalk by the narrow watercourse that separated us from the marchers.

The *muezzin* could be seen in the distance, standing on top of the minaret covered with decorative blue tiles, a mix of delicate Persian floral motifs and bold Koranic verses. Its tall cylindrical shape reached out to the sky, an arm straining to bring the holiness of Allah's spirit to Earth. Cupping his hands around both ears in concentration, the *muezzin* finished the noon prayers: *Allah o akbar,* God is great; *Ashhado Allah va la Allah,* I testify that there is no God but Allah. His haunting voice traveled through the empty street, filling hearts with the deep sadness of the day. As his prayers came to an end, men poured out of the Great Mosque chanting from the Koran.

Banners were carried in front of the procession by two young men with stubby beards, dressed in mourning clothes. First came the black banners, setting the mood of the day, with the familiar Arabic words written in contrasting white: *Qulou: laillaha illa Allah ve Mohammed rasoul Allah,* people proclaim that there is no God but Allah and that Mohammed is his messenger. A loud cry escaped from the spectators: *Allah o akbar!*

Red banners, for the blood of martyrs, were displayed next by the marchers. The green ones, symbolizing life, bore their names: Hossein, his family, his followers, all seventy men, women, and children, who were slain so brutally in the desert of Karbala while thirsting for water. A banner of plain white fabric, devoid of any lettering, was marched by us. It was also in the color of death, the color of a shroud.

The emblems came next, decorated with tassels in deep greens of the fields and blues of the oceans, which are the sources of life. Some were embossed with the word *ALLAH,* some with the names of the Imams. Large poles draped with green silk fabric and decorated with jewels bore the metal imprint of Fatimeh's hand (the Prophet's daughter). Two solemn-looking men, unshaven like the rest in a sign of mourning, held tight to the corners of a large painting and took small deliberate steps.

From the heavily decorated and draped picture frame, the serious eyes of Imam Ali, the most revered Shi'ite leader, looked over the crowd of mourners in every corner. He was wearing an impressive Arab garment, a black caftan, on top of a white shirt and a long black head piece that covered his hair and draped over his shoulders. The painted image showed the Imam's body reposed in a heavy wooden chair, strong and determined. A wide curved sword rested on his lap, dripping blood! I shivered in fear that it was the blood of the Jews, that it could have been my blood.

A sacred palanquin decorated with flowers and colorful fabric was carried on the shoulders of four men. On each side of the symbolic coffin, unshaven men carried framed pictures of the martyrs. A lone mourner struck brass cymbals one against another, creating a rhythm for the steady footsteps.

The bravest were in front. Shirtless, they displayed bold chests. Each wore a wrap-around sash, or a loose pair of black cotton pants. The scant clothing gave them little protection from the brutal midday sun. Right feet came down in unison on the first beat of the cymbals. The marchers flung both hands automatically over their left shoulders, clutching in both hands wooden rods attached to a bundle of heavy chains. Bloodied metal rested on tender skin for a moment. The metallic beat announced their next move: left feet in front, the chains going over the right shoulders to land on bare backs. Their bare feet contracted in agony as they touched the hot, paved road. They were the strongest believers. The blood dripping from self-inflicted dagger wounds on their foreheads told of their unrelenting commitment.

Beautiful horses were displayed as though ready for war; sharp swords and daggers hung from their sides. White doves dipped in blood rode on the back of the war horses in place of the soldiers who never had a chance to fight.

The *sineh-zans* came next. With each beat of the cymbal, they raised both hands, to chest level, then above their heads, building a momentum that ended with their open palms slamming on their chests with a thunderous sound. Women, watching tearfully, hit their chests with their fists or their heads with the palm of both hands while moaning.

Younger men dressed fully in black entered the arena with lighter instruments, followed by teenaged boys who beat themselves with only two or three chains. "Hossein is dead! Hassan is dead!" The flagellants chanted in unison as they carried their beaten bodies from the great mosque to the Shah Cheragh shrine.

Young girls wrapped tightly in black *chadors* were the only females allowed to mingle with the marchers. They represented innocence, purity, and compassion. The girls carried heavy containers of water and metal cups on their backs. They offered it to the soldiers of God, suffering in the unbearable heat, in contrast to the evil army that had allowed the holy men of Karbalah to die of thirst.

This religious enactment always fascinated me and everyone else in the ghetto. We were allowed to stand next to the Moslem spectators to watch the ceremony respectfully. Day after day, for the first ten days of Moharam, mourners cleansed their souls of evil by self-flagellation, acts of charity, and a state of constant mourning. Every day, I watched the parade in absolute awe, trying to understand all the implications of the rituals, enacted so fervently.

The history of Shirazi Jews had not been documented then. When I was a child, many of us were still lost in ignorance and illiteracy. Elders of the community, their stories frightening, were our only source of information and historical continuity. Again and again across many generations, the Moslem clerics had initiated attacks on the Jews as holy wars. The ghetto had been decimated time after time.

Our elders retold the stories of horror, remembering times when pogroms had been carried on through the ghetto. Lost in their deep sorrows, highly emotional Moslem men recreated in the Jewish ghettos the story of a war lost long ago. Wanting to avenge the dead, the mourners carried on a *jihad*, a holy war, against the Jews, to imitate Imam Ali who had shed blood for the advancement of Islam. The killing, they believed, would bring personal salvation and global peace. It would expedite the resurrection of the messiah, the twelfth Imam, who would reappear when all nations accepted Allah as the only God and Mohammed as the final prophet to replace all before him.

Although the horrific tales were etched on my memory, I still needed to believe in the goodness of the people living side by side with us. Somehow I wanted to believe that if I knew them better the rumors would prove false. I begged my parents to allow me to watch the parade on the night of Ashura, the last night of the mourning period. I had heard much about this night through rumors from those who had dared to be present at the ceremony. Mostly, we cowered in our homes, doors locked, never answering a knock, jumping anxiously at the slightest noise.

Only once, when I was six years old, did I have the chance to venture out on this most solemn night. The men were away working. We, women and children, were too afraid to stay at home by ourselves. Before dark that day, my grandmother, my mother, my unmarried aunt, and I left our house, which was too close to the parade route, for Aunt Shams's house. She lived deeper in the maze of alleyways in the *mahaleh* with her husband's extended family.

That night we were all bolder. Maybe the sheer number of women together gave us courage. My aunt and her sisters-in-law gave everyone black *chadors* to wear. There was one folded in half for me. We walked through the dark alleyways to another main gate, trying to look inconspicuous, walking solemnly like Moslem women.

The orders were not to talk at all. The hint of a Jewish accent could bring trouble. Trying to act invisible, the older women directed us to a large tree close to a gate so small that even I had to bend down to exit the ghetto. The tree provided a sense of security, allowing us to huddle against it and feel less noticeable. All this preparation and the anticipation of a potentially dangerous event caused my heart to pump blood faster even before the march started.

The total darkness of the street was eerie. A few street lamps usually broke the blackness with their yellowish glow, but on that night these were turned off. Women's black *chadors*, and the men's dark clothing made the darkness even deeper. The silence of hundreds gathered on the parade route added to the blackness of the night.

The flickering of dim lights in the distance announced the approach of the parade. Soon hundreds of men, their faces invisible in the darkness and their battered bodies wrapped in white burial shrouds, moved down the street. It was a march of the living dead. They shuffled their way to the tomb of the prophet looking for victims' body parts to take for Imam Zaman, the Imam of the "time to come." On the Day of Judgment, as it was told, limbs would come together to return the righteous men to the Garden of Eden. The symbolic act of gathering the bloodied body parts was to remind God of the sacrifice of the best, of the holiest. In return, God would resurrect the invisible Imam through whom man himself would be returned to life.

The human shrouds stretched in groups of twenty or more across the wide street, walking slowly, chanting Arabic verses from the Koran, reciting melancholy Persian poetry, announcing the night of Ashura in a haunting murmur. They carried long candles that slowly melted, giving little light. In the total darkness, the two sources of light became one; the

Earth joined the heavens. The twinkle of the small flames connected the street with the black sky of Shiraz, covered with stars.

As the last of the dead passed, our small group came to life. Moving away from the tree, we found our way to the small gate, bent down one by one, and merged with the greater darkness of the *mahaleh.*

## A Restless Year

That grim darkness of the *mahaleh,* not just of fearful nights but of poverty, disease and illiteracy, made an environment from which my father wished to free his children. He desperately wanted to prevent us from adopting the dialect, the accent, and the body language of our denigrated people, to let us grow up not in dirt alleyways but beside tree-lined avenues.

He supported his two brothers, who studied medicine in Tehran, and was proud of them as if they were his own children. They fulfilled his own dreams of learning a trade that could not be taken away, an accomplishment that neither I nor my siblings would ever match. Consequently, we grew up in constant need of his approval that never came, and, in the shadow of the ideal uncles, we struggled for love and approval that rarely materialized.

During my childhood, the visits of these beloved uncles created excitement in our monotonous lives. At the end of one spring term, they arrived from Tehran with special gifts for us: a box of pastel-color toothbrushes, and tubes of what I then learned to be toothpaste. I brushed and brushed my teeth with the minty paste, then I ran around with my mouth wide open to feel the rush of air against its coolness.

They also brought me a fancy white dress with wide ruffled straps, a most beautiful dress, perfect for my first-grade pictures. I couldn't wait. Aunt Fereshteh trimmed my bangs to get them out of my eyes, and curled my hair. I felt like an *aroosak,* a little bride, a Persian doll. I ran down the street to my father's shop, right next to the photography studio. I fluffed up the ruffles around the skirt, shook my hair to feel the long curls, and wished my aunt had not wiped the lipstick off my mouth. I felt as if I were a flower girl at Queen Farah's wedding to the Shah.

My father was melting bits of gold with a jeweler's torch to fuse a rose-shaped ornament on a bracelet. He looked up from underneath his metal face-shield with a look of surprise. "I can't believe your mother sent you out looking like this," he said. "Who saw you? Anyone you recognized?

*My first-grade picture.*

What will the community say about my daughter prancing around immodestly? Go home!"

I turned my back to leave, biting my lower lip, swallowing hard the lump in the back of my throat.

"No, wait," my father said. He removed his apron, turned off the jeweler's torch, hid the gold in a drawer underneath his bench, and asked my uncle to watch over the shop.

I tried to straighten my hair, feeling naked. The apprentices stared at me from behind the glass divider and smiled. I didn't like their smiles or my uncle's.

Baba put his jacket over my shoulders, chaperoned me home, and waited for me to wet my hair.

My mother giggled when she saw us. "I didn't think he would like that," she told me. "Not my fault," she told Baba. "Your sister did it."

I thought she was happy that my aunt's work had been for nothing. I kept the dress on since it was the only nice garment I had, and walked back to the studio with my father, this time conscious of people's looks and whispers, wondering if it was about me.

At the studio, I climbed on a high stool, crossed my ankles, and held the corners of the dress as I was told. The photographer's greasy head disappeared underneath the black skirt of the camera. I looked at the glass lens in the darkness, trying to sit up straight.

No one said, "Smile!"

A few months later, as I was passing by the photographer's studio, I saw my picture blown up to a poster size, hanged from a metal frame over the sidewalk for everyone to see. The black and white picture was retouched with shades of pink. There I was with my hair severely pulled back, zigzag bangs, where my aunt's scissors had slipped, and a very serious look. I was proud of it every time I passed by. My father too enjoyed the picture, even though the photographer had not asked his permission to display it. I enclosed the picture with the first-grade application forms at age six.

Because Mehr-ayeen was a snobby school that rejected most Jewish kids, our family and friends tried to discourage my father from applying. Although it was a public school, the principal feared that its proximity to the *mahaleh* would entice too many Jews; and, if accepted, they would tarnish its image as an elite institution.

The day Baba took me for a first-grade interview felt like Rosh Hashanah. I watched my father shave the stubble on his face and the bushy hair under his armpits, wash his neck and behind his ears. He put a piece of cloth on the tip of a toothpick and scraped the wax from inside his ears. He dressed in his dark brown Shabbat suit and polished shoes. Then he brushed back his newly cut hair, and I thought he was the most handsome father.

My mother gave me a sponge bath in the yard and braided my hair tight in the back. She cut my nails and checked them for cleanliness and made sure I was wearing clean socks and underwear. I put on my fancy dress with a shawl for modesty.

My mother's longing eyes followed us as we left without her. My father walked tall and erect. His mustache twitched as he bit his upper lip, trying to control his facial muscles that slipped into a smile.

I was torn between having to skip to keep up with his long strides or taking bigger steps.

"Act with modesty," he scolded. "It's improper to run like a farmer's girl after chickens."

I obeyed, taking little steps, but ran every few minutes to catch up. I was as excited as he was.

We crossed Moshir Fatemi Street, a newly constructed street that ran like an arrow through the heart of the *mahaleh,* dividing it in half. The construction had been costly and labor intensive. Since the Jewish families refused to drink from the city water running through ditches, they each had a well in their homes. While destroying the Jewish houses to make room for the modern road, the engineers faced the nightmare of filling the sinking holes where the wells had existed for hundreds of years. This unexpected obstacle added to the cost of the construction immensely, infuriating the workers who thought it a Jewish sabotage. At the same time, the project angered the homeowners, who were not adequately compensated. The Jewish community felt exposed and vulnerable as the ghetto was divided by a major thoroughfare, and was no longer within a common walled-in perimeter.

The new street, one of the very first paved roads in Shiraz, was jammed not only with cars and taxis but also with mules carrying food and spices and pedestrians trying to avoid bumping into each other. I could not possibly cross the chaotic street safely by myself.

My father and I finally approached the iron gates of the school. As we waited for permission from two gendarmes to enter and approach the office, I kept busy watching the activities in a small quilt workshop nearby. Two workers in loose pajamas bottoms and once-white undershirts rested their backs against the walls of the shop as they beat cotton, *boing, boing,* with a harp-shaped gadget. A cloud of cotton dust circulated in the dark shop as two other men on their hands and knees captured the cotton in a blue satin casing with large needles and rapidly quilted flowers and geometric designs onto its shimmering surface. I didn't see the guards coming back to let us in.

My father grabbed my arms. "You're covered in dust! Look at you!" He brushed my clothes with his handkerchief.

We went through the large doors. I stopped in the walled-in yard to look at the playground, the classrooms surrounding the courtyard, two stories of brick and glass. It was so big, so clean. We climbed the stairs to the office.

The principal was too busy to meet with us, a woman behind a small desk announced. She wore her hair in a low ponytail. The corner of her lips moved downward as if she had swallowed something rotten. She continued reading the stacks of paper on her desk without looking at us. I watched my father lose a few centimeters in height, but he did not acquiesce. He didn't seem to be surprised at the unfriendly reception. This was a country of haggling and bargaining, in which my father was a master.

"Let me visit Mr. Principal, for just a few minutes," he said with a bow and much humility. "I took the morning off, and the child's heart will be broken. I beg respectfully." He bowed again.

"Let's go, Baba," I begged. "I will go somewhere else. It's okay."

"Don't act like a stupid donkey," he whispered.

We waited by the door until the principal left his office. My father jumped, bowed in front of him again, and, holding his two hands together in respect, begged for a minute of his time.

The principal looked at us with a sigh of resignation. He was shorter than my father but looked tall. He pointed his finger at me. "She is too young." He turned to leave.

My father followed him, waving my birth certificate. "But she is six years old. I was told by your secretary that she had to be six. She *is* six years old."

"No room this year. We're full. Why don't you sign her up at the Jewish school? She'll be more comfortable there with your own people." He threw the words at us in a rapid blast uncharacteristic of proper Iranian behavior that demanded deliberate speech.

"No," my father said. "We are closer to Mehr-ayeen, and this is where I want her to study."

The principal stopped by the doorway, sighed again, and shook his head. He adjusted his tie and coat, looked straight at my father, and said, "Come back next year. We're full for now." He took a side glance at me and walked away.

My father didn't pursue him. "His father is a dirty dog," he spat. "A true Moslem would not do this, breaking the child's heart."

That was the last time I wore my nice dress. It was too fancy for everyday use; then I outgrew it.

The year I had to wait for my acceptance to the first grade was the longest year of my life. There was nothing fun to do. Paper and pencils were items of luxury, books nonexistent. I helped sweep the floors, clean the rice, wash the clothes, and all the other boring chores, which I hated and tried to escape as much as I could. That year, my lessons were of life, my teachers the people around me.

My mother was busy with my baby sister, whose severe infection kept her in the hospital more often than at home. Maman often sent me to my father's shop to get me out of her hair. I loved going there to watch my father and uncle Morad thread little pearls on gold strings and sew them on wide bracelets in the shape of roses. I didn't know then that their art would show up in museums during my adult life. I didn't know that there would come a time when I longed for a small piece of the jewelry I watched my father create.

In the back workshop, I watched three young men, my father's apprentices, polish silver platters and goblets for the customers. They enjoyed having me there, took turns putting me on their laps, spreading my skirt so it would not get mussed, holding me tight so I would not fall. Their hips moved up and down rhythmically.

My father disapproved of my wandering around the workshop, alone with young men. Many times, he took off his face shield, turned off his jeweler's torch, shook the gold dust from his leather apron onto a metal container, and steaming, came to the back. Not being able to tell me of his fears (no one ever discussed such matters with children), he dragged me back to the main shop and ordered me to sit up straight, with my hands folded on my lap. Every time, after fifteen minutes, I became restless and jumped up and down, putting at risk large glass containers of acids used to purify the gold and the silver. Finally, my father forbade my mother to send me to his shop.

Soon I was looking for other means of entertainment. My father's first cousin lived next door, and his daughter was my age. Mahvash was mischievous. Her carefree running around the streets of *mahaleh* with her skirt flying in the air appalled the neighbors. "Look at her running like a boy. The girl has no shame," they would say, spitting on the ground with disgust.

My father forbade me to spend time with her after hearing the comments from our neighbors.

Years later, Mahvash would surprise all her classmates by participating in the competitions for Miss Iran. The self-confidence to think herself beautiful, deserving, to be adventurous and allow her pictures to appear in

*Zan-e Rouz,* the premier women's magazine, was beyond our imaginations. Many looked down at the way she exhibited herself, and wondered if she would ever find a husband. A Tehrani man saw Mahvash on television and fell in love with her. He found her address in Shiraz and asked for her hand from her parents.

Mahvash married at age fourteen. She looked like a dressed-up queen on her wedding night. She had a big smile, and when she saw me, she winked and pointed to her hair that was piled up on top. She pulled me to the side later. "Do you see the glitter on my hair?" she asked, a twinkle in her green eyes. "A special hairspray!"

Mahvash moved to Tehran and had three children by the time I graduated from high school. She was widowed by age thirty-five when her husband died of a heart attack. According to the Islamic laws reinstated by Khomeini, her father-in-law was in charge of the inheritance and the children's welfare. Mahvash was lucky. Her father-in-law was a compassionate man who turned over the money to her and helped her and the children leave the country for the United States.

Mahvash and I found each other in Los Angeles when we were in our mid-forties. We had not seen each other for over twenty-five years. She was still beautiful—porcelain doll skin, green eyes, curvaceous body, the same mischievous half smile and twinkle in her eyes. In an outdoor café, I asked her how she remembered me as a child.

She lit a cigarette and blew the smoke away from me. "You went by the rules—too serious," she said.

Her full lips parted in a seductive smile. She took another puff from her cigarette and laughed. She told me how she had tricked a bus driver, when she was eight years old, to take her and her cousins to downtown Tehran to visit her aunt.

"Please, sir, we lost our money and our aunt is waiting for us for lunch. She is probably worried to death!" They rode on top of the double-decker, singing from the top of their lungs.

I imagined her letting the wind blow through her blond hair, laughing with delight. I would never have dared. "Did you really do that? Weren't you afraid?" I asked her.

"See! You are still too serious. Who was going to get us?"

That was the difference between us as children. She looked at the world as if it were a playground. I envisioned a bogeyman around every bend.

"We were kids," Mahvash added, smiling in her familiar playful way.

"And guess what? After having lunch with my aunt, she gave us money for the bus home." She took another puff from her cigarette and laughed. "I convinced everyone to buy ice cream, and once again we waited for the bus with no money. The same bus driver stopped and bought the story again, taking us home on his lunch break."

Mahvash was right. I grew up to be suspicious of people. Like my father, I feared their judgment.

Originally, Mahvash jeered at me. My mother had my fine hair shaved when I was five years old. According to common beliefs, shaving made the hair grow thicker and more abundant. All winter, I went around wearing a kerchief so I would not catch a cold from my bald head. All winter, Mahvash made fun of my ugly scarf and hairless scalp. Later, when she began courting my friendship, I was both intimidated and intrigued.

She used to tell wild stories about how her brother ate a razor blade wrapped in a piece of bread to show how brave he was, and that her mother approved, saying it was nothing but pure iron that his body needed anyway. She told me that it was good to eat raw pistachios. I believed her despite hearing the opposite from my mother, who thought they would give me worms. She convinced me to go with her to the synagogue, put my head on its closed door, and ask God to take away the life of a neighborhood girl, who had angered her.

"Did you do it?" she asked.

I nodded.

"No, you say it aloud. I wanna hear it."

I audibly cursed the girl, but silently asked God not to accept my words.

Mahvash and I roamed the narrow alleyways looking for something to do. She told me about a wonderful confectionery outside the *mahaleh* and about the unusual candies we could buy if we had money.

One day, Mahvash spotted the beggar. His name was Sakalak, but we called him Kachalak, the bald one. His baldness differed from that of other men I knew. A few had receding hairlines in front that gave them a high forehead. Others had a more advanced form that stretched the baldness beyond the forehead to the back of their heads. There was usually a small dip from the natural boundary of their foreheads to the newly created extension all shiny and smooth, surrounded with thick brown hair. Others had no hair at all and did not have to worry about growing a row of hair long enough to be glued on top of their hair with grease.

Kachalak's scalp was patchy. Long dusty strands of hair sprouted around his head. Though lifeless, the hairs did not droop over the bald spots around them but instead stuck out according to how he had slept on them the night before. The dirt in the air of the ghetto and his own natural body oil that was never washed away helped give his hair body and form. Parts of the visible scalp showed white patches as though a mysterious invisible organism was eating the brown pigments of his skin, and no doubt the brown borders around them would soon succumb to the sickly whiteness of the disease.

He did not seem to have a reason for shaving. The crawling whiteness had found its way around Kachalak's left ear to spread itself beneath the protruding cheek bone and his lower jaw before proceeding to the right side, weakening the roots of the hair follicles in its path. Kachalak was also becoming bald on his face.

I thought he was lucky to be blind and not witness his own miserable condition. In place of the dark eyeballs that everyone else had, there were blue lifeless orbs floating in the mushy whiteness of his eye sockets. One eye was often shut with sticky yellowish slime, which oozed from his tear ducts slowly, drying around the sunken eye and eyelashes and creating a feast for flies.

I had seen him many times before, when he visited my grandmother at our home to ask for leftover food and old clothes, especially close to the holidays when everyone was more generous. I could smell his sour body before he entered the yard.

My grandmother sent me scouring the house for leftover food and my dad's old clothes. I resented my grandmother's generosity; her gifts would bring Kachalak's wasted body to our doors again and again, spoiling the thoughts of the holidays for me. I laid the food and clothing a few steps away from him and hastily locked the door behind him. At the time, I didn't know that he pushed his way into the house and that my grandmother was trying to get rid of him by giving him something quickly.

On the day that Mahvash and I encountered the beggar, he was sunning himself on a torn piece of carpet in a busy crossroad close to the public water spouts. He had a tin can in front of him with a few *rials* in and around it. I was revolted by the sight of *the thief,* as I used to call him, for who would want a perfectly beautiful day to smell of rotting live flesh?

Mahvash was merely intrigued. She wanted us to circle him. "Watch him," she said, "He will know someone is close to him."

I watched him tap his wooden stick on the ground trying to find us.

With his slight stutter, Kachalak said, "Give, give to the poor!"

As if being blind and bald was not enough, he had a speech impediment, too. I remembered someone saying the beggar had slight mental retardation. I tried not to act scared in front of Mahvash.

"Let's steal a couple of these *rials*. We can buy some candy with them. He is blind. He won't know what we're doing," she whispered in my ears. Before I could react, she bent down and picked up a few.

I imitated her. A volcanic sound of rage exploded from within the mound on the carpet. I was disoriented, and my heart pumped rapidly. I threw the coins down. I don't know how my shaking legs found the strength to carry me away. I could hear the blind man's voice for months after that screaming, "Get her, get her, *dofte mola Esghel,* the daughter of Mola Esghel." He screamed half in Farsi, half in Judi, the language of the ghetto.

I knew what he was saying—that he recognized me as my father's daughter. Not only had I humiliated myself, I had also shamed my father, a religious advisor and community leader.

I could not understand Mahvash's giddiness. She was as happy as ever, juggling the copper coins, giggling, and skipping all the way home. Her unbraided hair danced around her. I was horrified; Kachalak was my living nightmare from then on. Whenever he came to our house for his usual share of leftovers and old clothes, he eyed me with those drippy dead eyes. I hid in a hot closet, pale and shaking well after he was gone, fearing that he would one day murder me. Sometimes I hated my grandmother for being so kind to him.

A year later, tired of this nuisance among us, the community collected money and sent Kachalak to Palestine. In those days everyone believed that Israel was the solution to all problems, and that they would train the beggar to become a productive citizen.

We moved out of the *mahaleh* soon after, and I forgot about him until I began to tell my daughters bedtime stories of my childhood. As I recounted the event to them, I realized that the horror and the guilt that had brewed inside me for so many years had blinded me to the reason that a sightless man could have seen me so well. My laughing children knew that Kachalak was not blind.

After all that mischief, we still didn't have enough money for the candy. Mahvash suggested a scheme, "Let's go to your Dad's store and tell him that your mother needs money for groceries."

I did it. It worked. I think my father was too embarrassed in front of his cousin's child to say no. I had ten *tomans* of my father's hard-earned money burning a hole in my fist, feeling a certain thrill and shame at the same time. The call for adventure was stronger.

We went to the candy shop. Mahvash was right. I had never seen such pretty candy, shaped as apples, cherries, and pears. The friendly shopkeeper invited us behind the counter for a free sampling. Mahvash had warned me ahead of time, "He likes to stick his hands in little girls' panties." I had never heard of such nonsense, but I followed her advice and kept my distance. She took the money from me and chose the candies. We greedily bit into their velvety skins. Every piece tasted like sawdust mixed with sugar, but neither one of us wanted to admit the defeat. I spit mine out in a street corner when I thought Mahvash wasn't looking. In the pretext of having sticky hands, she knelt by the watercourse running by the side walk, and pulled the nasty mush out with two fingers.

Shortly after, the shame came back. I wanted to go home and give the rest of the money to my mother. Mahvash and I argued in the hallway between the two houses. She thought the rest of the money was hers, but I didn't remember such promises. I couldn't go home without any money. My mother would want to know where I had been. I was ashamed for wasting my father's money that had kept him working through late hours of the night.

I managed to secure most of the money from Mahvash. It was only half of what I had started with, but maybe nobody would know. My father did find out the truth that night. But when I told him Mahvash had some of it, he shook his head and with tired and sad eyes told me not to socialize with Mahvash again.

Then he screamed at my mother for not having enough control over me.

## The Price of a Woman's Education

I venerated Aunt Fereshteh like a big sister, a role model. Unlike other adults, she instilled self-confidence in me: "How beautiful you look in red," she would say—my favorite color even now. When my mother admonished me for slurping tea like a peasant, Fereshteh arranged a tea party for the two of us. We sat cross-legged in front of a samovar and practiced sipping like Persian princesses.

*Cleaning* ghooreh. *My mother and two brothers clean sour grapes.* Picture courtesy of Nahid Gerstein.

As I quietly mourned a rejection from the first grade in the summer of 1959, Aunt Fereshteh eagerly awaited her acceptance to the medical school. The Shah, trying to emulate the standards of the country that had returned the kingdom to him, ordered the establishment of Pahlavi University in Shiraz, an American-style institution with a reputable medical school. To keep up with the West, Pahlavi University imported American and British textbooks to be taught by Western-trained teachers.

One night that summer, my grandmother, my aunt, and I were walking home with plastic baskets filled with romaine lettuce, green onions, fresh dill, and cilantro, when we heard the names of the accepted students announced from a transistor radio. Arab tourists in white caftans fanned themselves on the rooftops of a motel, and a teenage boy sold spicy potatoes cooked with fried onions and tomatoes from a pushcart.

At my aunt's begging, we waited by a kiosk and listened to the radio. She was accepted to the medical school. I clapped. My grandmother didn't look overjoyed. Fereshteh's laughter attracted the other pedestrians. Two young men with fuzzy hair on their upper lips gawked and moved their hands over their crotches; older men with stubble and loose-fitting pants gathered around us as if for entertainment. We picked up the baskets and made our way home. My aunt and I were flying high. Such an unbelievable achievement for a woman, what a wonderful escape from an oppressed history! Excited, we both ignored my grandmother's grumbling.

I didn't hear any discussions about my aunt's college plans until a few days later. My mother, grandmother, my aunts, and three or four of my cousins helped with the yearly ritual of cleaning sour grapes. We spread a plastic cloth on the cement floor of our basement and put pillows all around the walls. My grandmother opened the Passover closet and took out baskets and containers.

My father and uncle had left very early to find the best bundles of sour grapes, and soon two donkeys limped their way through our yard. Sour grapes covered the entire room in a large pile, and I couldn't wait to get my hands dirty. It was work, yes, but it was also a ton of fun, although one couldn't tell by looking at the adults. My grandmother asked my cousin Farnoosh to be the first to walk in the room. Her steps were light; the work would finish early.

The yearly ritual involved separating the grapes from the vine and discarding the spoiled ones, then washing and air drying them. Every year, my father hired the same heavy-set man to squeeze the juice. In a huge barrel, he stepped on the grapes with his bare feet, his loose-fitting pants rolled up over his knees, and his "stuff" jiggling around inside with every heavy step he brought down.

We forced the pulp through cheesecloth and bottled the juice in huge, flat-bottomed glass amphorae. The first batch was for Passover. Then we put the Passover dishes away and used regular containers to store the sour juice for year-round use.

Ecstatic and playful, that day I made the biggest trouble for myself. During the lunch break, my aunt spoke excitedly about continuing her education at the medical school the following year. Morad was the first to object. "Stop dreaming about such nonsense. A woman's job is to get married. Plus, who is going to pay the expenses?"

Other than the two uncles in medical school, no one in the family had finished high school. My aunts and grandmother joined in to remind Fereshteh of the role of marriage and children in a woman's life. My father moderated, trying to keep everyone calm.

During a moment of silence, a rest from shouting, I couldn't stand my aunt's crying and took the opportunity to add my own opinion. "Of course she is going to college," I said. "It's free for women. I heard it with my own ears."

Uncle Morad looked at me as if realizing for the first time that I existed. He jumped off the ledge he was sitting on, and made his way to me in two huge steps. His big hand went up and landed on my face. Too surprised to cover my face in defense, too stubborn to cry or touch my burning skin, I didn't look at my mother or father. Instead, I looked straight into his eyes.

Looking directly into a person's eyes implied lack of social graces for adults, but for a child, especially a girl, it connoted defiance. He looked at my dry eyes with his own, bloodshot with anger. He tossed me over his shoulder and carried me through the yard, through the little alley, through the second set of doors, and put me down on the ledge next to the open doors of Mori-Jaan's house. Then he smirked, went back into the house, and closed the door.

I sat there, numb, shaken, and empty. I was scared, too scared to look at the open doors to my left, too scared to think what my neighbor's ferocious dog would do to me if he found me there all by myself sitting in the dark, damp hallway. I don't know how long it took for my father to win my release. When he finally came, all the blood had drained from my face and limbs. I was cold and limp. He carried me into the house, and I went quietly back to cleaning the grapes and stayed silent amid the noisy conversations around me. I don't remember any reactions from my mother. I sought neither her help nor her comfort. Even then, I knew that she was more helpless than I was.

My aunt was one of the very first Iranian women to enter medical school that year. I was very proud of her, a stubborn woman capable of overcoming many obstacles to reach seemingly impossible goals. She went on to continue her education in the United States, but she never did get married. Most men were intimidated by her intelligence, her education, and her title.

### Khanom-bozorg

I became closer to my grandmother during the year I awaited an opening in the first grade. Where my mother was meek, Khanom-bozorg was strong and resourceful. She was my teacher in life before I had any formal

*Khanom-bozorg.*

education. My grandmother often enticed me to clean the rice with a promise of a story. As she and I inspected piles of rice on a round brass tray, she entertained me with my favorite tale, that of her first marriage. "I was only nine years old," she said. "Your great-grandmother, Bibi, would hold my hand and take me to my fiancé's house."

There, my grandmother's future mother-in-law asked her to sit by a pile of vegetables and herbs and clean them for dinner to see if little Tavous was a good worker and if she was not *zaban-deraz*, a girl with a long tongue who answered back. My grandmother remembered her fiancé, a man in his twenties, playing childish games with her as she sat on his lap. The young bride, however, was restless in her new home, homesick for her mother. "As soon as they were busy, I ran away." My grandmother covered her toothless mouth with her hand and laughed with delight. Through the maze of alleyways, my little grandmother ran home like the strong wind that blew between her many braids.

Every time she escaped, Bibi screamed, beat her chest in exasperation and cried, "You're ruining your reputation! Who is going to marry you now?" Finally, the family returned her one day saying she was not suitable for their son.

*Khanom-bozorg and one of her sisters, Khanom, were briefly
reunited in Jerusalem after the Iranian Revolution of 1979.
Khanom died shortly after. My grandmother died the following year.
I am very sad that despite my father's efforts, I couldn't obtain the
picture of my grandmother's best friend Joon-joon.*

I quietly cheered my grandmother's defiance and strong sense of self
that freed her from an unwanted marriage at a young age. I desperately
wished that her spirit of independence and stubbornness would also run
through my veins. But sometimes, I also resented her for torturing me unknowingly.

A late summer afternoon, when the temperature had already fallen, my
grandmother sat on a low stool in the yard, curing tobacco leaves in salted
water. I squatted next to her, watching her rinse and hang them outside on
the laundry lines. She said, "Don't touch," before turning her back, which
made me more curious. I tasted a piece floating on the brown water. It was
salty, grainy, nasty, and burned my tongue. I screamed, jumped to my feet,
and spat on the ground.

"Didn't I tell you to keep away?" my grandmother said.

"Is it poisonous? Is it poisonous?" I asked in a panic, not able to get rid of
the taste in my mouth no matter how many times I spat. There was no reply.

"Is it poisonous? Am I going to die?"

*Khanom-bozorg with her older sister Khatoon-jaan (left). My father searched for this picture for over a year, knowing how much it meant to me. A most courageous woman, my great aunt sold her own dowry to provide for my grandmother and her destitute children after my grandfather died.*

"Go wash your mouth with clean water."

"Am I going to die, Khanom-bozorg? Am I going to die?" I said, panic-stricken.

"I don't know," she answered, her eyes gleaming. "We'll see." She winked.

Put in the same situation, my mischievous friend Mahvash would have laughed. Not me. For the rest of the day, I watched for signs of death. Nothing happened. At the end of the day, when I could not keep my eyes open any longer to keep death away, I decided I was going to bed and if I awoke in the morning, then I knew it was not poisonous, and if I didn't, then I wouldn't.

The next day, I woke up still breathing, and my grandmother asked if I wanted to go shopping. She was anxious, she told me. She needed to get fresh air, to see people. I loved the chance to leave the ghetto in the safety of her flowered *chador*, to explore the unknown. The world outside our immediate neighborhood frightened me. My parents, family members, and children my own age told me repeatedly that evil lurked outside the gates of the *mahaleh*. Genteel-looking grandfathers enticed young chil-

*Evil Eye Pendant: the large stone symbolizes blind eyes; the white shells represent closed eyes. The square gold piece used to encase a salt cube to deter evil. My mother pinned this to all her children's clothes when we were babies.* Pendant courtesy of Nahid Gerstein. Photography by Jon and Jennifer Crockford.

dren with drug-covered candy and kidnapped them to slavery. Nice old ladies, covered modestly in *chadors*, asked for directions, and made the children disappear. Kidnappers from other cities, Arabs from other countries, and those they hired from the local community, cornered children in quiet alleyways and took them by force for prostitution.

These scary stories made my excursions with my grandmother even more valuable. I especially loved going shopping with her. Even in those days, I knew the power belonged in the folds of the little knitted purse wrapped around her waist. In our outings, she often bought me a chewy taffy bar that took forever to eat, and, when I was finished with it, I had taffy drool all over my shirt. Or she treated me to a long piece of paper rolled tightly, glued and filled with sugar. Sometimes, when she stopped by the bakery to buy a few *noon-e chaee* for breakfast, she bought me a raisin cookie dripping deliciously with oil.

That day I thought only of a treat as we walked down the busy street. Unusually quiet, my grandmother cocooned herself tighter in her *chador*. I left her in her own world and enjoyed the sounds of shopkeepers inviting the customers in: fruit stands, selling long yellow Persian melons piled up in a neat row, the bakery, tempting me with chickpea cookies, *zulbia*, and *koolooche masghati* arranged in skillful pyramids.

Khanom-bozorg allowed me to linger by the kiosks and to explore displays: head coverings in Indian motifs, bright tribal colors, or simple black ones for praying. We passed by a salesman, his merchandise displayed on the sidewalk: plastic shopping bags and colanders, naked dolls, and striped balls.

"Look, look at those dolls," I said excitedly. "Can we look, pleeese." We stopped. I touched one. "Aren't they wonderful? Aren't they beautiful?" I looked at their little naked bodies and dreamt of sewing little dresses for them; maybe Maman could help. There was always a little extra fabric left over from a dress made a long time ago. Maybe she could even knit a little jacket with the leftover yarn, I thought.

I looked at my grandmother. I hadn't ever noticed so many wrinkles around her eyes, which were set in deeper than usual—sad eyes. I was surprised to see that she didn't have her teeth in; she never appeared in public without them. I ignored that and knowing that it was inappropriate for a child to be greedy and demanding, I still slowly lifted my head and, in a small, very small voice asked her, "Could I, Khanom-bozorg, could I have one? They are very cheap," I reasoned.

She looked at me and absentmindedly asked, "You don't have any dolls, do you?"

My heart pounded like an iron pestle smashing turmeric sticks in our stone mortar. "No, Grandma, you know I don't." She asked the shopkeeper how much it was.

"Five *rials*, only." He pushed the toy into my hand.

I prayed. I would be a good girl. I would do anything for that doll with yellow hair and blue eyes.

"Let's go," Khanom-bozorg said, turning her back.

I was used to the methods of bargaining. I assumed that was the game being played. So did the shopkeeper.

"Okay, come back, four *rials*." But my grandmother kept going.

"Khanom-bozorg, it's cheap," I cajoled her.

"Yes, and you don't need it."

"Cheap Jews!" The shopkeeper screamed at us. People turned around and stared. A few laughed.

I wanted to go home. I thought she took pleasure in my shock, and I didn't want her to see my tears. I held my head up, swallowed hard, and didn't say a word, fearing that I would lose control and cry, not realizing that tears might have convinced her to buy me the toy.

I followed the little floating flowers of her *chador* moving fast past the kiosks and the hotels that housed Arabs during hot Arabian summers. From their billboards I had learned my first Arabic word, the word for hotel. A few Arabs with their long, white summer caftans sat on platform beds on the roof, watching the street. We passed by my father's little jewelry workshop and didn't stop. Now we were very close to the gates of the *mahaleh*, and had only the teahouse to pass. The men there especially scared me. I hid myself in the folds of my grandmother's *chador* and I wished for her to speed up. We were almost home.

A few men with mischievous looks on their faces sat outside the teahouse drinking chai and smoking *ghalyan* under the shade of an old tree, next to a meandering stream. The city allowed the water to run through the open gutters of the main streets to help shopkeepers wash and cool down the sidewalks. To my horror, my grandmother slowed down, trying to release me from the tight grip of her *chador,* as though I was a fly on the flowery fabric, and started to talk to them.

"Come on, come on, what's your problem? Got to talk to these people. They're in our neighborhood. It isn't good for them to think the Jews are disrespectful. Just a little small talk." She held her *chador* tight around her face and prostrated herself to the laughing faces. "*Salam*, what a nice day!" She greeted them in her heavy Judi accent.

"Yes it's a nice day, but it's even nicer outside the city in the mountains, cooler. Say, a few of us are going to Babakoohi, wannacome?" He talked in poor Farsi without taking a breath in between words, then grinned, revealing tobacco-stained teeth. "What do you say?"

"I hope that your kindness will always be great," my grandmother *taarof*ed. "I have to go home, but thank you." I wondered if they would

dare ask a woman of their own faith to go to the mountains with them. I
didn't know why my grandmother, who demanded much respect for herself in the synagogue, would invite such disrespect. I wanted to go home.

"What about the little girl?" They laughed. Now the situation was truly
grave. I just wanted to leave. The gates of the *mahaleh* were visible and
promised security. I tugged at her *chador,* trying to give her a reason to
leave.

"She is not worthy of you," she *taarof*ed again. I had always thought
that there was a bit of truth to the custom of niceties, and I was horrified.
I pulled on her *chador* again, trying to turn myself invisible in its folds.

"Do you want to go?" she asked, laughing at my fear, trying to peel me
from her body covering. My heart ached. My legs took off. I covered my
ears not to hear the laughing voices, trying not to see anything but the
gates. When I finally stepped down from the smooth, hot pavement down
to the dirt road under the arch, I realized that my face was cold and wet. I
hated myself for crying. I had lost the battle.

After our day out, my grandmother was sick again, too exhausted to
get out of bed. She couldn't catch her breath. My father took her to a well-
known, American-trained doctor.

When the doctor asked my grandmother what was bothering her, she
responded, "Everything!"

The doctor prescribed many bottles of pills, and Khanom-bozorg took
them religiously for a few days, but she still hurt. My mother squeezed
watermelon juice for her, but it was too *cold* and made her weak. I had
learned by then that there was a second kind of temperature for all food.
*Cold* sapped the energy; *hot* gave it back. There had to be a balance or one
became ill. My father went to the bazaar and purchased a collection of
herbal teas: white tea and green tea, tea made of tree barks, and tea made
of flowers. I stood on a stepstool and watched my grandmother make her
potions. She felt cold in her bones and that meant that she needed *hot* tea
to give her energy, to revive her spirit, to put heat under her chilled skin.
She chose the bark of some magical tree, combined it with cracked fruit
of wild bushes, and boiled it with crystallized sugar. I strained it for her in
a cloth; even with all the sugar, it tasted bitter and repulsive. To balance the
*humors* in her body, she drank the foul tea with dates and dried mulberries,
with soft *halwa* made of rice flour and the hard one made with sweet date
syrup. Nothing helped. Her body was out of balance. Her stomach hurt;

she was cold in her bones, dizzy in her head. And now I had a stomachache too from feasting on the dried fruit and the sweets without the tea.

Her women friends stopped by every day to bring new remedies. What about tattooing? Khanom-bozorg already had large green dots tattooed on her forehead and wrists to alleviate her unknown pains and aches, but the magic had worn out. What about letting out the dirty blood?

No, no. My father wouldn't allow that. Absolutely not. He was going to take Khanom-bozorg back to the American-trained doctor.

The word "bloodletting" horrified me. I imagined relatives gathering around my grandmother cutting her skin with razor blades, opening her veins with my father's sharp knife when he wasn't around.

My father warned his mother before leaving the house every day: "*Mava,* my life should be sacrificed for you. Don't do it. On my life, on my kids' lives, promise you won't do it. You'll expose yourself to disease, risk your life." The ritual constituted voodoo, forbidden by Jewish laws, he empha- sized, appealing to my grandmother's strong religious beliefs.

I took a sigh of relief; my grandmother would live.

My grandmother's sister Khatoon-jaan came for her daily visit one day, but didn't enter the house right away. Esghel-*khan* home?" she asked.

No, my father had left early that day for work.

She bent back, holding her blue *chador* tightly around her with one hand, and with the other motioned to someone. Khanom-bozorg's best friend Joon-joone-bandi appeared at the door, her usual jolly self, and, be- fore I could defend myself, she put two juicy, drippy kisses on both sides of my face, her white mustache tickling and repulsing me at the same time.

A short woman with a fat stomach followed the two women into the house, her middle clanking and swishing. "No men at home?" she asked.

"No, no men," I said.

She took her *chador* off and there was a bucket where I had imagined a fat belly. Had I known the contents, I would probably have run to my fa- ther's shop, screaming and warning him of the mischief, but instead, I fol- lowed them to the main building and went upstairs to tell my grand- mother her guests wanted her to come to the yard. I thought Khanom- bozorg looked pale; that my grandmother could be scared of anything that day didn't cross my mind. Khatoon-jaan piled up a few pillows by the wall and helped Khanom-bozorg sit on one and fluffed another to support her back.

The brass knocker hit against the front door again in urgency. My mother, who was working in the kitchen at the end of the yard, must have opened the door. My two married aunts arrived flushed from their quick walk. Relieved to discover that nothing had happened yet, they threw their *chadors* on the limb of the rose tree and sent me to the kitchen to see if my mother had prepared the large omelet with the hard-to-find eggs that they had brought with them. They fed Khanom-bozorg every single morsel that I hadn't picked on the way from the kitchen.

"Eat, eat," Khatoon-jaan said as she rolled up my grandmother's sleeves and bared her thick, hairy legs.

The leech-lady gathered her skirt around her. She knelt on the floor, and ladled the thick brown silt from her bucket onto my grandmother's right arm and then the left. I watched black slug-like creatures attach themselves to her as if they burrowed into her flesh. In just a few minutes, they bloated and grew fat. The women inched their way to my grandmother, asking if enough blood was sucked out. The leech-lady scraped the creatures off and let them fall into the bucket, where they vomited my grandmother's pomegranate-colored juices.

Khanom-bozorg's eyes rolled back and she slumped over the pillows. The three women rushed to her side, massaging her body, her toes, her legs, her shoulders, her hands, and her arms. She closed her eyes and called for my father. I ran to the kitchen and made mint tea, sweetened with honey. Khanom-bozorg opened her eyes, her color still white, her hands trembling. The women covered her with blankets, but Khanom-bozorg's fingertips were blue, her body cold and heavy. I wanted to go to her and hold her but I was afraid to touch her. What if she died?

When my father came home for lunch and saw the women gathered around the pile that was my grandmother, he was terrified. "*Mava, Mava,*" he called his mother. "What have you done?" he asked in Judi.

Later we learned that he had gone to all the butchers, begging to purchase a cow's liver, which he threw directly on hot charcoals. Then he slowly fed my grandmother as if she were the child and he the parent.

The following day, Khatoon-jaan and my grandmother's best friend visited to inquire of her health.

"Not good!" Khanom-bozorg moaned, still under the covers. Someone must have cursed her, she said. That was it—pure, unadulterated evil eye.

The other two nodded. Khatoon-jaan said that the women had to take matters into their own hands. From her bundle, she retrieved the bark of a tree, the size of a half coconut, put a few drops in its curve and, with a back of a teaspoon, rubbed it for a few minutes. A white paste oozed out, which she tenderly rubbed on Khanom-bozorg's forehead.

Joon-joone-bandi drew a puff from the waterpipe, held it for a second, and, as if she was whispering a secret, she blew it into my grandmother's ears. "A doctor! He is nothing but a coat and a tie," she said. "That's what your son respects, and what good came out of it? What did he do for you that we could have not?"

Khatoon-jaan rearranged pillows around Khanom-bozorg. "Is women's wisdom for nothing?" she asked. "All these years, we took care of everyone, but now we are discredited."

My grandmother agreed that the women needed to take charge. The three discussed a list of women to be invited to a private ceremony at the full moon. She gave Joon-joone-bandi the task of finding a soothsayer.

My father didn't oppose the idea, although it deviated from Jewish beliefs. He allowed it for its psychological impact, he told me. At age six, I had never heard that word before. I knew it had something to do with my grandmother's mind, that if she felt cured, she would be okay. I knew I shouldn't believe in such nonsense: a bunch of old women getting together for hocus-pocus. My father didn't want me there, but I begged. Such fun! I had to be there.

As the daylight disappeared a week later, the guests entered our yard without knocking and made themselves comfortable on a Persian carpet in the middle of the bricked backyard. The orange trees looked like creatures with arms and legs. I sat on my mother's lap, wrapped her skirt around my legs, and wouldn't move. Women sipped sweet fruit-essence drinks and took turns on the waterpipe, drawing smoke from its long wooden mouthpiece. *Bblllla,* the water gurgled at its blue glass base, from which a gold-painted, surly Ghajar king stared at me, dressed in his fineries and crowned with jewels and feathers.

A woman tapped rhythmically on the back of a brass platter. Others joined her, clapping, making music with their hands. Joon-joone-bandi slowly raised her thick body with the pulse. She wrapped her *chador* around her waist, twisted her wide bottom around, clasped her hands over her head, snapping four fingers at each other to make a crisp, crackling noise like charcoal burning in a brass brazier. Her surname "bandi" was a reflection of her job, weaving strings to hold men's pants up at a time zippers were not commonly used in Iran. A widow, having hired other poor women to work for her, she made a small fortune. She pulled a long bundle of strings from underneath her *chador,* attached it to her front, and thrust her hips, singing a song about my father's virility. The women roared. My mother giggled. I was astonished.

"Come on, Joon-joon," my grandmother laughed for the first time in months. "Stop it! There're young girls here."

Slowly, the light dimmed in the yard. The full moon crawled to the center of a star-studded sky. I had fallen asleep in my mother's lap in the comfort of the women's chattering. I woke up with a start from a deep silence around me, fearing that I was left alone. My mother rubbed my back to calm me, then I saw the man's shadow moving on the courtyard wall. I noticed that the women had pulled their *chador*s tightly around them as the soothsayer approached our circle. He held a canvas bag thrown over his shoulder. His eyeballs looked like watermelon seeds folded in fleshy droops around his eyes, reflecting the secret of something extraordinary, something unconnected with this world. Although his eyes were black, I thought of them as somehow connected with the stars.

Khatoon-jaan put the brazier filled with hot charcoals in front of the fortune-teller. He slowly undid the cord around his bag to reveal small bundles wrapped in old cloth and tied in small knots. He touched them one by one, turning them over, getting a feel for their shapes and weight. He finally picked one and slowly unwrapped it. We looked at him, mesmerized. The fire crackled and sent flames and amber in the air, its light blinding me. Then I saw it. He held a shiny block of metal in his bony hand.

"Is it silver?" I whispered to my mother.

"Shh! It is tin."

The other women looked at us disapprovingly, "Sshhhh!"

"Tell me about your problems," the soothsayer asked my grandmother as he wedged a thick, round vessel into the middle of the coals.

My grandmother's eyes glimmered with anticipation, I thought, or maybe with hope. She rubbed her hands again and again. She wet her lips, dry and cracked, with her tongue. Khatoon-jaan put a glass of willow essence into her hand, which trembled as she took a little sip.

"I don't know what to say." My grandmother started her monologue without pausing to breathe between the words. "I was all fine, no problems, all healthy." She sighed. "Then, all of a sudden, out of nowhere, I am hurting all over. I can't sleep. I can't eat well. Everyone says my color is no good." She poured out the words in rapid succession and sighed again.

The fortune-teller's vessel turned red from the heat. He broke off a small piece of the metal, looked at the moon directly above, mumbled a few prayers, and dropped it in.

"Everyone says I was hit with bad eyes," my grandmother said.

The fortune-teller nodded as he held his vessel with a thick cloth on top of the fire and swirled it around.

One aunt mumbled, "Yes, of course. That *is* the truth."

My grandmother went on, "I've heard that you're good at finding out the source of this evil."

Adding small pieces of tin to the pot, the soothsayer said, "You're right. I'm the best."

I watched the metal melt and shine. It still looked like silver to me.

The magic man looked at my grandmother, "Are you ready? Let's hope that the evil isn't so strong that it can hide its identity."

Khanom-bozorg nodded.

"Say a prayer and concentrate on your pain."

The only prayers I had ever heard my grandmother say in Hebrew were the *shema* and the *brakha* over the candles. She imitated the voice of men rising to the balcony at the synagogue, distorted and unintelligible. Khanom-bozorg mumbled some prayers, pleading with *khodaye bozorg,* the Great God for mercy and help.

"*Ya khodaye bozorg,*" a woman repeated.

"In the name of the Great God," the rest of women echoed.

"Cover your faces," the only man among us ordered. "We don't know how strong this evil is. Close your eyes." He held the side of the vessel with a metal grip, and, averting his eyes, poured the molten metal into a ceramic bowl filled with water, and jumped back. There was a huge bang as the liquid metal hit the cold water. Smoke gushed out and the bowl broke into pieces. "Pretty strong enemies you have!" he told my grandmother. "See what happened to the bowl?"

The women gasped, muffled their screams, and huddled together as if in the presence of a ghost. I scratched my mother's arms in the sudden confusion. She cried in pain and slapped the back of my hands.

The man searched the ground, found a piece of metal, and held it with a metal tongs for everyone to see. "Look! It is in the shape of a woman."

I focused on the shape to see if that was really true. I couldn't tell.

Khatoon-jaan pointed to a protruding part of the long object. "He's right. Look, she's smoking a waterpipe."

"Who could that be?" Aunt Shams asked.

All eyes focused on my grandmother. She lifted the piece and turned it around. Even I knew she was looking for someone she disliked. "That pagan! She is no Jew," my grandmother screamed. "This is Simin, the neighbor down the block. She came to visit the other day, when I had come back from the *hamam*. I should have known the way she looked at the braids around my face. I could see the jealousy in her eyes. She envies me because she thinks I have the time for such luxuries every week. She is the one who put the bad eye on me."

My grandmother was back. She was feisty again, full of energy and emotions, even hatred. The magic had worked. I tried to sweep the belief out of my head, not allowing myself to believe in supernatural nonsense.

The soothsayer packed, but before leaving, he reminded everyone not to leave my grandmother alone. "Watch her at least till this moon dies and the new crescent of moon appears," he warned.

Women whispered their remedies. The evil was strong. They had to employ all remedies. They consulted each other about the methods each had learned from her family. My grandmother spread herself on the carpet, a little smile hiding in the corner of her lips. Aunt Shams rubbed wild rue and salt all over her as she let a trilling noise escape her pursed lips to draw the evil out. She threw the concoction into the same fire in which the soothsayer melted his magic metal. Cracking noises accompanied a yellow flame.

Aunt Maheen rubbed a whole raw egg in its shell over my grandmother's legs, arms, stomach, head, all the areas hurting and aching. The women started to chant a secret hymn:

> For the giver of the evil eye who knows of it,
> and for the one who doesn't know;
> For the one who has arrived,
> and for the one who left town.[1]

A woman hid the egg underneath the dark cloth of her *chador*, and headed out to smash it against the wall of Simin's house. Other women washed Khanom-bozorg's legs in well water mixed with herbs and the

1. Quoted also in Laurence Loeb's *Outcast*.

roots of trees that grew only in the desert outside Shiraz. Two women carried the water to pour over the stairs leading to Simin's house. There was a sense of relief that I felt as well—a feeling of cleansing, of renewal.

Before leaving, all the women reminded my grandmother to be careful as the new month approached. It could determine her well-being for the entire month. The first time she saw the crescent of the new moon, she had to cover her eyes and to make sure the first person she looked at was happy, healthy, and lucky. That would help the spirits to make the month a good one for her too. That night, and every night until the new moon appeared, Khatoon-jaan and Joon-joone-bandi took turns sleeping with my grandmother, so she wouldn't be alone when in a deep sleep. In such a state, her soul and body were the most vulnerable to both human treachery and the jinns' malice. (Jinns are evil creatures that live beneath the Earth.) My grandmother was well for many months after that until the attention dwindled again.

During all my years with her, I watched Khanom-bozorg cover her face with both hands every time the new moon rose in the sky, calling for this person and that person so she could look at their faces. "Smile, smile, Farideh, so I can look at your face," she told me if I was the appointed one that month. If she had a bad month, she pointed her finger at me, "See what you did! Didn't I tell you not to be grouchy?"

I laughed at my grandmother's antics for years—such nonsense. Then, many years later, when I had grown children of my own, one quiet evening my American husband and I strolled in our Norfolk neighborhood. I looked up and saw the beautiful crescent moon peeking behind the trees. I turned my head to point it out. Instead, I saw the funeral home at the end of the block. My husband felt the sudden change of mood in me. "What's wrong?" he wanted to know.

How could I tell him that my grandmother's superstition had seeped into me, so suddenly, after so very many years? I felt dazed the entire month. I kept a close check on my family members. The very last day of the lunar month, I sighed with relief. The danger had passed. Since when did I believe in superstitious nonsense? I was appalled at myself for allowing the thought to cross my mind.

The phone rang right before sunset. My sister-in-law's asthmatic father had died. He was in his home entertaining guests. He went to the bathroom to wash his face and couldn't catch his breath. With no one around to help, he had a heart attack. So, that was it. Was my grandmother correct after all? I became a believer. I never again opened my eyes after seeing the crescent of the new moon until I was sure my glance would fall on a happy face first. I had become my grandmother.

I always thought that the belief in the supernatural helped my grandmother and other women who lacked education to gain control over a world that was unknown and mysterious to them. But another reason, at least for my grandmother, was to gather people around her. After my grandfather's death, she feared loneliness. She worried that her children might get busy with their own lives and forget her. So she found creative ways to have the family visit her.

Even now, my sister Nahid and I laugh as we remember a day when we helped my grandmother sew the covers on a quilt. I was sixteen, my sister four years younger. Two French doors were left open to bring in the sun and the smell of potted geraniums from the balcony. A handmade quilt with geometric designs on blue satin was spread on top of a white sheet, tinted with a blue hue, still warm from the sun. The three of us sat on a red Kashan carpet with designs of flowers and palmettes. One leg tucked underneath, one planted on the floor, my sister folded the sheet neatly over the quilt as if she were framing a picture in ivory. She secured the fold with a safety pin, expediting the job of my grandmother and me, who hemmed the edges with large needles and long matching thread.

We threaded Khanom-bozorg's needle for her, made her a sour cherry drink, and ran down the street to buy a fresh bottle of skim milk (she never drank milk that didn't have that day's delivery date). We would do anything she liked in exchange for her memories.

She spoke of times when we were children and of the era before we were born, recalling family episodes and the way of life. She spoke of the houses in the *mahaleh,* separated with tall walls, but connected through flat mud-covered roofs, where one could travel the entire length of the ghetto by jumping from one to the other. "Do you remember it at all?" she asked me.

I remembered Aunt Fereshteh holding me to keep me from falling off the roof as I picked green apples from the top of our neighbor's tree that hung over our side.

My grandmother was astonished. "Oh! You remember that?"

"Yes, a guy in that house converted to Islam." By virtue of his new religion, he became the first in line to inherit his uncle's fortune. He was rejected from the community, of course. His Jewish wife and children were sent to Israel by her family so he could not take the kids. In revenge, he took a wife from an anti-Semitic family and moved his in-laws to his house as well. From then on, they threw stones at us whenever we tried to pick the top apples. Our neighbor later regretted his decision, not being able to cope with his new lifestyle, but it was too late. The punishment for rejecting Islam was death. Although the Jewish community never forgave him for enabling a Moslem family to live amongst us, it came to his aid and secretly arranged for him to be smuggled to Palestine to join his wife and children. After his disappearance, the family he left behind cut down the apple tree.

One reason that the community was angry at our neighbor was that connecting roofs were the last route of escape during pogroms. By giving his house to a hostile Moslem family, he had also given them access to our roofs, jeopardizing our safety.

The terrace roofs were also our summer retreat to a world above the dust and heat of the narrow alleyways. During the hot summer nights, we slept on the rooftops on mattresses spread on bamboo mats. There were no fences. Parents feared that their young children might wander off in the pitch darkness that engulfed the ghetto at night and fall off the roofs. In the women's section, I was always squeezed between my mother, grandmother, and aunts to ensure I wouldn't wander off. But, despite the parents' vigilant watch, every year the sad stories of a child or two who had fallen to their deaths circulated in the *mahaleh*. Or maybe the stories were made up to scare us into behaving.

The desert temperature fell rapidly at night and the gentle breeze flowed freely over the rooftops. The air was fresh and fragrant high above the old city in contrast to the stagnant air mixed with fine dust and the smell of animal and human refuse in the unpaved alleys. With no industrial or light pollution in the skies of Shiraz, the clear sky was a magnificent panoramic backdrop for the stars shining brightly against its blackness. Neighborhood women found each other in the light of candles and gossiped while cracking watermelon seeds between their back teeth. Men spoke of the day's business, their fears of the unfriendly neighbors, and the events in the Jewish community.

The flat roofs were delightful but also problematic. On rainy days in spring, or snowy days in winter, large patches of the ceiling collapsed in the common room, forcing the entire household—my grandmother, uncles, aunts, and us—to sleep in one room until the weather was sufficiently warm for repairs. Then, a mixture of mud and straw was hauled to the roof on the workers' backs, spread evenly, and packed by running the *ghaltak* on top.

A *ghaltak* was a heavy cylindrical stone. It took two men to control its roll. It was often shared by many neighbors and stored on top of a strong joint where the walls met. Pieces of stone and wood braced it when not in use.

Picking up the story as we sat sewing the quilts, my grandmother said that in those days (this is before I was born), the city of Shiraz opened its water reservoir to run through the gutters once a week. Plumbing wasn't available. The Jews stored the water in open pools often shared by many families in a common courtyard to be used for laundry and washing dishes.

On a chilly day at the end of fall, the water ran through the Jewish ghetto in man-made canals and poured into the pool. The women of my grandmother's family and the neighborhood had gathered for a wash-day. There were about thirty women, grandmothers who directed the activity, mothers who did the wash sometimes with the help of professional washerwomen, young girls who helped run errands and hang the clean clothes on the trees or wires running between them. Wrapped in their *chador*s, these women sat on low wooden stools around the pool, a wash basin in front of each. They rubbed the clothes on the back of their hands or against the fabric itself. Most Jews used pulverized branches of *choobak* bush to wash the clothes instead of soap, which was made with unkosher animal fat.

As women gossiped, sweet aromatic *sharbat* was passed around to refresh everyone. Once in a while a mother picked up a crying baby and let it suckle underneath her *chador*. Young children played in the dirt with sticks and pebbles. The boys played *alak-dolak:* They laid down little sticks that they hit hard to make airborne and then hit them harder with a larger stick and watched to see how far they flew, a dangerous game with the young ones around. The women shouted at them to keep away. The boys finally left the scene. My father, a young boy then, went with them.

The voice of women sharing stories was the only sound to be heard. Rushing to finish the clothes before dinner, they didn't notice the absence of the boys, who had found the door to the roof open. Filled with mischief, the boys hopped from one roof to another. Someone suggested rolling the *ghaltak*. They released the catch and rolled it on the roof. It was fun at first. Then the heavy stone found a life of its own. Picking up speed, it flew off the side of the roof toward the area where the women and children had congregated.

When the *ghaltak* hit the ground, it miraculously missed the entire group below. It hit the side of the pool, broke the tiles, and rolled into the water with a tremendous sound mixed with the screams of women, children, and the horrified boys who watched the scene from above.

Agha-jaan Bakhshi was a neighbor of my grandparents who was famous for his musical ability, especially as a violinist. He was at home that day taking a nap, enjoying the warm rays of sun coming through a window facing the pool. The commotion woke him from a deep sleep. Groggy and shaking, he screamed. "What happened? What happened?"

A woman screamed back with a shaken voice, "*Ghaltak* fell into the pool from the roof."

Because there is no "the" in Farsi and the language is gender-free, in his grogginess, Agha-jaan thought "*ghaltak*" was somebody's name. "Pull him out of the water. Did anyone pull him out of the water?" Agha-Jaan asked.

"Too heavy," another woman answered in the confusion.

Still disoriented from his sleep and horrified that the women had not taken "*Ghaltak*" out of the pool, Agha-jaan jumped out of the second-story window to save it, thinking that it was a child. He broke both legs and arms and had nothing to comfort him, not even his own music, as he was bed-ridden for months.

Nahid and I felt sorry for poor Agha-jaan, but my grandmother told the story in such a hilarious way that we held our stomachs and roared, missing the first few knocks at the front door. I looked out the window. "It's only cousin Yunes, visiting," I told my grandmother so she wouldn't worry about covering herself in a *chador*. I turned around to go downstairs and let him in.

My grandmother screamed, "Wait, wait!" In a swift move, she jumped into bed, took her false teeth out of her mouth, and deposited them on top of the watermelon seeds. "If he sees me sewing, the entire family is gonna think I'm well. They don't know how I suffer in pain every day! All alone! All by myself, with no one to look after me."

By the time Yunes and I reached the room, my grandmother was moaning through her bare gums, her face pale, her hair disheveled, her hands shaking, and her speech slurred. She would have been convincing even to me had I not been laughing with her minutes before.

Of course, Yunes used our newly installed telephone to call all the aunts, who came rushing in taxis and stayed all day massaging her back and her legs. My mother made special stews and drinks for everyone. The cousins dropped by one at a time to see how our grandmother was doing. They propped up my grandmother on comfortable pillows as they talked and gossiped. On their way out, each aunt turned to Nahid and me to tell us what terrible grandchildren we were for not taking care of our grandmother. We had giggled the entire time, disregarding the somber mood of the room as their mother lay suffering. Each aunt looked at my mother as they spoke to us, including her in the collective blame. They couldn't be there. They had their own lives. How could my mother allow her mother-in-law to deteriorate so very badly? Shame!

Nahid and I escorted them downstairs, closed the front door, knelt on the floor holding our stomachs, and laughed so hard that tears streamed down our faces. In the kitchen, my mother clanged the pots together as she washed them. She softly mumbled curses to no one in particular.

## The First Grade

My father visited the principal of Mehr-ayeen School again without me six months after our first visit. I don't know what transpired between them, if he raged or gave a gift, or if he took a more influential person with him. I was enrolled for the following year.

For the first month of school, my father proudly walked me to school every day in my new gray uniform. He stopped by the bakery and bought a slice of sponge cake for my snack. In America, I have learned that sponge cake is a symbol of Passover, filled with cholesterol from as many as twelve eggs that make it fluffy. To me, it is still the sign of my father's love, on which I gorge myself every Passover without any self-control.

On the first day, I was surprised to find two other Jewish girls in my class, neither of whom I had ever met. I knew all the children in the *ma-haleh* at least by appearance. I knew the boy with the football-shaped skull whom we called *khiaree* or cucumber-head, who played a game of sticks every time I passed by him, hitting me on the head. I knew the snot-crusted faces of the many children playing in the dirt of the unpaved streets, who my mother complained never got sick while her clean children did.

Meena was my best friend next door, of whom Mahvash had been jealous enough to convince me to pray for her death. I knew the kids with a lisp, the ones with crossed eyes, the ones with sores on their legs that were a feast for the flies, and the albino kid, of course, with glassy eyes. So many kids had problems that I assumed that was the way of the world. I knew the little boy from an entertainer's family, who dressed up as a girl to dance at happy occasions. I knew all the girls in a permanent state of curved spines, who didn't go to school and carried little babies on their hips. I knew all the boys my age who were *pa-do-ak,* a word literally meaning, "running legs," who were hired to run errands for shopkeepers. At school, for the first time, I realized that there might be Jews who lived outside the ghetto. Wealthy Jews.

Accompanied by her well-dressed mother, Fariba arrived late on the first day of school, wearing a beautifully tailored uniform. The fabric was a rich gray color, I noticed with jealousy, made of soft wool. I wished I could touch it. My own new cotton uniform felt dull and scratchy. I felt that there was a wall between us that was too high for me to leap over and meet her. Our Moslem teacher, Mrs. Khatami, jumped from her seat to greet them: "*Salam,* hello, Mrs. Doctor, welcome."

So her father was a doctor. Money and education wiped out some of the Jewish dirt, I thought—first lesson of the day. She made another girl move so Fariba could have an aisle seat, which her mother said she preferred.

During the first break, Mrs. Khatami introduced her to a few choice students, including an American girl. Mary's hair was yellow, a hair color that I had never seen and thought ugly. Her eyelashes were light, almost white, not giving much protection to the glassy, light-blue eyes. Her skin was the palest I had ever seen, other than the albino boy in the *mahaleh.* My grandmother would have said that she was "without salt, bland." I thought, "just washed out." And she spoke Farsi with a funny accent, displeasing to my ears.

She was popular, nevertheless. Mary and Fariba shooed away girls who were mesmerized by the unusual look of the *farangee* among our naturally tan skin and dark hair. I didn't try to approach them.

That day, my mother took time off from the busy kitchen to collect me. I was disappointed. I had hoped to see my father. Maman's hands looked rougher than usual, her dress thinner and cheaper. The vacant look in her eyes was the same. Fariba's older sisters picked her up with hugs and kisses, I noticed. They brought her an English language practice book. I heard them whispering that they were going to teach her the language. I felt a pang of jealousy. I wanted to learn English too.

Our teacher told us to bring three notebooks and two pencils to school the day after. "Don't come to school without them," she warned.

I felt as if she was only looking at me.

"You'll be punished, I promise." She shook her index finger at us.

Punishment, I had learned already, meant standing in the corner of the class on one foot, the way Eshrat was reprimanded that day. I told my mother on the way home that I needed to stop by a kiosk and buy the school supplies.

She was rushing to prepare dinner. "Wait till your father gets home," she said. I nagged my mother about the matter all afternoon.

When he came home, Baba gave me money to buy *naan* for dinner before a fast starting at sundown. "What about the supplies?" I asked.

"Get out of here and buy the bread," he commanded, "before it gets late."

I went to my mother again and asked if I could use the money to buy supplies.

She shrugged.

I went to Meena's house and asked her to accompany me to the kiosk a few blocks away and bought half of what Mrs. Khatami had requested, saving the rest of the money for bread. On the way to the bakery, we ran into my father and uncle Morad, wearing pajama bottoms, V-neck undershirts, and plastic flip-flops. How could they embarrass me like that, showing up in their lounging clothes?

"Where's the bread?" my father asked.

I showed them the notebooks proudly. Morad hit me on the head with the palm of his hand, screaming about how irresponsible and self-absorbed I was as Meena and the people on the busy street watched. I took the supplies back and asked for my money as my father watched from a distance. The owner deducted cash as penalty for the return. This time, my father himself, pajamas and all, rushed to the bakery to purchase the *naan*.

My teacher was not upset to find that I didn't have notebooks or pencils. She had expected it; that was the reason they didn't want kids like me at their school. As the seating was rearranged once more for Fariba and Mary to keep each other company on the same bench, the teacher moved me to the back of the class to sit with a trouble-making girl from the poor Moslem side of the city. "You're a nice quiet girl. Have a good influence on her," she demanded. "If Eshrat makes trouble, you'll be punished as well."

My parents reminded me years later how I went home everyday crying and not wanting to go back to school. Eshrat tortured me all year, pinched me whenever she thought I was taking too much room, stole my sponge cake, and hit my hand when I was writing and ruined my handwriting. I was afraid to complain. Although a *verag* at home, I was timid and quiet at school, fearful to voice my discomfort. My parents didn't try to find the reasons for my uneasiness. Once more, I learned not to count on them for protection.

"You used to be a good student," my teacher admonished me one day, "look at you now. You've become just like Eshrat and I was counting on you to change her!"

The second Jewish girl in my class, Golee, was a short, chubby girl with light, curly hair. Her father was also a physician. One day, as we lined up with our folding cups for milk, courtesy of the United States government, she started bragging about how her father loved her and always wanted to be the one to put her to bed. He caressed her back, and, every night before he left, he put his hand in her panties, massaged her private parts, and licked his fingers before leaving. She was surprised to find out that none of our fathers did that. Her story circulated around the school during recess and made her our pastime activity. We laughed and made her cry. She refused to go back into the classroom.

The principal called her older sister and demanded that Golee stop telling wild stories that corrupted the other girls, or else she would be expelled.

Golee's sister came to a group of us screaming from the top of her lungs: "You cruel, hateful, nasty kids. My sister would never say such lies. You've made up the story! You're evil."

I joined the others to answer her accusations with my nervous laughter. For the rest of the time I was at Mehr-ayeen, Golee never spoke to anyone her age, and walked around the yard alone at recess. Her only companion was her sister. I always wondered if she told her parents about the incident or if she too had learned to keep quiet.

I transferred to a new school the following year after we moved out of the *mahaleh*. My father rented the upstairs of our new house to an American family to make ends meet. My uncle's family, my grandmother, my unmarried aunt and uncle, and my family lived downstairs, occupying as much space as the two foreigners, a husband and wife, did on the second floor. I saw Mary visiting our neighbors one day as I sat on our outside steps. I said "*Salam,*" timidly.

"*Boro gom sho,*" she said with her American accent. She told me to get lost, assuming that I was pestering her like many Iranian kids who often followed the Americans on the streets, sometimes harassing them. She had never noticed me in her first-grade class.

Fariba and I never made friends. I didn't try and neither did she. She was of a different breed. She came from an educated family who traveled abroad often and had a nice home in an exclusive part of town. She probably was told to keep clear of those who came from the ghetto. She and I crossed paths in high school and again in college, where I struggled with English, which she spoke beautifully. She also knew French from her many trips to Europe on shopping excursions. I was still puzzled. How did a Jewish family become so wealthy and cultured? How was she ever going to find a Jewish husband from her social class? I heard that she married a Tehrani man after immigrating to Los Angeles.

As for Golee, we saw each other often at the synagogue and later in college. She always avoided me, never making eye contact.

## Leaving the Mahaleh

Midway through my first year at Mehr-ayeen, my father learned about a piece of land for sale in a faraway neighborhood. A well-known man, the owner had minor financial problems and needed to sell the land quietly, preferably to a man of little influence, who would not be among his circle of friends. My father and uncle Morad shared a small shop, making jewelry. The land was an impossible dream, but one they could not relinquish. They mortgaged the house and the shop. They borrowed money from the bank, family, and friends. The land was theirs. Building a modern home on a corner lot in one of the most progressive neighborhoods became their daily joy and pride.

By the time I was ready to register for the second grade, the house was half finished. The masons sat on the street chiseling stones all day for the

*A market place in the* mahaleh. Picture courtesy of Dr. Laurence D. Loeb.

outer facade of the house. The construction of a metal roof kept the main welding shop in Shiraz busy for months. No more clay roofs for us. No more leaks. No more patching and thatching. But, in the excitement, no one thought of slanting the roof to make the rain and snow run off easier. We still had to hire workers to shovel the snow off the flat roof every winter. Also, no one envisioned the heat absorbed by the metal roof during the hot summer months when the temperatures rose to dangerous degrees.

My father, however, foresaw the school problem for me and found one closer to the new house, hoping that we would move in the fall, before school started. That was not to happen. I had to commute to the distant neighborhood every day, and the hour-long walk made it impossible for my mother or father to accompany me both ways. My father walked me to school in the morning. He asked Mehdi, an apprentice at the shop, to pick me up at twelve o'clock.

I didn't mind going home with Mehdi. He invented funny riddles to make me laugh. He brought dried peaches for me, knowing that I was often starved on the long walk, and made a little game for eating the peaches.

There was a lazy boy who sat under a peach tree every day, he told me. Instead of climbing the tree, he laid underneath and screamed: *"Hooloo beoft to galoo,* Peach, fall in my mouth."

*One of the many alleyways in the* mahaleh. Picture courtesy of
Dr. Laurence D. Loeb.

"Did it work?" I wanted to know.

"Close your eyes and open your mouth," he said. "Yell '*hooloo beoft to galoo.*'"

When I did as he said, he put a small piece of the dried fruit in my mouth. It was delicious, but it was always too little.

"More please," I begged, closing my eyes and yelling the rhyme.

"Okay, but you have to give me a hug and a kiss first."

In the space of the five months he took me home, I gave away lots of tight hugs and kisses for the taste of the dried peaches. Although I found the entire thing a nuisance, I never thought much of it.

Once a man saw us in an embrace in the quiet alleyway leading away from the school. "Who are you, little girl?" he asked.

Mehdi said, "Don't tell him. He is a stranger, a Moslem."

But I was in a good mood, giggling and chewing the fruit. I told him my name, and when he said he wanted to buy some jewelry from my father, I gave him the directions also.

My father asked me that night if Mehdi had been bothering me.

I said "No."

Was I sure, he asked me.

Terrified, I denied any problems. Mehdi had made me swear I would deny the Moslem man's accusation or else I would get in big trouble. Baba picked me up from school from then on. About a week later, I came home to find him holding his head in his hands, looking exhausted. I felt as if I had been a deceitful daughter, a liar. So, I told him the truth.

"Okay, forget it," he told me. He then walked away absentmindedly, leaving me confused and disappointed.

Later that day, I learned that Mehdi had slipped while moving heavy containers of acid to wash the floor. The acid drenched his clothes, burning much of his body. The other workers rushed him to the hospital, but by the time they managed to secure a taxi and drive through the crowded streets filled with cars, bicycles, mules, and people, he was too far gone.

I felt guilt-ridden. Had I told my father the truth earlier, maybe he would have been fired and not died such a horrible death. Maybe if I hadn't told the stranger the truth, Mehdi would not have died. For some strange reason, I carried the burden of his horrible end as if I had committed an unforgivable sin.

He visited me in my nightmares, skinless, dripping with acid and blood, offering a dried peach in his deformed hand: "Open your mouth. Close your eyes: *Hooloo beoft to galoo.*"

*Chapter Four*

# A PLACE FOR ME

### Our New Home

The day finally came. We were moving out of the *mahaleh* to our new house—only thirty minutes from the Shah's residence in Shiraz, five minutes to the medical school. We were moving to an all-Moslem neighborhood.

There was total chaos in the morning as I prepared to leave for school. I would have preferred to stay at home, to be a part of the hubbub and fun of the move.

No! No one needed a child around. Not even if I could help with my little sister. No one was going to pick me up from school that day either. Could I find my way home?

Of course I could; I was a big girl; and the school was only a fifteen-minute walk to our new address. I was giddy with excitement. We were finally "moving to the street," a term used to describe those who left the ghetto.

After school, I joined the students lining up to march to various neighborhoods. I jogged gently in place, shifted my weight from foot to foot; the waiting was unbearable.

The teacher in charge of organizing the groups counted the students until she reached me, calling me by my last name as it was the custom, "Calm down! What are you doing here? Where is your father?"

I convinced her that we had truly moved—and yes, I knew how to get to the house after the line crossed the main street.

I was hungry and couldn't wait to have my first lunch in the new house. Uncle Morad was leaning against the door frame as I approached and was surprised to see me there. I was lucky, he told me, that he had stopped by to wait for someone from the city to connect the water and the electricity; otherwise, I would have come to a locked house. He had to go back and help with the move; he smirked and told me that since I was there—such a big girl and all—I would be in charge of the utilities connection.

I watched him as he walked away rapidly in long strides, and the smaller he became, the larger the house loomed over me. Our new house was a duplex, separated by frosted, sculpted glass doors that led to a winding staircase. I ran around the large rooms, enjoying the feel of the open spaces. I jumped up and down with no one to tell me to stop, screamed and enjoyed the echo of my voice bouncing off the bare walls. When I ran out of games to play, my stomach reminded me that it was past lunch time and there wasn't even a drop of water in the shiny clean pipes. Lunch was the biggest meal of the day, and the *sofreh* was usually spread on the car-pet by the time I got home from school. But in the new house, the pantry was completely empty, shining brightly from its new coat of white paint.

The man from the water department finally came, and, although he told me it was okay to stay, I waited outside as he connected the water in-side the house. But no one from the electrical company showed up that day, and, as the sun languidly dipped behind the buildings, imaginary demons hovered around me. Spooky, dark thoughts occupied my mind: What if the family decided not to move; what if they had forgotten me?

I heard the distant voice of the *muezzin* chanting the prayers at dusk. I went outside and sat on the front steps, but kept the door slightly ajar, ready to retreat and lock it if a stranger approached me. The light bulbs on the wooden beams lining the street came to life with a yellowish glow. I was afraid of the unfamiliar street, yet more fearful of the dark, empty house. Panic found its way into my stomach and bounced. I wrapped my hands around myself, my head on my knees, and played with my braid the way I used to rub my grandmother's before I went to sleep.

I sat there for maybe an hour before the neighborhood kids discovered me. First, there was a young girl with short, straight hair, from the house around the corner. She stood afar for a few minutes until she was joined by another one with curly hair and a darker complexion, then another, and another. When a large group had gathered, they finally walked over, ex-amining me, eyeing me with curiosity.

Was I really Jewish? one asked.

How did they know that, I wondered, and did I match the description their parents taught them, the specifications they had learned about the Jews? They circled me with wondering eyes. Their suspicion of the Jews wasn't surprising to me, because the first day at my new school, I had caused a near riot as I had tried to drink from the water spouts in the yard. A few girls had knocked me over the head, protesting that they used the water to make themselves *taher,* to clean before saying their prayers. If I made the waterspouts *najes,* they wouldn't have clean water to purify themselves. Other girls had joined the group, deciding if they should designate one spout for the Jews. Yet others thought the entire thing nonsense. I stood there paralyzed until an administrator broke up the group. She told us that it was unsanitary for anyone to put her mouth to the spout. "Make sure you drink out of your hand," she added, and then walked away, not quite satisfying those who believed that my touch alone defiled the water source.

Now that I was meeting Moslem girls from my new neighborhood, I wasn't quite sure if I should be happy or afraid.

Did we use the blood of Moslem kids for our Passover crackers, one wanted to know.

I shook my head, not knowing from where the outrageous idea had sprung.

A debate broke out between the ones who were certain that I was lying and were cautioning against getting too close to me, and those who didn't think a child could be that harmful, especially when they outnumbered me. We finally spoke about other matters. Which school was I attending? Where were my parents? How many people in the household? They too had more than their immediate family living with them, although the size of my family sounded a bit unusual to them. To take care of one's grandparents at home was customary—but aunts and uncles living in the same house?

We talked a bit longer from a distance. I assumed that they worried that my touch would defile them. I was afraid to ask for a piece of bread or a glass of tea. What if the food wasn't kosher? What if they poisoned it to kill me? Would they allow me to touch their utensils anyway? They surely feared that I would make them *najes.*

At some point, when the speculations had been exhausted on both sides, when our patience for arguments had ran out, they looked at the sidewalk in front of the house and thought it unusually wide—a perfect spot for hopscotch. The first girl, Zari, ran home and returned with a piece of charcoal. The second girl, Paree, found the perfect stone. We played game after game, laughing and screaming, fighting over nothing but the scores, and the fairness of the judgment: What if someone's foot had brushed the line? Or if the stone was still inside the square when it touched the line?

By the time the two trucks overloaded with carpets, pots and pans, bedding, and tired faces showed up in front of the house, there were two separate games going on with half the neighborhood children clapping and encouraging the kids hopping on one foot, hitting the stone from one square to another.

My family, horrified to see so many Moslem kids in front of the house, shooed them away. Dismayed at the drawings on the new sidewalk, Morad sent me to find a rag and wipe them out. "The last time! The very last time I'm going to see you bring all those Moslem kids to our home; they will become brazen and learn our comings and goings and rob us clean," he spewed the words at me.

My hunger came back. I was starved now that the fun was gone and the regular life of discipline and chastisement had restarted.

My sleeping baby sister in her arms, my mother giggled in her usual style of exonerating herself from responsibilities of adulthood. She used the plural "we" instead of the singular "I" to communicate a participatory neglect. "We kept asking what had happened to Farideh-oo," adding the usual Shirazi accent of "oo" at the end of my name to ensure my third person position, as if I were not in the room.

No, there was no food in the house; they ate before leaving; they didn't know where anything was. Who told me to come here instead of going home anyway? They had been so busy—such a horrible, taxing day!

I didn't ask why no one had been waiting at the school to take me home, if I were supposed to go to the old house. They had forgotten about me. It was as simple as that, and no one was willing to take the blame. So in the end, I was at fault; I had worried them; I wasn't at the house to help at least with the baby. How dare I ask for food when they were so busy moving the furniture with no light to guide them through the house? Someone asked, "Do you ever pay attention?" Another voice chimed in from within the darkness that I must have been too busy making trouble with the neighborhood kids to notice the man from the electrical company. Now someone had to scramble for candles. "When are you going to grow up?" yet another relative grumbled from behind the shadows the candles had etched on the walls of our new house.

I didn't dare ask why Morad hadn't mentioned me. I went through the packages as they were being unloaded and found a small snack bundle in the corner of the room that my grandmother had put aside for herself. I tore through it, greedily eating the leftover bread and cheese from the cloth wrapping as I sat on the bare floor in the dark, wishing for a hot cup of tea.

I was the only Jewish student at my new school until many years later when my sister Nahid was old enough to enroll, and the only Jewish child in our neighborhood until my friend Mahvash and her family moved to a nearby street. I had no choice but to make Moslem friends, well aware of the restrictions from both my family and theirs.

Baba, so suspicious of everyone outside the immediate family, couldn't understand my need for friendship. He himself had been scolded by the members of the Jewish community after his father's death whenever he had "selfishly" made plans with a friend for a picnic, or if he had strolled down the street with one. Was that a time he could afford *rafigh-bazi?* The Persian word has no synonym in English. It means the game of having friends, as if they were an addiction like gambling or smoking hashish. In return, my father tried his best to educate me in the lessons he had been taught himself, the codes of community life that he had been subjected to and had come to believe.

The more Baba watched me, the more secretive I became. Once my father observed me happily walking home with a few neighborhood girls, hopping at times, laughing at their jokes. He was incensed.

I defended myself: "It's not that I wanted to make friends with these girls, but they were going my way . . ."

"Then, just mind your own business and walk on the opposite side of the street. I don't want my daughter to run like a farmer's girl after the chickens. Lower your head and walk modestly. No hopping, no laughing like a fallen girl."

I told my friends that I had to separate myself from them on the street leading to our house, knowing that my father stood watch from the second-floor window, smoking a cigarette.

Baba's mistrust of the Moslems had a valid foundation. Not only had he witnessed the raid against the *mahaleh* as a child, but he had also seen his father beaten bloody as they walked home from the synagogue one Shabbat morning. The ghetto alleyways being muddy, they had decided to walk on the street although it was forbidden for Jews to be outside the ghetto on rainy days. My grandfather, the chief rabbi of the community, respected not just by Jews but by many Moslems as well, looked pathetic and humiliated—his caftan torn, his *kippa* a toy for the thugs, his long white beard smeared with blood and mud. My father had been too young and too frightened to protect him against strong and angry young men.

Baba had seen unprovoked violence against the Jews, who were hated for being meek and poor, yet despised when wealthy and strong. The week we moved into the new house, our neighbor's son raised a bright red, glass swastika in his bedroom facing our house. We couldn't escape its colossal presence: at night, it shone under a display lamp, and during the day, it glittered in the sunlight—sickeningly beautiful.

My friend's grandfather routinely dumped their garbage by our sidewalk, and one summer night, as we slept in our backyard, someone set fire to our pine trees. We could hear steps receding and loud cackles of laughter, and my father was convinced that Zari's brothers were behind the destruction.

I had my own experiences as well. The *hajee,* a title the grandfatherly-looking grocer had taken after pilgrimage to Mecca, rubbed his hands, sticky from handling dates, on mine as he passed a bag of lentils, making me feel queasy. I was disgusted at myself for being lazy and not walking the extra twenty minutes to another shop. But then, a Jewish merchant had also tried to put his hands under my skirt when I was looking at socks in his shop. I didn't tell my parents of either incident. I knew that the basic nature of people was the same beneath the divisive layers of religious beliefs. Baba himself had told me that whereas close family members left him and his young siblings to starve after his father's death, a Moslem man trusted him with his gold when he was a young, inexperienced jeweler, and saved the family from hunger.

I didn't find it possible to build a cage around myself. Instead, I found it ironic that my father, who struggled and sacrificed so much to get us out of the ghetto, was obviously missing the security of its tall walls and insulated community, where all faces were familiar, where he didn't have to keep on a mask of politeness, humility, and even servitude at all times to present the neighbors with the opposite of what he thought they expected of a Jew.

In our new neighborhood, my mother and grandmother stayed home to cook, clean, and receive visitors, mostly family and old neighbors from the ghetto who were curious about the house. Their outside interactions were limited to the area shopkeepers. Maman came back complaining every day. The man at the fruit stand didn't allow her to select her own because his customers wouldn't buy *najes* food if her Jewishness rubbed off on the fruit; he put overripe peaches and rotten apples in my mother's basket. The baker gave her leftover *naan* that no one else would take, and since everyone in the neighborhood had maids who stood in the long line for bread three times a day, the humiliation was heightened for her. She was lower than the Moslems' servants in stature.

My experience differed from the rest of the family, since I had a balance in my relationship with the Moslems. Abuses did happen, but so did friendship, love, and kindness. Members of Paree's family were devoted Moslems. Unlike our chaotic house, hers was always clean and orderly. Persian carpets covered the entire large common room; a brass samovar with a pot of tea placed on top stood at the furthest corner of the room from the door. Over the mantle, the usual portraits of the Prophet Mohammed and Imam Ali hung above the family pictures. Koranic verses embossed in silver and framed in Shiraz *khatam* hung on the wall asking for Allah's protection. Paree's father bowed to me and never looked at my face, protective of my modesty. Her mother wrapped herself in a *chador* even at home, never saying anything but kind words, asking about my family's health, praying for good grades for me, offering a glass of sour cherry *sharbat,* chai, and sugar lumps with rice cookies.

One day I visited Paree, knocked at the door, and impatiently waited for her to open before someone from our household could see me visiting.

"Shhh!" Paree asked for my silence as she moved aside to let me in. Her mother was in the middle of her noon prayers. We took our shoes off and tip-toed quietly to the corner, sat cross-legged, and waited for her mother to finish. She had a large white kerchief wrapped around her head and fastened under her chin with a safety pin. It covered her shoulders and most of her back. Bare-footed on top of a prayer-rug, she was now bending, now kneeling and putting her forehead on the prayer stone at the head of the carpet. She looked serene, content, at peace, the opposite of my mother, who was filled with repressed anger, hatred, unhappiness, and feelings of abandonment bubbling like molten lava inside her.

I wanted Paree's mother to be mine.


## My Space

I had imagined us having such freedom in the new house, without the eyes of the community scrutinizing our every move. I had envisioned open spaces for me and my family in a big house. Today I can say that I never lived in a place more confining.

When the house was under construction, I went with Baba often to check on its progress. Fascinated, I watched the Moslem workers from nearby villagers who had moved to the site, working, sleeping, and eating around the foundation of our house. They sat on the ground chiseling stones all day with long nails and hammers; fine stone dust covered their beards and eyelashes and gathered in clumps around their mouths, where they had coughed it out.

A bare-footed bricklayer hauled buckets of mortar up on a pulley; yet another man, with his legs hanging on either side of the wall, rested the bucket next to himself, scooped and slammed the mortar on the wall with a spatula, at which point the man at the bottom threw him a brick. He grabbed and set it tightly on the mortar. They were quick, efficient, and precise, building a wall around my house to give us our own private space, to free us from the claustrophobic ghetto.

As the house came together, I was ecstatic about my room on the right side of the foyer, about which I bragged nonstop to my unbelieving class-mates. One day, his pencil mustache twitching, Uncle Morad smirked and pointed it out to me on the blueprint, "That's *your* room. How do you like it?" I looked at him, then at my silent father, and again at the small space on the paper, and jumped up and down in delight.

Finally, Uncle Jahangeer heard Morad building up my expectations and told him to stop teasing me. My room was the only toilet downstairs. Morad was right, however, to tell me that the bathroom was mine, since I had the responsibility of scrubbing it every Friday until I left Iran in my senior year of college.

None of us were destined to have a room of our own. The dining room with no windows was Uncle Morad's, soon to be married and his wife added to the crowded house. A small room was my family's. My parents slept on the platform bed, my sister and I and soon two brothers slept on mats strewn on the floor. A large room connected with a smaller one accommodated my grandmother and her two youngest children, Uncle Jahangeer and Aunt Fereshteh—my uncle slept in the back room, the two women in the front room that doubled as the living quarters and dining area.

Years later, we accepted the modern idea of using the large foyer as a common room, conquering our distaste of being so close to a lavatory, but my grandmother cringed whenever someone used the toilet as we lounged in the hallway. She believed a toilet belonged in the backyard, far away from where we ate and slept.

Shortly after we settled in the house, the realtor found an elderly American couple to rent the second floor and help pull us out of the huge debt that my father and uncle had accumulated. The separate quarters with their beautiful curved staircase, large glass windows, living and dining rooms that stretched the entire length of the house, terrazzo floors, gold-embossed handmade plaster moldings, and wooden and glass built-in china cabinet seemed to have been designed from the beginning with the idea of someone else living in it. My father had also had a *toilet-e farangee,* a European-style toilet, built to replace the hole in the floor. There was already a bathtub installed in the bathroom with a hand-held shower that didn't cease to amaze us. I used to walk around the tub and touch it, enjoying the feeling of being so close to such unbelievable, exotic luxury. Unlike the mud-covered, charcoal-burning stoves in the gloomy kitchen downstairs, there was a gas stove upstairs, and a window opened conveniently into the dining room to pass the food. Our American neighbors brought a dishwasher, a washing machine, and a dryer along with their truck and large boxes of canned and packaged food from the States. They also had enough communication gadgets to fill an entire room. They ran a large antenna from the attic to the roof and spent much of their time at night listening to the ham radio, whose muffled beeping traveled through the walls and could be heard on rare occasions, when the house was not noisy and chaotic.

We didn't have a telephone until I was a college freshman. Uncle Beejan, who was doing a medical residency in the United States, periodically sent us tapes in additions to the letters that were always read and reread, kissed, and stored neatly high on a mantle out of respect. Since we didn't have a tape recorder either, the *farangees* lent us one. They excitedly let us use their machine and listened with us. We briefed them on the messages my uncle so painstakingly addressed to every single person in the house, including the children; therefore, it was fortunate that when he decided to speak to his sister, Aunt Fereshteh, in English our tenants were attending a dinner party. "Are the Americans spies?" my uncle asked.

Spies or not, they exposed us to a taste of American life. We never used their names to talk about them; we rather called them *Aamrikaioo,* the Americans. The tall man, whose robust figure dwarfed the shorter Iranian men, lined up Baba, Morad, Jahangeer, and even some of the neighbors around the large traffic circle in front of the house and taught them the basics of baseball. They stood there with their large leather gloves, learning to throw and catch balls. Self-conscious, Baba chewed his mustache. The neighborhood kids stood around with their mouths wide open, ready to run after each stray ball; the women giggled and pointed to anyone who missed.

When our American neighbors sprinkled salt on the sweet watermelon, we made faces: "Yach, yach!" They boiled their corn instead of roasting it: "Ooo! How nasty!" we all agreed. They pulled some of the flowers out of our flower beds and planted tomatoes that grew large and fleshy, which they reaped when still green. They wouldn't listen to us that they would taste better ripening on the vine; instead, they lined them up on their window sill. My grandmother thought that maybe those strange *farangees* ate them green.

To our dismay, they bathed every day, wasting our precious resources. Yet most of us avoided their touch. They didn't wash their bottoms in the bathroom as Iranians did; instead, they wiped themselves. How disgusting! Americans held their dogs, the most defiled animal in an Islamic country, and even kissed them. They smelled funny. As Jews, we felt hurt whenever Moslems considered us *najes,* impure to touch because of our religion. Nevertheless, it was easy even for me to go along with the societal beliefs and to think of Americans as *najes* and cringe if touched by them.

Every Wednesday, our entire family visited my grandmother in the courtyard. If the weather was mild, they sat in a circle on a Persian carpet on the bricked-backyard. I played hide and seek with my sister and ten cousins. We chased each other with a water hose, threw shoes at each other, which had to be hunted later from underneath the bushes, from the tops of trees, and from inside the neighborhood yards. The women took turns smoking a waterpipe and cracking watermelon seeds. On these occasions, the Americans stood on the balcony watching us and laughing. They showed us their generosity by throwing candies or boxes of animal crackers down like the king and the queen of the Mardi Gras from a float, watching us scramble, push, and shove like animals for a piece of America.

## Out of Place

I don't remember much about my sister's birth. When I was four, I once saw my mother folded over the flower beds in the morning, vomiting mushed bread and cheese that smelled like rotten pickled apples. I ran to my grandmother and screamed, "Maman is dying!"

She laughed.

Then, my sister Nahid was born, but I couldn't play with her as I had hoped. She was back in the hospital with a severe infection shortly after her birth; and I was jealous because Maman spent her time with the newborn. I don't know who took care of me then—probably my grandmother. I don't know if I cried, if it mattered to me that at a time when I rarely saw my father, who worked into the late hours of night, my mother was not around either. Early in the morning, Maman left for the hospital on her daily visits to Nahid. Upon returning, she cried softly as she cooked, and she wouldn't eat her lunch because a big lump was always blocking her throat. Unaware of the seriousness of my sister's illness, I kept away from my grieving mother as if she were a stranger, afraid to enter her morbid sphere.

A deep sadness hung in the air. The birth of a second daughter wasn't a joyful occasion to begin with in a culture that prized boys. My sister's illness that would lead to a physical imperfection added to the agony of our parents' lives. A female's destiny was marriage, and what did a girl have to offer but a good name, beauty, and physical flawlessness? Later, as an adult, I learned that my mother had miscarried a child late in her pregnancy after I was born. "A son!" she sighed. She thought hard work, bending and carrying heavy objects contributed to the death of the fetus. Sometimes she blamed the miscarriage for my sister's problems; maybe her womb hadn't had the strength to produce a healthy baby. But then she said that it was her fate. Later, the family discovered that my mother's brother, Shimon, had undeveloped arms, a hunched back, and crooked short feet. My ma-

*The mausoleum housing the tombs of Esther and Mordechai in Hamedan, my mother's birthplace.* Picture courtesy of Farsinet.com.

ternal grandmother Touran blamed Thalidomide for the deformity. But my father's family and even my father blamed my mother's genes.

Later, as an adult, I learned that my mother had insisted on giving birth to this child at a newly built hospital to avoid a dirty midwife. But, ironically, as the result of unsanitary conditions at Morsalin Hospital in Iran, Nahid suffered from osteomyelitis, which began from an infected umbilicus at birth. Poor diagnosis and medical mistakes exacerbated the infection that had nested in Nahid's hip. She was given massive doses of antibiotics to help fight the infection, followed by surgery to drain the affected area. Despite the efforts, the top of Nahid's right femur was eroded by the infection, which would leave her with a hanging hip and a severe limp.

Walking at one, she had a barely noticeable discrepancy in the length of her legs. By age three, she was walking on the tip of her right foot to gain

*The tombs of Esther (left) and Mordekhai (right) in Hamedan.* Pictures courtesy of Hadi Rabbani.

a few inches for balance. This image of my sister became etched on my mind: a ballerina with big dark brown eyes, pointing with one leg only, looking at the world for answers to her plight.

When she was six, Nahid's body dipped to the right exaggeratedly. My father came home one day after a meeting with her surgeons. "I am taking Nahid to Israel," he said, his eyebrows drawn together. "The doctors here are suggesting to immobilize her leg. That would be a terrible fate for a young girl," he added with tears in his eyes. For the first time, I saw my father cry. He and Nahid left for Tel Ha-shomer Hospital in Israel and spent much of that year away from home.

By this time, my mother had given birth to my brother Freydoun, who was now four; she was also pregnant again. But she insisted on accompanying Nahid and my father to Tehran to bid them farewell on their journey to Israel, and also to visit her family, who had moved to the capital to escape the insufferable anti-Semitism. When Baba and my sister left, my mother's brother Eliahou insisted that we should stay longer, visit my mother's hometown, Hamedan, and make a pilgrimage to the tombs of Esther and Mordechai to pray for my sister.

I remember most of Hamedan like an old black and white movie, fuzzy,

*A sukah decorated with hand-painted tapestry, built by the small Jewish community still living in Hamedan.* Pictures courtesy of Hadi Rabbani.

out of focus, an amateur production that had yellowed with age. More than anything else, my mother wanted to visit the Jewish ghetto to check on her old friends. My uncle kept reminding her that many years had passed and that most of the community had emigrated either to Israel or to Tehran as her family had. Yet, she had to see the place she had longed for since her wedding, so that was our first stop.

My mother's demeanor changed quickly as she recognized her childhood arena. She put her hand on her mouth and giggled, her voice cracking in joy. Once in a while, she skipped, forgetting her stomach, the size of a round watermelon. "Remember," she asked Eliahou, "the day we made a big pile of snow? Remember?"

Eliahou winked at me when he noticed my astonishment. His long black eyelashes couldn't hide the tears. His big bony frame wrapped around my mother. "Yes, wasn't that fun?"

"Remember we made such a big cave inside the pile of snow and asked our little brother to stand on it . . ." She couldn't continue for a minute, giggling so hard, her eyes teared. "Poor thing fell inside and all the snow . . ." She bent in laughter. "All the snow fell on him and we had to dig him out. . . . Oh, so much fun!"

This was a side of my mother I had never seen! I was embarrassed by her behavior, wanting her to act with dignity. She tittered as she bounced and skipped on the dirt-covered alleyways, forgetting the baby in her big stomach. "Let's knock at this door and ask if Moneer is still living here," she said. "She was my classmate, you know. There it is!" She covered her mouth to squash a cry of joy.

There was a tiny dilapidated door in the ruins of what had been once a large community. A brass knob was calling my mother. She hit the door with it, chewing her fingernails as we waited. Eliahou put his arm around her.

"Yes!" The door opened a crack to show a wrinkled face framed with an old flowery kerchief above stooped shoulders. "What do you want?"

"Is Moneer here?" When she saw the astonished look on the woman's face, my mother pointed to herself. "Don't you know who I am? Rouhi. Don't you remember? I used to come to play with Moneer."

The old woman crinkled her eyes; she pursed her mouth like the tied knot of a cheesecloth around mushy cheese, hung to drain.

"Moneer finished high school, went to Tehran to become a nurse, married, and left for Eretz Israel. Everyone's gone. There are only a few Yehudim left."

My mother's eyes darkened. She had finally come back home to find that it was not home after all. "So is life," she sighed, "we will never find each other." She stood there even after the door closed.

Eliahou took her hand and in a quiet voice said, "Let's go for ice cream."

At the garden café, we sat down under the shade of cypress trees on a brick patio. I had tasted ice cream a few times before but never served in such a fancy manner—shaped into white and brown balls and presented in footed glass bowls. I wondered how someone had formed such perfect balls and didn't want to ruin their shapes with my spoon.

"It's melting," my uncle warned, "you better eat it now." I wanted to know why one of the balls was brown. "Chocolate!" Eliahou said as he watched me. I gobbled the treat in rapid gulps and then sat there with a sticky mouth looking longingly at my uncle's dish, which my mother forbade him to share with me.

I remotely remember spending the afternoon in the luscious hills of Abbas Abad on the outskirts of Hamedan where families picnicked under the trees. The gurgling of the waterpipe, the smell of the kebab, the laughter of faceless people were everywhere as I kept bending over, trying to capture the gold in the glittering sand. I felt humiliated when my mother finally told me that the gold dust was nothing but a mirage. I wanted to go home then, but Eliahou promised the delight of visiting the tombs of Esther and Mordekhai the day after.

The following day, I was shocked at the sight of the building. "This is it?" We had come such a long way to see the drab, square brick monument. Maybe if my uncle had not built up the trip to be such a fantastic adventure I would have not been so disappointed. I hadn't expected a palace for a burial ground, but a Persian monument decorated with blue tiles, like the mosques colorfully scattered throughout Iran—in Esfahan, Shiraz, Tehran. The Moslems had conquered Persia much later; nevertheless, the Achaemenids had Romanesque columns; images of beasts, flowers, and soldiers carved in stones decorated their palaces and their tombs. I expected to see a glittering gold or silver dome marking the burial place of our courageous queen. Instead, there was only a plain building with a dome. Rather than the hands of Persian artisans and stone masons, strong winds, rainfall, and ice had shaped the sand-colored bricks through the last two millennia.

"Is this truly the burial site of Esther and Mordekhai?" I asked Eliahou in disbelief. The poor sat cross-legged on the grounds, their lunches of yogurt and flat bread spread over kerchiefs. A few vagrants squatted on the worn-out steps, their greasy fingers extended through the sleeves of their patchy overcoats, gesturing for alms.

The *ziarat* was meant to be the highlight of our trip. Every year, Esther's story was retold in all its awesome details: love, treachery, and heroism. The most beautiful women of each region had been brought to the king's palace so he could choose a new queen. The beautiful Esther had groomed herself for King Akhashverosh, her black eyes red from crying, her spirit gloomy for having to leave home. But her uncle Mordekhai, her only family alive, had encouraged her to be brave. Maybe God was placing her in this fate for a greater purpose. Among all the virgins, the most beautiful woman of each province was ordered to the court by the royal decree; but a Jewish woman was chosen to be the queen of the most powerful man, the King of the Persian Empire.

Then, after she held a position of respect and power, Esther had endangered her life to stop the murder of the entire Jewish community by the evil vizier Haman. How could she then be buried in this simple place? If not as a Jewish heroine, then as a queen she deserved better. I thought of the room in the ruins of the palace, Takhte Jamshid, outside Shiraz that I was told was hers. The large room was made of the finest stones, polished to such degree that they reflected the queen's image as mirrors do. The king wanted his queen to be surrounded by her own beauty. Where were such fineries then for her tomb?

A strong sense of longing overtook me. "I want to go home," I whimpered. "I want Baba."

"He is in Israel with Nahid. You know that," my uncle said.

I was at an awkward age, with a scrawny body and chicken legs. I had never been away from my father for such a long time, never spent so much time with my mother. Baba had been away for only a few days, but I already felt that I had forgotten his features. Now that the excitement of the trip had died in disappointment, I especially needed the comfort of a familiar place, where my father's clothing hung in the closets, where the scent of his cigarettes was a part of the house.

I refused to enter the mausoleum, crossed my arms and puckered my lips, expecting the filth to be also in the inside. Holiness couldn't exist in squalor, I thought. My mother covered my hair with a kerchief and pushed me up the broken steps. We entered through the threshold of the heavy wooden doors. The room was dimly lit from the natural light of a skylight. The sweet fragrance of rose water surrounded us, mixed with the smoky smell of candles burning in remembrance. A large dome in the middle of the room was covered with silk fabrics in bright colors, some with gold threads. Women crowded around the sepulcher crying, some beating their chests, a few spread even more cloth on top; all lips moved in silent requests, quiet prayers. A younger, worn-out woman held tightly to the bars crying and had to be forcefully peeled off to make room for the crowd behind her.

In a carved opening in the wall in front of us, a Torah scroll stood upright in its round silver casing, decorated with velvet fabric and gems, crowned with silver. My mother and I bent to kiss it. I prayed for my sister's healing and for her and my father's safe return. I don't know what my mother prayed for but our faces were covered with tears as we stood up.

I had not seen the tombs yet. They were hidden underneath the offerings. I knelt by the bars, removed the layers of fabric and stared down into the deep room underneath. Two simple gravesides were lit artificially. The rest was darkness. My uncle bent over and told me that those who wished very hard could be transported to Jerusalem through a secret passage underneath.

I closed my eyes and willed to be in Jerusalem with my father and Nahid. I imagined being transferred down to the gravesides, musty and dark. I reached to find the walls to the tunnel, slowly making my way through its dark, narrow, muddy sides. I could not see anything. I cried for my father, "Baba, Baba." I called for my sister, "Nahid, where are you? Do you see me?" An echo came back, and I was trying hard to hear the words, but a hand grabbed me by the shoulders and removed me. My time was up.

I wrote to Nahid every day when I returned to Shiraz, telling her of my experience in Hamedan and of the little events of our lives. The two of us became very poetic, dwelling on the sorrows of the unimaginable distance that separated us, in the florid tradition of Iranian poetry bemoaning heart-wrenching separations.

Nahid had not attended school yet and could not read or write. My father read my letters to her and wrote her responses. I looked for beautiful postcards of two birds for her—to give her something to look at when she did not understand written words. We called ourselves two *bolbols*, nightingales, the symbol of pure love in Persian poetry. I sent Nahid long letters and postcards with the picture of colorful birds: tropical parakeets, whimsical ones, fanciful like the birds in the Iranian epic, *Shahnameh*. My favorite ones had a sprinkle of glitter on them. Always, I put those in envelops so their sparkle would not diminish during their journey to Nahid.

When my little sister came back from her surgery, she still had those big dark eyes, but she was not dragging one leg along either. She could not walk. Nahid was in a body cast. She could move only her arms and her head. They put her on a single bed in my parents' room, with the headboard by the window. My baby brother's circumcision ceremony had been delayed by a week so my father could be back. During the party, when Nahid stretched to look at the guests in the backyard, she fell off the bed and broke the leg in the cast. That day, my father told me that I was in charge of her, that I should not leave her sight unless someone else was there.

This is how I became my sister's guardian the summer before sixth grade. I taught her the curriculum for the first grade so she would not be a year behind. Even though the lessons were just writing and math, I resented the task because it meant not having as much time to read for myself. Often, I told her to go to sleep, while I picked up a story to read. Nahid wouldn't allow me: "Read it to me too." I dragged a mattress next to her bed on the floor and lay next to her. I told her stories from *Shahnameh* in the imaginary mythical land of Touran; I told her the tales of Vikings on the cold seas, although I had never seen an ocean, or even a lake or a river. Sometimes I forgot the stories in the middle. Nahid would not accept that. "Just make them up," she demanded. Sometimes Nahid told me about the orange groves she had seen in Israel, or even the ocean, or the airplanes she had flown in. I had never seen a plane. The two of us made travel stories and flew to exotic places like America in our imaginations. Sometimes, I made up stories about the rumors of little girls being kidnapped on the way to school. We stayed up all night in fear, although we were safe at home, locked in one room.

The situation didn't get much better when Nahid was out of her cast. She had to relearn walking at age seven with braces tightly holding her right leg in place, her shoes heavy and cumbersome. My sister was brave. She never asked, "why me?" My grandmother bought a calf's hoof every Friday, filled it with water and made my sister drink the stinking fluid. A wise-woman had told her it would strengthen the weak leg, already looking much thinner than the other. When family members came to visit, our aunts bent their heads close and whispered about Nahid's problem. "She shouldn't go out," they said. "She would be mocked and laughed at. She could be treated as street entertainment."

People did stare at my sister; women pulled their *chadors* tightly around themselves and gawked. Kind ones said, *"che heife,* what a pity!"

My grandmother asked her doctor if Nahid could ever carry a baby and give birth. Many in the family whispered that with such deformity, no one would ever marry her. My father worried what would happen to his daughter without a man in her life.

Nahid passed the exam for the first grade and was allowed to enter elementary school at the second-grade level. As the principal gave her the results, she looked proud and confident. School, however, was not what she had dreamt. Having never attended school, Nahid still had a hard time shaping the more difficult Persian letters. When she failed to produce a perfect letter "K" at the beginning of the word *kam-kam* (ironically meaning "little by little"), her teacher slapped her. I was pulled out of class to calm her down. She stood outside her classroom sobbing. Her teacher, seething with anger, hit my sister hard on her head in front of me, aggravated by a seven-year-old's lack of control over her emotions.

To make matters worse, Nahid couldn't go to the bathroom by herself. She could not untie her braces or squat over the hole in the ground. I had left a hospital bed-pan at school for her. It was a novelty to all others who had never seen one. It was a clear sign of humiliation and lack of privacy for my sister, who had to use it in an open hallway, and an embarrassment and an inconvenience for me to be called constantly to take her to the bathroom. Wishing so much to escape my own sense of humiliation, I couldn't wait to leave for high school.

That year, I was in the sixth grade, my last year in the small elementary school, Tavalali. As the senior class, we were making plans to disperse among various girls' high schools, excited in anticipation of meeting a larger group of students. A new teacher at the school, Mrs. Mojtahedi, was in charge of the sixth grade. Short black hair in wild curls surrounded her round face, shiny from excessive makeup. She wore black eyeliner around her eyes that were lost in her raised cheeks and painted lips with the reddest lip color I had ever seen. Due to her unusual obesity, she struggled to make the smallest movements and created so much body heat that her makeup melted and smeared. The regular chairs weren't big enough for her, so she brought her own and didn't bother to move out of it other than to leave for a break, at which point she asked one of the girls to guard the chair instead of taking her own break with the threat of punishment if she failed. Very early on, she assigned students to help with teaching.

She designated me to teach history and geography because I managed to answer a few questions. Maps were not available for geography; historical events were not discussed. Instead, students took turns reading the assigned pages from the textbooks, then the teacher told us to memorize the long passages word for word by copying them a few times. Sometimes, there were no written tests. A student was called in front of the class to regurgitate the material and was corrected if a word was out of place. Points were deducted for misplaced words rather than distorted meaning.

I had difficulty memorizing verbatim, so I took advantage of the situation and gave tests that required thinking. "How do you interpret Nader Shah's behavior? Was he a good king who brought unbelievable wealth to Iran? Or was he a madman who allowed his soldiers to kill, rape, and steal, and who blinded his son with his own hands in fear of losing his power to him?"

Mrs. Mojtahedi eyes often closed behind her dark sunglasses, a smile fixed on her face to fool us into believing that she paid attention to every detail.

My classmates were incensed. They would rather have memorized the entire passage without thinking. Where did these questions come from? they wanted to know. They weren't written in the textbook.

I didn't mind the complaints. I ignored them and enjoyed being in control immensely, even if for a short time.

A few weeks into the school year, my father's sisters and their children came for their regular Wednesday visits with my grandmother. The sun had already set; the weather was cool and pleasant. This was the usual time for catching up with gossip and everyone's problems, since telephone services were unavailable. My grandmother chose a section of the walled yard under the tall sour orange trees and next to the flower beds for the gathering. I helped my mother carry a Persian carpet outside. We spread a plastic cloth over the middle of the carpet and brought the food. Everyone sat cross-legged around the *sofreh* in front of the spread of fruits, nuts, seeds, Iranian cucumbers, and watermelon slices. I tossed a few lit charcoals into a round wire bowl attached to a long string and whirled it in a circle to make the coal burn hotter. I put them on top of the Persian tobacco leaves in a metal crown on the peak of my grandmother's hookah. An aunt took the first puff, ensuring the tobacco was burning right, and passed it to my grandmother. Everyone started the *taarof* ritual, proffering food and exchanging niceties.

My grandmother told an aunt, "Come on, peel a cucumber. Why aren't you eating?"

My mother offered a plate of apples that she had peeled and sliced. *"Befarmaid,* please have a piece."

A few aunts ate watermelon seeds. Each threw one after another into her mouth, positioned it between the top and bottom teeth in the side of her mouth and cracked it open, spitting the shells out. I served limeade in tall glasses on a silver platter with the patterns of Achaemenid soldiers with shields and arrows engraved on it.

The women started to *dard-e-del,* to speak of the ache in their hearts, of their new preoccupations and worries. One complained about her husband, who spent too much time with his friends; the other worried about her only daughter who was suffering from a skin condition on her legs, getting worse despite all the doctors they visited and many ointments and pills; the third was troubled about her oldest daughter. A nice man's family had gone to their uncle requesting him to be an ambassador of good will and to ask her parents for her hand in marriage. The uncle told him that they would not give their daughter to a Kohen. Being from the tribe of the keepers of the Temple, the Kohanim were to be given special respect. Fearing that a regular husband and wife dispute would set the wrath of God upon their daughters and themselves for disrespect to a descendent of the temple priests, many families didn't give them their daughters. That hadn't been the case with my aunt's family. In fact, they had hoped that the man would ask for their daughter. They thought the uncle had done this out of malice and were bewildered what to do since the customs didn't allow them to approach the family and correct the mistake.

Much to my surprise and horror, my mother for the very first time joined the conversation to *dard-e-del*. "I have a complaint with this family," she started to say.

My grandmother stopped smoking her waterpipe and swatted the air with the back of her right hand in a gesture to stop her.

"No, no, no," one aunt said. "Let her talk. Who else can she talk to? Her family isn't here. We're her family. She is a sister. Let her tell us of the pain in her heart."

I had a very bad feeling about this. Why was my mother doing this to herself? Didn't she know better than to complain to them about themselves? Maman looked at the aunts one by one and finally said, "I'm being treated like a maid. I have to cook for your mother, wash her clothes, iron her sons' shirts, and she still complains about me to my husband. Your mother goes to him and tells him I didn't take her watermelon juice right away, didn't buy fresh milk everyday. What I am I to do? I have kids to take care of. I am always tired. I do everything for your mother, my husband's mother, but I am always told that it is not enough, not been done the right way."

I was surprised that they had allowed her to talk for such a long time without interrupting her. I thought maybe I was wrong. There was a silence for a second, then they all attacked her simultaneously—an emotional massacre. I didn't have the heart to watch how my mother had set up the trap for herself. So I went to the kitchen to get a fresh pot of tea for everyone, hoping that the food might soften them. I came back too late. My mother looked smaller than usual leaning onto her left side, her hand pushing against the ground for support. My aunts looked sweaty and red from the battle. My grandmother smoked serenely.

Morad's wife had a smile on her face, since her sister-in-law's defeat was her victory. She looked at me as I passed the small glass tea cups and exploded: "Who gave Farideh the authority to fail these kids?"

I was taken off guard, not realizing that the conversation had switched from mother to daughter. Unfortunately for me, one of my classmates was my aunt's niece, who had complained to her after receiving a failed grade in history.

My uncle's wife looked at me with fire in her eyes and pointed her index finger at me. "She has no conscience, making life so hard on them. I bet she can't answer the questions herself." Then she turned her head to me and her tongue slithered. "Do you know any of these things yourself? You're the dumbest of them all, but you act like a queen."

I looked at the aunts. They were still cracking the watermelon seeds and sipping the tea I had steeped for them. I bent over and picked up some of the dirty dishes to find an excuse to leave the assembly and got a glimpse of Geeta, Morad's wife, sitting on her knees now.

"You get good grades for licking your teacher's behind," she screamed.

I felt as if I were the pit behind our house where the neighborhood kids practiced their stone throwing. I looked at her with fixed eyes. She was turning red now, angry for not getting any reaction from me, no tears, no shaking, just nothing.

"Instead of being good to the other kids by giving them simple questions, you are being hateful," she added. Then she turned around and spat in the garden.

I turned to the faces around me for sympathy. That was absolutely uncalled for. I didn't know what the school had to do with the family. She was right. I was not qualified to teach. I did enjoy giving tough questions. Which teenager wouldn't have? Her sister and niece should have taken their complaints to the school and the teacher. Plus, I was close family; my aunts barely knew the girl, but to my chagrin, everyone took Geeta's side.

"What good can come out of this?" one aunt asked. That was a family motto; keep away from anything controversial.

"Why would you accept this kind of responsibility?" My grandmother admonished me. "Is it good that people will curse after your last name and by extension we'll suffer from the bad eye that will be set upon us?"

I looked at my mother. She asked me to help her take the small dishes filled with the shells of watermelon seeds and get fresh ones. In the kitchen, she pinched my arm until it turned blue and screamed at me. "Am I not miserable enough without the troubles you make? Look what you have done! I will be hearing about this now for a week. Go to school tomorrow and tell your teacher you're not doing it anymore." She slammed the arm she was still holding against my body in a display of anger I had rarely seen.

The following day, Mrs. Mojtahedi made me tell her of the admonishment I received from the family when I resigned from teaching. She laughed and her long gold necklace jingled on her large bosoms.

I thought everything was going to be okay, but I was wrong. She had taught in the Jewish day school for many years and after this incident she enjoyed talking about it.

"How come you don't go to the Jewish school?" she said. "I was surprised to see a Jew in Tavalali."

"It's too far away," I said, knowing that the others were giggling.

"You don't speak like them. How come you don't speak your own language?"

She was referring to Judi, a Judeo-Persian language that was spoken only by the older generation or the Jews still living in the ghetto. We were all trying to disassociate ourselves from it in the hopes of integrating into the larger community.

"I don't know. We don't speak it at home." I said in a small voice, hearing more giggles in the back of class.

"*Shalomalekhem, shalomalekhem!*" She laughed imitating the thick Judi accent she had heard the teachers at the Jewish school use as they had greeted each other. The words were from the Hebrew *shalom alekhem,* meaning "peace be with you." "I've decided today that the Jewish students should not leave the classroom during the reading of the Koran and prayers. It would be good for you to learn." Then she smiled widely, smearing more of the red lip-color on her teeth.

I knew I was in big trouble. Moslem students started reading Arabic when they were in the second grade. Although I knew a few things about Islam and Moslem prayers, I had never practiced *namaz*, the daily prayers that others knew so well. Not only were the words unfamiliar, the body language, kneeling, putting hands over ears, and bowing at the right time, were important and insulting if performed wrong. I had heard my classmates mocking the Sunni Moslems' method of praying. *Namaz* was an exact art, I had come to realize.

I asked a good Moslem friend to write the instructions for me and, to my father's disbelief, covered my hair, bared my feet, and went through the motions, proclaiming Mohammed as the God's messenger. My father knew an argument with the school would evoke more hostility and kept quiet. As for reading of the Koran, I soon realized that the very first section of each *sura* was the easiest to read, so I managed to raise my hand quickly and ask with enthusiasm to be the first to read the sentence that starts all writings in Islam: *"Bismilahe rahmane rahim,* in the name of the divine merciful God."

That year, my last year in the elementary school, the pressure built up in the house, where interpersonal relationships were becoming more complicated as our numbers increased. My father's brother Morad and his wife had two children by then. The arguments became more intense now that every squabble among the children became a reason for the adults to fight.

One day, my grandmother gave me a piece of watermelon in the kitchen. Morad's wife complained that I ate a big piece and didn't leave enough for her children. Plus, she should have been offered first. Morad and my father fought when they came home that day, Morad taking his wife's side, my father, my grandmother's side. Soon, my father's shirt was torn off him, the bloody imprint of Morad's nails on his bare chest. We huddled behind him. Baba tried to close the glass doors on his brother. Morad shattered them with his fist, sending glass nuggets flying over me, too stunned to cry or scream. The overt hatred and animosities nibbled at the self-esteem and happiness of my siblings and myself like locusts on green wheat kernels in spring. There was no way out.

From time to time, someone in the family tried to break away from the suffocating atmosphere. Jahangeer, by then a well-known dentist, found his own apartment and moved out for a short time, but my grandmother cried that the family was falling apart and blamed my mother. She besieged my father to keep the family together for the sake of their father's spirit. Jahangeer came back, and he and my grandmother moved into the upstairs apartment, which had been without a tenant for a while. My mother still cooked and the entire family ate the meals together downstairs, but my uncle had some autonomy over his own life. He bought a refrigerator, the only one in the house, and my grandmother guarded it against those of us downstairs. She considered the area a sacred space, where her son would eventually bring a wife and establish a family.

On Fridays, my only day off, I swept and dusted the second-floor apartment, scrubbed and washed its tiled floors and the bathroom under the watchful eyes of my grandmother. She didn't understand that I wasn't interested in the material goods, the silver cutlery or the china. Like my siblings, I only stole food items, a tangerine from the tree in the backyard, a handful of pistachios from the neat bundles hidden in the back room, slices of American-style bread that my grandmother carefully tucked away behind dishes in the upstairs kitchen cabinet.

The issues of ownership had become complicated. Both Morad and my father considered the house to be theirs, wanting the other to move out. We begged my father to leave, but it was a matter of power and pride, and he didn't want to be the loser. Morad and his family moved out to an apartment after many open fights. I visited their place with my grandmother once in a while, who called it a disgrace that they had been booted out. They moved back.

Personally, I had a difficult time finding an escape. I lost myself in foreign books, renting instead of buying them to stretch my money. I tried to avoid every family member as much as possible, visited friends after school, and didn't come home until dark. My father didn't know because he came home even later, working, enjoying his new business in poultry farming. But I still could see my siblings being abused and again kept silent so we would have quiet, so there would be no blood drawn. No matter how I tried to insulate myself, the conflict found ways to seep into my life like the rain that had brought our mud roof down so many times when we lived in the ghetto. Morad started regularly calling Nahid *shashoo,* the one who is drenched in her own pee. We were open to insults. Nahid was slapped when she was busy with her homework and didn't go out to socialize with the aunts; she was slapped when she forgot to announce that the mail had come in. The hatred grew and festered like a giant wound immune to any known therapy. The air in the house became poisonous, but I kept silent, and so did my siblings.

My period started that year amidst the unrest, the bickering, and the absolute lack of privacy. And as that year came to end, I had a déjà vu of my first grade. I wasn't able to register for the school of my choice; its principal told me that there were already too many Jews enrolled. I had to ask Jahangeer, who was a respected dentist in town and knew influential people, to intercede on my behalf, as he would again six years later to help me change majors in college. As I was ready to start junior high, I was an awkward teenager, feeling confused, hurt, unwanted, lost, and helpless to save myself, my sister, and my brothers.

## A Piece of Chocolate

As I had never before seen animal crackers, I didn't know about other American sweets either. What we called chocolate in Iran was a chewy caramel-colored square candy wrapped in colorful, glittery paper, more like saltwater taffy. I am surprised children didn't choke on its sweet rubbery texture. Many times I had to put my finger down my throat to retrieve the goo that blocked my air-tunnel. Still, all children loved the troublesome candy, and every time I had a few rials, I ran to the little kiosk a block away to buy a handful. They usually lasted a few days because they were so difficult to eat. Maybe that was the purpose of the formula, to make children eat them languidly and frugally, to learn patience as they took little bites, knowing the fine line between savoring its sweetness slowly or choking on it.

At the end of my sixth grade, Baba came home from work one day with a treat: small milk chocolate bars with fluffy, smooth sweetness inside—made in America. He gave me two. Boxes of the sweets were donated to the *Sohonot*, the office of the Jewish agency a block away from my father's shop, to be distributed among the underprivileged Jewish children. I gobbled up the first bar, inhaling it, not bothering to chew. It was the most delicious thing I had ever tasted in my life. The second one I ate slowly, taking the tiniest bites every day, until it became hard and crumbly in the pocket of my black uniform. Although the chocolate was no longer edible, I kept the crumbs and smelled them once in a while. When I washed my uniform, I was careful to go around the pocket. My mother finally got hold of it when I wasn't around. She took the inside of the pocket out and washed it a few times, grumbling that the chocolate had embedded itself into the fabric. I was furious at her for washing away the sweet smell of the chocolate, and didn't know why.

I tried all different chocolate bars when I moved to America. Many looked like the one I remembered, but none tasted so good. I know now that I don't really like chocolate. I hadn't cherished the crumbs as food. The gift of chocolate by the American humanitarians made me realize for the first time in my life that there were people somewhere far away who knew I existed and who cared about me. They had reached out to me. I hung onto these anonymous American benefactors as my saviors for many years. At that moment, I knew that I was going to leave and find a new home, my very own place in the world. I knew that there was hope in my future. For the first time, I started to dream of America.

## Chapter Five

# MARRIAGE: A WOMAN'S DREAM

### Khastegaree: Marriage Proposals

Around 1908, when my paternal grandmother was nine years old, her mother Bibi took Khanom-bozorg to her future husband's home to clean *sabzee* for an herb stew, peel cooked potatoes for *shamee*, pluck a chicken for Shabbat, draw water from the well, and scrub clothes over her hands with homemade soap. Those were her tests to prove to her mother-in-law that she could be a good housewife, a trainable worker. She passed the tests, but was divorced two years later at age twelve for having run away too many times. Each time my grandmother escaped her in-laws' house, Bibi hit her own chest in exasperation and returned Khanom-bozorg to her husband's home, but eventually she was refused. Who needed such an unruly woman? Discarded, my grandmother learned to turn wool into thread with her homemade spindle and to weave socks to make a living.

Turning fifteen, my paternal grandmother, whose name "Tavous" means "peacock" in Persian, was given in marriage to my grandfather. This time, she didn't protest. Her new husband—well-known and respected in the community—had lost his wife after their third child was born. Tavous was sturdy. She had strong legs, wide hips for childbearing, and strong hands for raising children and running a household. She remained married to my grandfather until he died, raising his three sons from a previous marriage as well as eight children of their own.

When my turn came for marriage, the rules had changed somehow— women weren't married off at such a young age, but the old rules stood that they had to be clever housekeepers, be modest, and be accepting of the elders' role in arranging marriages. In keeping the traditions, I learned

*My maternal great-grandmother, Dina Salem. Her*
*husband's early death made her destitute, forcing her to*
*marry off her daughters very young.*

to clean *sabzee* and chop it too; I knew how to shell fava beans for *baghela polo,* and how to wash fresh tobacco, salt, and dry it for my grandmother's waterpipe. I helped wash the clothes by hand and press them with a charcoal iron. I polished everyone's shoes on Fridays for Shabbat. I could clean the lining of the cow's intestines and the four stomachs and stuff them with a mixture of cilantro, short grain rice, and split yellow peas.

I also spent quite a lot of time beside my father in his jewelry workshop, watching him string pearls on gold threads and sew them on a solid piece of gold hammered into the shape of flowers. I frequently sat beside my great-uncle, Daee-bozorg, in our backyard under the shade of the rose tree as he rinsed gold and silver particles from the rubbish that came from my father's shop. I listened to the stories of his adventures in Baghdad while he melted the gold dust and poured it into iron casts. He told me

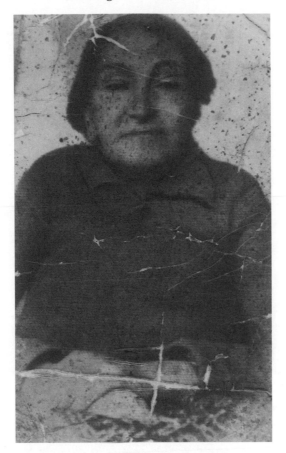

*Dina's mother, Adina Sabba. Her successful merchant husband was murdered in an Iranian village for being Jewish. His death brought financial devastation to the family.* Most of the family pictures were collected and preserved by Nahid Gerstein.

Biblical stories too as I crouched next to him and watched him weigh flour for Passover *matzah*, shadowing him whenever he was around. He showed me how he built a mud *tanoor* for baking the unleavened bread and, unlike other adults, he enjoyed my questions; I loved his stories.

Until I was of marriageable age, around sixteen years old, I acted as a son to my father and followed him on his business ventures into poultry farming, helped him experiment with hatching chicks and feeding them at home. I traveled with him to Tehran and watched him conduct his busi-

*Dina's mother-in-law, Hamineh Saed. She diligently helped the Alliance school in Hamedan.* Picture courtesy of Alliance office in New York.

ness. Therefore, my world was dramatically different from that of the women I knew. The bond between my father and me lasted for many years and didn't break until my brothers were older, and I became more assertive.

The first time the *khastegaree,* the marriage proposal, came for me, I was only twelve years old. I was at the movies with my mother to see an American comedy, *Chitty Chitty Bang Bang.* Wearing a new brown dress with yellow flowers, I yearned to run and make its flowing skirt twirl, but I knew girls had to be modest and squashed my desire to skip from happiness. As we waited in the newly opened indoor theatre, an old woman in *chador* approached my mother and whispered something in her ears, while her eyes focused on me.

My mother threw her chin up, indicating a negative answer in the Iranian fashion. "No," she said.

Still staring at me, the old woman replied, "He's from a good family." I

*A synagogue in Shiraz. Mothers lined their daughters on the front row of the balcony, or right outside the windows in the yard, for a good viewing by eligible bachelors.*

hid behind my mother's skirt. "You don't know what fate will bring. You should consider it. You don't want to wait too long," she warned.

"I was married young myself. I don't want my daughter to have the same fate," my mother said. She gave her refusal finality by turning her back and walking away. Then she looked directly into my eyes. "I could have given you to them, you know. That's what happened to me."

I kept quiet, but my heart ached. I felt helpless; I crossed my arms to hide my small budding breasts. Feeling flushed from the stranger's gaze, I tried to hide behind my mother until the lights started flashing and we entered the movie hall.

The incident led to two major squabbles with my extended family. I was ruining my posture, they said, by covering my chest with my books, by hugging the bag of groceries, or by crossing my arms. A family member's fists usually landed on my back to straighten it out, and although the shock worked momentarily, I stooped as soon as the pain subsided.

Despite the fact that I had become reticent, one family member or the other constantly reminded me of my past *veragi*. With my new attitude, they gave me yet another hated title: *kaleh-shagh*, stiff-necked and stubborn. The elders particularly scolded me for refusing to act as they wished when in public. Saturday evenings, Jewish women gathered at the large traffic circle in Meidan-e-Shah, which displayed a gigantic statue of the Shah on horseback standing on top of a monument. Roses, geraniums, water fountains, benches, and modern lighting decorated the tiny park. Women greeted one another. *"Shavua tov,* a good beginning for the week ahead!"

Each family chose a corner, spread a small Persian rug, and pulled out sandwiches and drinks, waiting for the men to join them after services at the synagogue. My grandmother always told me to go for a walk, and if I refused, she took me for a stroll herself. I blushed and tried to make my-self as small as possible until my father's or uncle's fist came down on my back. Since this was a place for matchmaking, the family expected me to be gracious, but I wouldn't smile and often refused to go through the cus-tom of exchanging niceties, embarrassing and infuriating them.

When my aunts came to visit my grandmother on Saturdays and Wednesday evenings, I helped my mother serve tea and biscuits, water-melon slices, sour cherry *sharbat,* and romaine lettuce with pickled veg-etables or mint syrup. In fine weather, they sat on a Persian carpet on the bricked backyard, under the citrus trees; at other times, they gathered in a circle in the family room, sitting cross-legged, smoking waterpipes, and cracking squash seeds with their back teeth. They gossiped and asked for advice. Once in a while when I entered the room with a fresh pot of tea, they went quiet. Then, my grandmother would say, "Farideh, go outside for now and close the door."

I left, turning to close the door just to see the women's faces fixed on me. On those days, a new marriage proposal was being discussed. Some-one had approached my grandmother in the women's section in the bal-cony of the synagogue, another had made a call to my uncle's office, a third had stopped by my father's shop to say hello. Whoever was ap-proached by a suitor's family felt proud and became the defender of that family's good name and fortune. Resentful and angry, I chewed my nails and felt the bile in my throat with each incident.

Whether I could accept it or not, I knew that high school was a time of marriage for many women. One by one the school administrators dis-missed my classmates upon hearing the news of their engagements. Most parents wanted their daughters to marry young, when they were more desirable. In those days, I was curious why so many teenage girls went willingly to the slaughterhouse—which was my view of marriage.

## Feathers and Hair

Cousin Ziba married shortly after high school. The day of her wedding, women of the family divided into two groups; one group celebrated with my cousin, while the other plucked the chickens for the festivities that night. The more prestigious women, including my grandmother, the mothers of the bride and groom, some aunts, and many prominent women of the community, leaned against large pillows on Persian carpets in the living room of my aunt's house, decorated for a pre-wedding party. Some of the younger female cousins passed around trays of sweets, limeade, and *sharbat* as older women showered the bride with candy, covered their mouths with their *chadors* and ululated, *"Kililili."* The second group of women—my mother, myself, my sister, the washer-woman, and her daughter—sat on low stools behind the party room in the brick-paved backyard to clean mounds of chickens.

A short distance away, under the persimmon tree, the *shokhet* said a *brakha,* plucked a patch of feathers from underneath the neck of the chicken, pulled the head back, slit it, and then threw the body on the grass to do its dance of death. Next, the father of the bride gathered two or three throbbing birds in each hand, holding them by their feet, and dropped their warm carcasses in front of us to pluck.

Weddings tested a young woman's skill in cleaning chickens. Since refrigeration wasn't available, chickens had to be cleaned quickly and cooked right away, leaving the pluckers little time to bathe and dress for the wedding party.

I felt hurt that I was excluded from the party room, missing the fun and treats. As I grew older, my fate, my role in the family, became more tightly connected to my mother as an outsider, as if I still swam in the amniotic fluid that had protected me in her womb, but now it offered no warmth or safety. Instead, its cloudy stench kept me at a distance from the other daughters of my generation, those cousins who should have been my equals, my friends and confidants.

Khanom-bozorg came by, noticed my look of disappointment, and told me that I was doing a *mitzvah* by plucking the chickens for a wedding, that

I would be blessed with good luck, a good husband. I didn't want to get married; I hated the hard and dirty work. I knew that by the time the chickens were feathered, gutted, and cleaned, I would not only be covered in chicken feathers, fat, blood, and excrement, but would also smell like a barnyard.

I kept at the work, sulking. A large surface of the carcass had fine feathers, easy to pull, and I could get through them quite fast. The larger feathers, however, embedded deep in the flesh, were the most difficult, particularly on the wings, where the delicate skin tore easily. Even worse was the fatty backside of the chicken, where the long quills often pulled out and splashed fat and blood on my hands, arms, legs, hair, and clothes, where the fine feathers clung, making me look so silly that everyone smirked. Sometimes, the quills broke and I had to trap the imbedded piece between the edge of a small knife and my thumb to pull it out, careful not to cut my finger. My mother's hands, however, were already rough from housework and the knife made only a small dent on her thick calluses.

While I worked on my third chicken, I realized that the ceremony down the hall was a *bandandazi* party. As the *bandandaz* entered the room with her little basket of thread, we heard a wave of ululation. We echoed the celebratory cries while plucking. I had seen this particular woman before. She held the end of a string between her teeth, looped it and put it close to the skin. With her other hand, she pulled the opposite end of the thread and swiftly removed the hair from women's legs, arms, faces, and armpits. Its growth and darkening being synonymous in women with their loss of childhood beauty and innocence, body hair obsessed Iranians, and its removal appealed to Middle Eastern men, who preferred a youthful appearance in their women.

Plucking the chickens, I listened to the noises from the party room. The ululation went on; water gurgled in the waterpipes, and once in a while I heard a subdued moan from the bride when the *bandandaz* pulled a particularly stubborn hair.

The chickens were almost done when the small groans became heart-wrenching screams that all the noise from the ululation could not muffle. Horrified, I started to rise from my stool to help Ziba, but my mother pulled me down with a knowing smile on her face. What was going on? No one seemed to want to talk about it. Instead, my mother and the rest of the women joined in, drowning the screams in their own sounds of ululation.

I had learned not to ask questions, but I didn't have to wait too long for the answer. My mother left briefly to fetch water. We had to wet the feathers once in a while to keep them from flying. Then, one of the cleaning people (whose low-class status freed her from the inhibitions of the "high-class" people) bent over and, using a derogatory word, whispered, "They're doing her private parts!" Then she giggled hysterically, covering her mouth with her feather-laden hand.

There I was cleaning the chickens while the aristocracy of the community plucked my cousin's pubic hair! I couldn't get Ziba's image out of my mind, legs spread in front of women who themselves were covered modestly in long *chadors*, having the hair plucked all the way down to her private area. Angry and worried, I plucked recklessly, ruining the skin of the next few chickens.

The removal of the body hair didn't bother me, since I had seen the *bandandaz* working on women's faces, legs, and arms; I had seen naked bodies of married women with shaven private parts in the *hamam*. Rather, the public nature of the ceremony terrified me, the loss of privacy and self-determination; this initiation into a culture of conformity appalled me, although it delighted the other women.

I was only fourteen, a year older than my mother at her wedding, and three years younger than my cousin. Instead of accepting the custom as a show of support and camaraderie, as many women did, I felt lost and feared that my life could spin out of my control as I grew older and became a woman.

A few weeks later, I asked Ziba about the ceremony. "It hurt like nothing I've ever experienced. Even the *bandandaz* said she had never seen anyone bleed so badly." She spoke with a pride I couldn't understand.

For years, I analyzed the ritual, trying to understand why Ziba's mother and grandmother had allowed it, especially after having experienced it themselves. The realization sank in slowly and bitterly. All mothers helped to perpetuate the cycle of misery for their daughters, I concluded. For a long time, I wondered if my mother too was going to drag me with her into darkness; I wondered if I had to break the bond between us in order to free myself.

Thinking of Ziba's mother, and of her grandmother, who was also my grandmother, passing the customs of torture to the next generations appalled and horrified me. Their joy in linking their chains to the younger women made me feel lonely and powerless, for the plucking of both the feathers and hair plainly symbolized our mothers' subjugation.

At the end of the party, my grandmother stopped by to see how the chicken cleaning progressed. She blessed me, "I pray for the same happiness and good life for you."

And I, who had learned to shut up, once again lost control of my tongue. "May it not be God's will!" I blurted.

In the silence that followed, looks of horror spread over every face, including my father's as he happened to walk by to check on us. I felt sorry for both my parents, since a daughter's wedding day was the ultimate desire for Iranian Jewish parents. Still, I just didn't want it, not this way. But which way? I recognized myself as an oddity, a loner, a defiant girl. My heart went out to my parents. I was sorry that they found me an embarrassment, but I also feared my own fate. What was going to become of me—the one who didn't belong?

A decade later I would move to the United States and marry an American man. At my own wedding, I so adamantly wanted to distance myself from my past that I took care to exclude all rituals of my heritage from the ceremony. I walked down the aisle American style; I offered neither Iranian stew nor aromatic rice for the reception party, and I was glad that the chickens weren't plucked by anyone I knew. The poultry came from neat packages that did not even look like chickens—breast of chicken stuffed with wild rice was on the menu for my wedding.

Today, partly through my writings, I have come to peace with my past, and if I have any regret about my wedding, as beautiful as it was, it's the fact that I allowed my fear and disgust of some customs to erase all others. But in May of 1977, my fiancé and I selected music with an Eastern-European flavor, and I was actually pleased that my aunts weren't there to sing *vasoonak*, the traditional Shirazi Jewish wedding songs. I was jealous when my grandmother became the center of attention at my wedding, smoking her *ghalyan* with Iranian tobacco. She covered her hair with colorful silk scarves for modesty, sat cross-legged on the floor, sipped mint tea with a sugar lump in the back of her cheek. Taking puffs of her waterpipe, she entertained her American grandchildren with the gurgle of the water at its base. Men ran inside for cameras.

When they were gone, my grandmother put her lips to my aunt's ear, signaled toward me, and in a loud whisper, asked, "Has she taken care of the stuff?"

For a moment, I didn't understand what she meant. When I realized the meaning of her words, anger went through my body like a jolt of lightning. The memory of Ziba's wedding flooded my mind. How could I have forgotten? But I composed myself and, with a smile, replied, "Yes, definitely," and in a small voice she could not hear, "for generations to come."

## A Viewing

During my college years in Iran, *khastegaree* rituals changed in many ways to accommodate the more educated generation. Yet many elements remained unaffected. Since public *hamams* were not in use by the upper class who had moved out of the ghetto, the synagogue became a focal point for hunting brides. During the holidays, many families scrambled to have their daughters sit closer to the main sanctuary (the men's section), either on the front row of the balcony or in the yard, to be seen by the young men inside. Still, the most likely judges were the other women, who viewed the new crop and passed the information to families on the lookout for their sons.

As the Shah's government encouraged education abroad, more Jewish men enrolled in the universities in the United States. Rarely did these men marry Americans. Most were shocked at the sexual freedom in the United States. Declaring that "there were no virgins in America," many returned a year later suffering from culture shock and loneliness, looking for wives to take back. Since time was of the essence for these students, their families made the preliminary arrangements. A few wanted brides as young as possible. Many requested their choices to be limited to those women attending a certain high school. Some preferred women with higher education, particularly students of a humanities major—not medicine or engineering.

I studied English literature at Pahlavi University in Shiraz, frustrated by living in two different worlds. My American and British teachers spoke of individual freedom and rights, of the power of critical thinking, free expressions of thoughts and exchange of ideas. Yet daily I went back to our half-communal household, to a world of patriarchy. It was one that I understood less every day, a world whose rules were rapidly becoming foreign to me.

After the Iranian Revolution in 1979, Americans often asked me why the Iranian people accepted such a radically different government. I told them that if one person in each family had felt as I did, that would have been enough reason for the older generation to revolt against the government for separating them from their children by offering Western education. If half of Western-educated men and women had felt as I did, that would have been enough for them to reject the West, which alienated them from their culture, weakened their roots, and drastically altered their identity.

In 1973, I was finishing my sophomore year in the university. At the end of the second semester, as exams approached, I often spent extra time at school to avoid confrontations with my family. The weather turned extremely hot. Lacking deodorants, I went back to the house every day at noon to take a shower before returning to school.

One day as I gathered my books in a hurry to make the 4:30 bus, my grandmother approached me with an evaluating look. "Good, good. I was going to ask you to take a shower myself. I see you're dressed nicely," she said. "Make sure to use the sidewalk on the right side of the street and walk very slowly."

I looked at my mother for an explanation. She giggled and looked away. I went to a second-floor window and saw what I suspected. There they were, women of all ages waiting for a one-person show, a drama whose sole actress was me. The watchers had spread a Persian carpet on the sidewalk, set up a few chairs, brought tea and even a waterpipe. I could imagine the conversations:

"No *khanom!* You should sit closer," one probably said.

"This is a better place for you; after all you are the one to make the decision," another responded.

"Come, come sit here. It's under the shade of the tree. It's cooler here," a third woman offered.

My hair dripped wet. I always allowed it to dry in the hot dry summer air, but now I regretted having washed it, since a woman's wet long hair was considered seductive. I contemplated grabbing the scissors to chop my hair off. I thought of going downstairs and releasing my anger by hitting my grandmother and my mother hard on their chests, breaking the cultural rules of seniority and respect. In the end, I did neither. I was going to miss the bus, and the exam was more important than my rage. I collected my books, held my head up, smiled, and walked out of the house. I noticed a commotion in the little circle down the street as someone announced my appearance and more women came out of the house. I wondered if the entire extended family had come there to see if I were a suitable bride. I looked back. My father leaned out of the upstairs window, smoking; my mother and grandmother stood at the door watching.

My grandmother motioned me with the back of her hand: "Go, go. Don't keep them waiting. It isn't polite."

I wore my comfortable shoes, no high heels for such an occasion. With no one around to beat my back as I held my books tightly to my chest, I slowly crossed the road to the opposite side, took a long breath, and broke into a run. I managed to get on the bus in time, flushed, sweaty, and out of breath. I sat there for a few minutes with my fists clenched in anger. But the episode had been too funny. Soon a small giggle escaped my mouth, which I didn't try to hide from the rest of the surprised passengers.

When I returned from school, no one was amused.

My grandmother fumed. "You embarrassed us. You embarrassed me! How am I going to hold my head up now?"

My father was disgusted. "A girl doesn't run like that—after all those years that I taught you to take little steps!"

"He's a college-educated man. He just came back from America." My mother said. "He could take you away."

America was more enticing than ever. Maybe if I had been approached differently I would have accepted the offer. Maybe not.

That summer, I agreed to meet the suitor in person—just to tell him off. He apologized, saying he had no idea of our families' schemes, but I was too angry to care. More than ever now, I knew that I didn't belong. I had to find a way out.

*Chapter Six*

# MY NEW WORLD

*Leaving Iran*

The struggle to leave Iran was the most difficult endeavor of my life. Six hours short of finishing my bachelor's degree in English at Pahlavi University, I realized that I would soon run out of excuses to avoid marriage, that my graduation would expedite the transfer of control over my life from my father to a husband, and that I would be trapped forever in the same cycle of life as women before me.

Also, the political climate changed rapidly. During my last year at Pahlavi University in the fall of 1974, I felt a shifting mood among my Moslem friends. In this American-style university, many women put aside their latest Western clothing, covered their hair, and discarded their French makeup; men grew stubble and exchanged their American jeans for black pants and dress shirts without ties. Adherence to strict Islamic teachings, and, as a consequence, hatred against the Jews and the West, bonded the young and strengthened their resolve against the rule of the Shah. The sword of Islam became the weapon that would eventually destroy the Peacock Throne.

Whenever I joined a circle of my Moslem friends, the conversations stopped; secrets circulated to which, as a Jew, I suspected I wasn't privy. One by one, all but two Moslem friends stopped talking to me. Although she was from a religious family, my dear friend Firoozeh still kept a close relationship with me. Her sister studied in a religious school in Ghom, the city that became famous later for being Khomeini's hometown. Once she told me that her sister awaited a man who would change the country. When I inquired about the man's identity, she realized she had let slip a piece of information to which I, as a Jew, was not entitled. She didn't repeat that mistake.

During the exams, I would meet Firoozeh for tea in the morning before we headed to the library. One day as I said goodbye to her, I casually mentioned, "I'll see you tomorrow." A look of surprise crossed her face. She told me she couldn't and maybe I should study at home too. Her attitude puzzled me, since she knew I lived in a multi-family house, too chaotic to allow me quiet time for studying.

When I arrived at the library the next day, somber and watchful students stood in small groups around the campus. Few Moslem students occupied the usually packed library, but Firoozeh waited for me by the door. I asked her if she too had noticed the "weirdness" that hung in the air. She didn't respond; instead she insisted we abandon our regular seats by the windows and choose a space between the stacks. Firoozeh fidgeted, looked around, and couldn't concentrate on the subject we studied. She was distracting me; and I almost wished she hadn't come when I heard the loud shouts. Frightened, I jumped, but Firoozeh pulled me under the table as rioters ran through the library, throwing chairs at full-length windows. Large sheets of glass sliced the air. Firoozeh led me outside through a back door, and we talked our way through soldiers who had barricaded the school with drawn guns and bayonets. Through iron fences, I watched the Shah's army rip the clothes off women and batter my classmates.

My architecture professor stood next to me screaming, "Not on their heads, please don't hit them on the head."

At first, my body shook uncontrollably, and then I was listless and cold. While the brutality of the troops appalled me, I found the alternative theocracy more frightening. Logically I knew that my friends deserved a better government, while personally I knew that the shift of powers potentially could destroy Jewish lives. I had to leave as soon as possible.

Firoozeh found a taxi, pulled me out of the frenzied crowd, and, when we reached the house, told my mother that I was in shock. She even stayed to help me get in bed. Although she couldn't trust me with a warning about the student riots, Firoozeh endangered her own safety to ensure mine.

Most of my Jewish friends avoided the public arena to avoid the political unrest and the growing anti-Semitism. Their homes became the only places of refuge as they reevaluated their changing relationship with the world outside. For me, however, life in the house became more unbearable. The *hamam* had been my only quiet sanctuary in the house. When my grandmother, my parents, my siblings, my aunts and uncles, and my cousins took their afternoon naps on hot summer days, when the heat melted the asphalt on the pavements, I locked myself in the *hamam,* taking long cold showers. This was my private time of solitude, of reflection and peace. On one of these serene afternoons, Morad pushed the bathroom door open and watched me as I stumbled toward the door to close it. Slippery with lather and with the shampoo stinging my eyes, still I could not help but see his gleeful smile. From then on, the *hamam* became a place of fear, where I took showers with my underwear on, a chair wedged behind the door. Sometimes I took a bucket with me to the bathroom, which I filled with water to wash the soap off as I stood behind the door guarding it.

I hated myself. The water lost its magic to soothe me; instead I felt dirtier after each bath. Whenever my uncle smiled at me, looking at me appraisingly, I shuddered, blaming myself. I would learn from my mother that after a fight with my father, Morad had opened the bathroom door on her as well. Revenge, a man's way. But Morad had miscalculated me. I had learned to keep silent. Fearing another round of arguments, I didn't share the information with my parents. I withdrew inside my body. Bitter, angry, lost, and abused, I needed to distance myself from everyone I knew.

My need to depart quickly became urgent. Initiated by the Shah's sister, a new law included women in the Shah's White Revolution army. We were candidates to serve as soldiers and teachers in remote villages for two years. My fear was realized later as my classmates were called to duty after graduation. I had only a short window of time to run. To serve the country by force wasn't exactly my idea of equality. I could vote; I had to vote, but only for one seat assigned to a Jewish congressman who was already preselected by the Shah. Such liberties I could live without. I was twenty-two years old, but because I was a woman, I would never have the right to apply for a passport without the permission of a male guardian.

Fortunately, in the winter of 1974, my father applied for passports for himself, my mother, my siblings, and me to travel to Israel to visit my mother's family. The situation became complicated, however, when my grandmother requested to accompany us. My father considered taking one of the cousins to assist with her needs, and then other cousins asked to join as well. Finally, because my father didn't have the will to hurt any family members by refusing them, we gathered such a large entourage that the journey became impossible.

When the trip fell through, my mother smiled in resignation, although she had tears in her eyes. She hadn't seen her family since they had emigrated to Israel seven years earlier, and her father was elderly and fragile. "This is it," she said. "I'll never see Agha." That was the name she called her father.

She was right. At the time, I was mad at her for not picking up her passport and demanding to go by herself. I wasn't going to wait as she did for someone else to make decisions for me.

My passport had collected a year's dust in an office downtown when I showed up to claim it. I tried to hide my apprehension and guilt for cheating the system and defying my father's authority. Bored faces looked at me from behind metal desks and piles of yellowed paper. A guard in a khaki uniform looked at me suspiciously, surprised to see a young woman. I recognized an older man, gnawing on a pencil, gave him my sweetest smile, and introduced myself. "Do you remember me?" I asked him. "I was here with my father."

He barely let me finish the sentence. "Of course, of course." He jumped out of his chair, turned to the clerk and asked him to find Miss Farideh's passport in a filing cabinet. "Don't you need the others?" he asked.

"No, my father is sending me to America by myself to visit an uncle." I satisfied his curiosity, making sure he knew I was being protected by my father here and my uncle in the States. I smiled at him once more, glad no one I knew could see my flirtation. He double-checked my father's permission. I paid the cost of the orange and blue stamps that he pasted on the back pages, waved at him sweetly, and stepped out, dancing in my head.

I still had to obtain a visa and there wasn't an American consul in Shiraz. A close Moslem friend, Shahnaz, knew people in Tehran and tried to find a way for me to skip town for two days without arousing suspicion. My father wouldn't allow me to sleep away from the house, afraid that I would compromise my reputation. In college, I had slept over at a Jewish friend's house only when my father was away. Obviously, going to Tehran was impossible.

Again I was lucky. That week, when I stopped by the Iran-America

Society, the principal called me to his office. "Didn't your uncle want to visit the States? Tell him that if he is still interested the consul will be here next week."

I didn't give Jahangeer the message, but I was waiting for the consul myself hours before the doors opened. He looked twice as big as any Iranian man I knew, spilling out of a student chair in a classroom. I sat in front of him, trying to control my quivering, at the same time fearing that if the flimsy desk chair collapsed under his weight, he would be too angry to grant me a visa. This was it; my entire future was in his hands.

He looked at me for a long time before addressing me. "Do you speak English?" he asked me in Farsi.

I nodded. "A little," I said in English. The blueness of his eyes unnerved me, so I stared at my clasped hands on my lap.

"Why are you here?"

"I need a visa," I said. Was he wondering why a young woman would appear in front of him unescorted?

"Why?"

"To visit family and friends, to improve my English." My face flushed. I was sweaty.

Minutes later, I walked out with a shiny stamp granting me a visit to the United States to visit family and friends for three months. I had saved my monthly stipend from the government for being in the top one percent of my class. Firoozeh, my close Moslem friend, lent me another 2,000 *tomans,* all her savings. Since they wouldn't accept checks, I walked into the office of Iran Air with all the cash in my pocketbook and bought a one-way ticket to New York City. Then I told my father.

"No!" he said.

He couldn't do anything about it, I told him, since he had legally given me permission by applying for a passport. He fumed, screamed, threatened, but there was nothing he could do but to imprison me in the house. He demanded to see the passport and the ticket and went through my clothes and books to find them, but they were in a friend's locker at school.

Uncle Jahangeer intervened. "A trip to the States might be a good thing for Farideh. It will raise her status, make her a better candidate for a good marriage," he said. "Our brother Beejan will watch over her."

Having the blessing of at least one member of the family, Baba gave up. "Just a month," he said.

"A month," I lied.

Before the trip, Baba went through my bag after it was packed and pulled a winter coat and a sweater out. He repacked the bag with summer clothes only, folded each item neatly, and grumbled that I didn't know how to pack. I watched silently, and when he stuffed my panties and bras in the corners I promised myself that was the very last time anyone would have so much control over my life.

I arrived in New York for the first time on July 4th, 1975. As the plane circled over New York City, I could see pleasure boats on the Hudson River, people water skiing, the sun shining through the Statue of Liberty's crown. I would never return to Iran, I thought. I was out. I was free. I was scared.

That year I didn't go back. Beejan, my uncle who lived in the States, convinced my father to allow me to finish my bachelor of arts degree at Old Dominion University, not too far away from his home. I also met and fell in love with my future husband. Norman's youngest sister and I had been pen pals for over two years. My sister Nahid had visited the States, hoping that American orthopedists could repair the discrepancy in the length of her right leg. She met my future sister-in-law and asked her to correspond with me so I could improve my English. When in America, I called my pen pal to meet her for the first time. She was away, but her brother was visiting from school. Their mother begged Norman to do a *mitzvah*, a good deed, and take a poor Iranian girl out for dinner. I was impressed by him because he wouldn't enter my uncle's house until he learned to pronounce my name. We became good friends, wrote to each other, and he walked me through my culture shock that first year, at the end of which we considered ourselves engaged to be married.

When Uncle Beejan called my father for his permission for our engagement, my proud father cried like a child. I was his. My uncle didn't have the right to decisions concerning me. He begged his brother to send his daughter back, like I was a package given for safe keeping. It was bad enough that he had kept me much longer than anticipated. Beejan was in a terrible bind, because my father had raised and sent him to school at a great sacrifice to himself. He helped me study in the States in order to partially pay his debt to his brother. To keep a balance between his loyalty to my father and fairness to me, he bought me a round-trip ticket and told me that I had no choice but to return to Iran and ask for my father's blessing; otherwise, he said, he would withdraw his legal support and I would be deported. Meanwhile, my father hoped that if I came back, I could be convinced to stay, to get married to a man of his choice, and to forget about life in America.

I returned to Iran; I had no choice but to go back and face the family once more. I had a round-trip ticket in my hand and a renewed passport. At worst, I could take the flight back, I comforted myself, as I watched the ocean disappear underneath the Iran Air flight home.

As we reached the mountainous region bordering Iran, a returning student asked, "Isn't it wonderful that it's so easy to get an exit visa? They're really trying to make it easy for students to return for visits. I sent my passport to the embassy in Washington and had it back in a week."

I checked my passport—no exit visa.

"Do you have your grades?" The same young man asked me.

"No, what for?"

"You can't get a return visa from the American embassy without them." He looked at me with critical eyes.

I felt stupid. I was stepping into a trap. My heart pounded as the passengers broke into singing a nationalistic hymn. We were flying over Iranian airspace. I was light headed, my breathing labored, the mountains closing in on me. At the time, I didn't think it important that the returning passengers had chosen a song about their love of Iran, not the national anthem that glorified the Shah.

The Tehran airport was filled with jet-lagged passengers, some welcomed by the entire extended family, grandmothers covered in *chadors*, little girls carrying flowers, young women in mini-skirts, men in ties and suits standing stiffly and holding back tears of joy. The modern conveyer belt went round and round with our luggage, but two porters kept the passengers away, grabbed all the suitcases, piled them on top of huge carts, and collected tips before handing over the bags. Exhausted from the long trip and irritable from jet-lag, older male passengers with designer ties and younger ones in American blue jeans screamed and shoved their way to their suitcases. It wasn't proper for a woman to squeeze herself between all those shouting men fighting for luggage, so I stood on the side, confused, helpless, and dazed. On the Iranian soil for just fifteen minutes, my reserved nature was back already. "I need a man!" I thought, surprising myself by acting like the vulnerable woman that I had left behind a year ago. I was relieved to see my father walking toward me.

Baba had aged and looked fragile. I felt guilty for having been the cause of his worries. He hugged me and wouldn't let go, sobbing in front of the gawking crowd as if I had been resurrected from the dead. If I were so alive, I thought, why did I feel so dead inside? What was wrong with me? Why couldn't I be happy like all the other students laughing and hugging their families? I had missed my father, the familiar sounds and sight of the country I had tried to escape from, but, at the same time, I didn't want to be back. A woman and a Jew, I didn't belong to my country of birth. I didn't want to go back to a house that had never been home.

To my surprise, when I returned to Shiraz, the entire family was at the house, aunts, uncles, and cousins, their arms open in a warm welcome. Being my usual cynical self, I wondered who had arranged it and what their reward was. The women ululated as if I were a bride coming to my husband's home for the first time, but my mother stood in a corner, pale and teary. I took a few big steps, hugged and kissed her. I had missed her vulnerable look. I felt guilty for failing her with my return, for I had freed a part of her too by my escape. I had done it for both of us.

Pregnant a year earlier, Maman now held my baby sister, whom I was seeing for the first time. Suffering with chronic high blood pressure, she had been forbidden by her doctor to have another child. I could have lost her with this last pregnancy. I wanted to be alone with her and my siblings, who had grown and changed in my absence, but the extended family pushed me toward the kitchen in an orchestrated manner.

I stood on top of the high step leading to the sunken kitchen. There was a calf lying on the floor, its legs held tightly by four men. Our eyes met, big black eyes, scared eyes, and I felt an affinity with the familiar look. Time stretched. We stared at each other's eyes as a hairy arm reached over with a sharp knife and sliced through the long neck that was pulled back tightly. Blood gushed out and showered the walls, the ground, and my shoes still dusted with American soil. I held my neck tight, trying to push the words out: *no, no,* but my vocal cords would not obey.

*Kililili,* women ululated.

My mother giggled over my shoulders. "I told you she wouldn't like it," she said to my father.

I knew that I was given the greatest honor, a man's honor, and that Baba was trying to make up for an incident the previous year. At the same ceremony, performed for Jahangeer who was about to get married, I had stepped unknowingly into the kitchen at the moment of the sacrifice.

When my grandmother screamed that I took the blessing away, I left teary under the disapproving gaze of family members. A year later, my father was trying to make up for his silence and to buy me back, but I didn't want the blessing.

I felt as if the event was an omen, and that my fate was sealed with that of the animal. I forced myself to watch the butcher as he blew air under the calf's skin with a wooden tube to separate it from the flesh. My grandmother supervised the distribution of pieces. The liver went to an uncle who had married my parents, the kidneys, the heart, and the brain to various aunts. With each piece leaving, I felt as if my own body was being torn apart. We kept the legs and some of the muscles.

My mother made kabob for us, but I couldn't eat. It was cannibalism, eating my own flesh. My grandmother broke the legs with a hammer, took the hooves off, and made my favorite stew. My broken legs; I couldn't eat.

My father walked around with his hands clasped behind his back, smiling. We would have a visitor the following night, a suitor, and he would be the one. American-educated and handsome, he was the right man. "Wait till you see him," he said with confidence. "He's been anticipating your arrival for months."

I went to the bathroom and threw up. The man came the day after with his father and uncles. My father, uncles, grandmother, and I joined them, sitting around the salon upstairs in stuffed chairs. My mother offered fruit. He obliged, took an apple, and slowly, methodically, peeled it in one piece to show his mastery, his good manners, and then he offered me a piece. I thanked him and put it down on a plate.

My father offered him his black-labeled Johnny Walker on ice and a piece of salted cucumber. *"Besalamati!"*

"To your health," every one responded.

I refused a cold drink. I took a cup of tea and set it on the table. This wasn't my life. I wasn't living inside my body. I watched myself from above, my hair in a short bob around my face, hands folded on my lap, eyes fixed on a windowpane, an artificial smile on my lips, politely answering questions. Who was that woman? Was it really me?

That summer, I never unpacked my suitcase. The second day I was back, I opened it, took out a pair of jeans and a T-shirt to wear, left it closed in the corner of the room, and went to visit a Jewish friend, Taraneh. My body language must have changed, since most people on the street mistook me for an American. Some tried their English on me. Others spat. My friend and I walked down the street, stopped by a café, and asked for Pepsi.

The waiter spat on the floor. Didn't we know it was made by the Bahais? he asked. He didn't sell anything made by the Jews or Bahais—such filthy people! He looked at us suspiciously as if trying to figure out if either one of us were a non-Moslem.

I asked my friend about the political situation in Iran. In the fall of 1974, the year before I left for the United States, the uprising against the Shah's government had been apparent. The engineering students had thrown two soldiers from the Shah's elite army who studied at Pahlavi University out of the library window. Another four students were blown to bits as they assembled a bomb in their dorms. Army officers, suspected of disloyalty to the Shah, disappeared silently. I assumed that the situation had worsened during my absence from Iran, but Taraneh said, "Everything is fine."

In the library riot of 1974, I had seen Taraneh in the crowd as well. But as I left that day, horrified, she stayed behind in a show of solidarity. This wasn't a matter of religion, she had told me angrily the following week, calling me a coward. She argued that as Jews we had to protest the Shah's brutal rule.

I had thought Taraneh out of touch then as she was now, two years later. I didn't think noticing a change in people's behavior was purely my sensitivity. Such displays of open hostility and religious bigotry would not have happened in this particular neighborhood. Anti-Western and anti-Semitic sentiments weren't unusual in a religious section of town, but they were surprising in the heart of shopping and entertainment areas, where restaurants relied on money spent by the Westernized segment of the community, where most shopkeepers were Jewish. I wondered if it was possible that the Shah's government had lost its tight grip on the people, enabling them to openly display a hatred that had been just underneath the surface when they were afraid of SAVAK, the Shah's secret service listening to their every single word. As Jews, we had always avoided involvement in political issues, but political was quickly becoming personal in our lives.

As my friend and I said goodbye at the side of the road, a cyclist passed closely. Eyes bulged out, he extended a hand to touch us, lost control of the bike, and brushed an old woman draped in a black *chador*. The woman screamed at us, "Whores!" She shook her covering as if trying to shake off the touch, an invisible filth. "Look at you, walking around without *hejab*, stirring up the men, and now I am defiled because of you." She spat at us before turning her back, still mumbling curses.

I told Taraneh that the situation seemed to have worsened in the year I was gone, that the smell of a revolution was in the air, and I asked her if she could see the change.

"Not really," she said. "You're sensitive because you just returned from America." She was almost apologetic as if it was her fault for choosing that particular café.

When I returned home from visiting Taraneh, I tried to convince my father to sell everything and move. I told him that a revolution hid in the wind, promising to churn the hatred of the Jews deep within the Iranian psyche. I pleaded, "Sell the farm, the house, get your money out of the bank, take the family to Israel or America before it's too late." My Moslem friends had changed during the last few years, I added, electrified with the anticipation of a holy man who was going to lead them to create a just country according to the laws of Islam, where they thought every Moslem was going to live in financial equality and freedom. There would be no room for the Jews under this new government. There had been warnings from the Israeli embassy; he knew that, I reminded him. I was going to leave and he should too.

Baba laughed. Did I think he was a child, an inexperienced youth? His beard wasn't white from working in a flour mill, he told me. He had seen riots and uprisings, and eventually he had seen all of them squashed. He had lived through pogroms in his childhood, famine and war in his teenage years, a Marxist revolt as a young adult, and hatred and humiliations during the Arab/Israeli wars. "This too shall pass," he said. "These are good times for Iranian Jews, never better. Take my word for it," he told me.

"I don't want to be here," I told him. "I'm leaving."

"Why do you want to be a wandering Jew?" he asked. Those years under Mohammed Reza Shah constituted the best of years, the pinnacle of the Iranian-Jewish revival. "Where would your younger siblings go," he asked, "if you, as the oldest child, set such an example for them? Africa? China?"

Baba had arranged another date for me. He was being very modern, letting this man I didn't know take me out to a restaurant.

I sent my fiancé Norman a letter asking him to send me my transcript so I could obtain an American visa. He called a week later, but my father picked up the phone and hung up without talking. From my mother's giggles and innuendoes, I suspected there had been letters for both my father and me. First I looked in the garbage and then broke into my father's briefcase to find them. I wrote Norman that I couldn't get out. I explained that the American consul wouldn't see me because I didn't have my grades and that my every movement was being watched.

That week, my father's favorite suitor showed me the house of his dreams. We were going to live with his parents, his two brothers, and their families in a house with four separate apartments and a common yard. My father was excited. I cried. The man took me to a fine restaurant. I drank the water, moved the food around the plate, and worried that I couldn't secure a visa, that my ticket would expire soon.

My father demanded that I should pick one of the suitors. "These are all the men left that you haven't said no to," he told me.

My mother came to me with red eyes, a bruise on her arm, and a shaking voice. "Who do you think you are to keep yourself above everyone else? Is it good to live so far away from all your family? Is that what you want? Do you see what has happened to me without the protection of my family?"

She wouldn't look into my eyes. Her words weren't hers. I wanted to remind her that she was the one always telling me to leave. Why wasn't she standing by me now that I was struggling so hard to fulfill her dreams of escape? My hands clenched tight into a fist. I wanted to beat her chest, to bruise her breast so badly she would never heal. I wanted to hit her, to scream at her for sacrificing me to a marriage custom that had already taken too many victims. I wanted to beg her, "Please help me even though your mother didn't help you."

But in the end, no words came out of my mouth. My fists relaxed. I turned my back. I had only myself now, me and the ghosts of all the women whose stories were embedded in me.

### Bibi

As soon as I returned to Iran, my grandmother and I fell into our old pattern of mutual love, dependence, and underlying resentment. Being the

*My paternal great grandmother Bibi.*

force behind the ideal of family togetherness, she criticized my choice to leave more than anyone else, often calling me irresponsible. She told me that I would be the cause of my father's death. Insignificant gestures enraged her. Whenever I took my shoes off at the door with one resting on top of the other, she screamed, "Line them up! Have them face the room." She warned, "Otherwise you'll have bad luck. You'll become a wanderer."

At the same time, she was ingratiating. Knowing that my father wasn't giving me even a *rial* (intending to curb my movements), from time to time she passed me enough money to catch a taxi or buy stamps. In return, she expected me to drive her to doctors' appointments and to her daughters' homes for socializing. She expected me to keep her company, to take long walks with her, or help her with sewing the covers on the quilts. But

I didn't feel like the old days. I was restless and teary. My thoughts drifted constantly to possible plans for getting back to Virginia.

The year before I left for the United States, I had copied a few lines from *Walden* and pasted the sheet on the wall by my bed. Every night before I slept, they reminded me of the essence of Thoreau's essays, that as an individual—a new and delicious concept in my vocabulary—I had the right to my own life. Every morning when I woke up, I touched the slowly yellowing paper, and the words reinforced the idea that even if I were wrong, my mistakes were more right than those the family could make for me. Many times my father asked me to translate it for him, thinking that it was a love poem. I refused. It was mine and only mine—and yes, in many ways, it was a love poem, an ode to myself, celebrating self-reliance and independence.

> *I went to the woods because I wished to live deliberately, to front only the essential facts of life, and see if I could not learn what it had to teach, and not, when I came to die, discover that I had not lived. I did not wish to live what was not life, living is so dear, nor did I wish to practice resignation, unless it was necessary. I wanted to live deep and suck out all the marrow of life.*

Thoreau's lines sustained me and fed a stubbornness that powered my will to leave.

Now, in the summer of 1976, I had left the quotation in America along with my books. I began to doubt its message as I observed the suffering I was causing my parents and my siblings. I desperately needed someone, something to hold me, to assure me that I wasn't making the biggest mistake of my life by severing all ties to my past, by seeking that independence that I had thought was my right.

I sat beside my grandmother one day that long summer, threading the needles for her as we attached the covers on the blue quilt. She sighed through her toothless mouth. Her kerchief slid to her neck and exposed her braids, white and faded orange. I resisted the urge to hold and rub them for comfort as I had done in my childhood before going to sleep. She hadn't colored her hair with henna on the days leading to Tisha'B'Av, a time of mourning for the destruction of the Temple in Jerusalem. She sighed again and asked me if I remembered her mother Bibi. Every time we were alone, Khanom-bozorg would tell me stories of our past lives—

maybe to keep my mind off my problems, maybe to keep me connected in the hope that I would become another branch on the family tree.

How could I not remember Bibi?

My great-grandmother had lived with her son, my great-uncle Daee-bozorg, in a small house shared by his extended family. The house was slowly renovated but Bibi's second-floor room remained the same, a dark, windowless cave. After we moved out of the ghetto, I walked the long distance between our new house in a Moslem neighborhood and Bibi's in the *mahaleh* once a week, taking food and clothing for her. Khanom-bozorg was a devoted daughter, checking on Bibi every day. She would visit or send one of the children or grandchildren to run her mother's errands. Whenever I complained of the chore, my grandmother reminded me that I had been Bibi's favorite child of my generation. She had held me in her arms as a baby and walked me through the streets whenever my mother had been busy. Although she was fastidious about cleanliness to the point of obsession, she didn't mind taking care of me as a baby, even when I wet her lap.

Nevertheless, I always balked doing errands from our new house to her place in the ghetto. I dreaded the long, forty-minute walk through still-unfamiliar neighborhoods, the sexual remarks made by young men in the dark winding alleyways, and the obscenities exchanged by the prostitutes at the gate of the *mahaleh*. To avoid entering Bibi's room, I asked Daee-bozorg's wife if my great-grandmother was in, hoping not, so that I could leave the package. Bibi was always in. I stood on top of the stone stairs in the open hallway, staring into the pitch blackness until Bibi saw me.

"Come on in. My life should be sacrificed for you," Bibi called me in with her shaking voice coming through the darkness.

"Bibi-joon," I addressed her using the word "dear" at the end of her name. "I am putting the package here at the door. I've got to go."

"Come in! What are you afraid of? No one is going to eat you. I've missed you. Come in. Your eyes will get used to the darkness. Come in. I've not seen you for a long time. My heart has shriveled in your absence."

I would walk into the dark, taking tiny steps, trying to balance the food, holding onto it tightly in anticipation of a fall. When my feet touched the bedding on the cobblestone floor, Bibi reached with her bony hands and took the package from me, and holding my hand, helped me sit on the mattress. She caressed my hair and blessed me. "May God reward you for your act of charity. May you find a good husband and have healthy children, *ensha-allah,* God willing."

At age nine or ten, I didn't want a husband; I couldn't think of children. I drew back from being petted by her rough hands. I didn't like her juicy kisses. I wanted to get out, to breath the fresh air, and see the light outside. Bibi often picked up a stone from the floor and threw it at an invisible mouse. Terrified, I would draw my feet up on the bed and hug my knees, wondering if the mice were brave enough to jump on the mattress.

Looking down at my stitches, I told Khanom-bozorg, "Yes, I do remember Bibi." After a long silence, I stopped sewing and lifted my head to see tears at the corner of my grandmother's eyes. Not knowing how to react, I asked what Bibi's name, Zaghee, meant.

"The blue-eyed one," my grandmother said, surprised that I didn't know the meaning of the old Farsi word.

Bibi's piercing blue eyes were an anomaly among Iranians, who were either mesmerized by the color or considered it unlucky. Her full lower and narrow upper lips opened to a complete set of teeth that amazed people who had never seen anyone keeping a full set of teeth into old age. She had a large nose for her petite face; her frame had shrunk and her spine was slightly curved. I remembered her well. An aunt brought Bibi over once a week. My mother washed Bibi's clothes as my grandmother and aunt bathed Bibi in the *hamam.* Serving the three women a pitcher of sour cherry drink in the bathroom, I almost dropped the tray when for the first time I saw my great-grandmother naked, her chest flat like a child's with skin stretched over defined ribs and little flesh.

My mother told me that Bibi's breasts were "cut off, diseased."

I wasn't frightened by her figure, just fascinated. After all, nothing about Bibi was common. She was the oldest person I had ever known. After her bath, my grandmother groomed Bibi's long white hair with a wooden comb, but let Bibi braid it herself in numerous strands. Then Bibi put a scarf on her head and wrapped a long black piece of fabric around it like a turban, covered herself in her *chador,* and sat in the sun with her eyes closed to take in its warmth. She ate little, didn't talk much—only to bless everyone in gratitude—never wanted to stay long. As soon as she entered the house, she longed to go back to her own room, but Khanom-bozorg kept her the entire day.

Khanom-bozorg said that her mother lived to be a hundred and ten years old, ten years short of the magic number every Iranian Jew wished for their loved ones, because she was righteous, because she had suffered. I wondered how one's suffering made her closer to God. My own suffering was distancing me from all I had believed.

My grandmother sighed again and continued to list Bibi's virtues. "She was fastidious about staying clean. She wore separate sandals to enter the outhouse, and wrapped her clothes tightly around her, so that they wouldn't touch the walls. Afterward, she washed her arms to the elbows, her legs to the knees, just the way Moslems purify themselves before praying." My grandmother wiped her tears. "Poor Bibi ate very little. She said she didn't want to grow food for maggots."

Although I recalled Bibi vividly, I didn't know much about her life. Her body had shriveled down to a child's size by the time she died in 1963, when I was ten years old. Unaware of her death, I went to school that morning. When I returned home for lunch, I saw my grandmother, father, and aunts washing their hands and feet at the door with the water from a jug my mother had left outside, the custom for Jews returning from the cemetery. No one told me anything. As always, I had to decipher information by listening. By then I had learned not to ask, not to try to take part in the adults' conversations. I heard an aunt tell the family how she was taking Bibi for a medical check up, when my great-grandmother collapsed in the courtyard and was gone, "an easy death. She was blessed." I felt cheated for not being able to express my grief, to speak of her as everyone else did.

My mother once said that Bibi's longevity was a direct result of her drinking a shot of *aragh* sprinkled with pepper every morning.

Incensed, Khanom-bozorg disagreed, "No, that was to keep her nerves steady. She had a hard life."

I had always wondered but feared to ask what could have tortured my quiet Bibi for so many years. On this summer day, watching Khanom-bozorg so tender and vulnerable, I asked. The answer was as long as all her other stories, as indirect as all conversation in Farsi.

Bibi Zaghee married a wealthy man, Esghel Ghalgeer, who made a living by retrieving silver and gold from the dust at the jewelers' shops. My father was named after him. Being relatively wealthy, Bibi's husband had bought his stunning wife a pearl necklace that was the envy of every woman in the ghetto. Petite, fair-skinned, and bright-eyed, Bibi had enchanted her husband, who would do anything for her, except live long enough to raise their son and four daughters. Although a girl, the youngest, Bagom-jaan, "I say you are my life," became Bibi's dearest child.

Like my mother, women in those days married before puberty and were continuously pregnant. When my Aunt Shams started her period before her wedding night, my grandmother beat her head with both hands: "It isn't time yet, not yet. What am I going to tell the groom's family?"

The Iranian custom of that time dictated that a woman's first blood was to flow in her husband's home. Therefore, when she was still a little girl, Bagom-jaan's extraordinary beauty sent the families of numerous men to ask my paternal great-grandmother for her daughter's hand in marriage. After the groom was chosen, Bibi spent days preparing for a special wedding for her favorite daughter and spent money that she didn't have to prepare a feast. Bagom-jaan was breathtaking in her beautiful wedding gown, her long black hair shone from underneath the sheer veil, and her youth and innocence were the crowns that adorned her head. She was a rosebud ready to be opened.

After the wedding, men escorted the bride and the groom, who rode donkeys through the narrow alleyways of the *mahaleh;* women walked behind them, clapping and singing *vasoonak:*

> The alleyways are narrow, yes; the bride is beautiful, yes!
> Don't touch her mane; it is decorated with pearls, yes!
>
> Don't take the bride through the alleyways; they are muddy,
> Just as the bride's lips are clearly rosy.

The entire neighborhood gathered on the flat roofs of their homes, ululating as the bridal party went by, showering them with sugar candy flavored with rose water. With the beat of their *tonbaks,* the Jewish musicians met the entourage at the groom's house and ushered the couple to their *hejleh,* decorated with silk fabrics and greens. The family sang until their voices gave up. Then they left Bagom-jaan and her husband to enjoy each other's company and waited outside, still clapping and singing along with the musicians, waiting for the bloody cloth.

The groom came out in a short while. The family sang even louder:

> Our bride is a child; early at night she is sleepy
> From the *hejleh,* the groom appears, satisfied and happy.

The groom didn't look happy, and my great-grandmother panicked. What was wrong? The bride was surely a virgin; she was but a child. Bagom-jaan was suffering from severe cramps, the groom informed the family. Bibi rushed to her daughter's side trying to comfort her, but no one realized the seriousness of the problem, and Bagom-jaan died on her wedding night. Bibi tore her necklace and the pearls flew in the air and scattered over the dead child. Her true pearl was going to sleep in the cold of earth rather than in the warmth of a wedding bed.

Bibi never recovered from the shock. She had to be peeled off the pile of dirt in the Jewish cemetery. After pulling out fistfuls of her hair and throwing them on the grave, she beat herself on the head and chest until she fainted. Her grief was too deep to be consoled. Week after week, she fasted and prayed for Bagom-jaan, but her grief wouldn't dull. She spent her days at the gravesite, crying, grieving, and eating little, trying to fast as many days as possible. After the thirty days of formal mourning, when her pain was still as harsh as the first weeks, Bibi still visited the grave every day, beating her breasts with a large stone, asking for atonement from God, for forgiveness from her beloved daughter, believing that her sins had brought death to Bagom-jaan.

Sick and depressed, Bibi was taken to a doctor, who was horrified to see her breasts lumpy and bruised. "Cancer!" he told the family. That week, he admitted Bibi to the hospital and surgically removed both breasts, with which my great grandmother, the beautiful Bibi Zaghee, had last nursed her favorite daughter.

When Khanom-bozorg finished her story, I was numb. At the same time, I had an uncontrollable urge to see my great-grandmother's room once more. I wasn't being logical. Visiting people was understandable, touring the rubble of a room wasn't. My parents didn't understand my request. I didn't quite know myself why I needed to visit a room that I had dreaded as a child. My grandmother's story had jolted me. Hurting inside, feeling trapped, I sensed that I couldn't go forward unless I stepped back in time and understood the women who had come before me. I needed to touch Bibi; to touch a woman who I was told—over and over—had once loved me unconditionally. I had to connect my own pain with hers.

I knew Khanom-bozorg was doing me a big favor by arranging my visit to Bibi's room before it was renovated to sell the house. Since both her mother and brother were dead, the experience had to be painful. We entered the small courtyard. I remembered it as the place where my grandmother's brother, Daee-bozorg, had erected a large *tanoor* every year before Passover to bake *matzah* for the community. The uneven ground, once covered with broken pieces of bricks, was leveled and tiled. No more ovens were going to be built there, and Daee-bozorg's kind face would not greet the nieces and nephews every Passover with the promise of a whole egg baked on a *matzah,* a treat my sister Nahid and I gobbled in excitement. There was a buzz around the Jewish community about imported machine-made *matzah,* every piece looking exactly alike, square with sharp edges. Daee-bozorg's round, uneven, unleavened bread was going to be a part of history.

I climbed up the narrow stone stairs, trying to keep a balance on their slippery surface. Where once there had been hand-made grooves, the stairs were now worn out like the shells I had seen on the shores of Virginia Beach, smooth from the constant beating of the waves. From the open hallway, I could see the heavy wooden door. I pushed it with both hands and secured it with a stone, the way Bibi kept it open to get fresh air. The room wasn't as dark as the one in my memory. The bedding was removed, but a small charcoal brazier, where Bibi heated her food, made tea, and warmed the room in winter stood on tiny brass feet. Seeing the empty ledge built into the wall, I remembered how Bibi's bottles of herbal teas, lighting oil, and *aragh* once sat on its stone face, their shadowy figures frightening me.

Walking across the dirt and stone floor, I smelled my great-grandmother. I broke down and sobbed loudly, frightening everyone. The women ran upstairs to see what was going on. I was mourning. I hadn't had a chance to grieve for Bibi when she died; now I couldn't restrain myself.

As I stood in Bibi's room, I could feel her presence, her suffering and guilt for having sacrificed her daughter to a tradition that was too strong for the mother to have resisted. I felt too the spirit of my little great-aunt

*There was a party in our house for the double births of my first brother, Freydoun, and my aunt's son, born around the same time. Khanom-bozorg (standing) gives orders to the cook, working in a makeshift kitchen in the backyard. Bibi suns herself in the right corner. The woman sitting in front of the cook is my grandmother's sister Khatoon-jaan.* Picture courtesy of Nahid Gerstein.

Bagom-jaan, her fear on the night of her wedding, and her pain as well. I said a silent goodbye to them, stepped out of the room, and closed the door behind me.

### A Match for Me

I don't know at what stage in my life I found the traditions unacceptable and why. I often wonder if my mother's position as an outsider and her perpetual unmet desire to leave influenced me to feel detached from life around me, from her, and from the customs as an extension of her bondage and possibly mine.

Even now, in the twenty-first century in the United States, my younger cousins and their children who escaped from Iran after the 1979 Revolution, abide by the cultural rules of the country they abandoned. An educated cousin married a woman his mother found for him in Iran and brought over. Repeatedly I hear from friends and family that with the arrival of each new group of Iranian women, men rush to marry them before "their eyes and ears are opened" to the freedoms of the West. Some of my young educated cousins have been here since childhood, don't read or write Farsi, don't remember their country of birth, yet wait for their parents to find them proper husbands. The men may date Americans but mostly marry Iranian women whom their parents recommend.

Naturally, in the summer of 1976, my father and the rest of the family were shocked at my disobedience and single-mindedness at daring to demand control over my own life, and I still don't know how I became so stony, unyielding, and defiant.

A month after my return to Iran, my father called for a family *moshaverat*, the gathering of elders to make important decisions. I served them tea and cookies as my grandmother, uncles, and father sat around the room reviewing my suitors. Then my grandmother asked me to leave. In a rare show of disagreement with his mother, probably to prove his flexibility and modernity, my father asked me to stay, to review and evaluate the suitors.

"They're all wrong," I told him.

My father chewed his mustache, always a sign of his anger. "Not the right answer," he said. He wanted to know what kind of information I had deciphered from them; how their family lives were; how much money they made; what kind of cars they drove; how much education they had.

"None," I said. "I didn't ask those questions."

"Do you think that there will be a man created to your specification?" He added that he couldn't lift his head in front of the family out of shame, the shame of having a daughter out of control. He turned red in anger. When chewing his mustache didn't comfort him enough, he bit into his knuckles.

My grandmother agreed that I was disrespectful to my elders, destroying myself, losing my charm and beauty by not eating and by crying excessively. "Look, what you've done to yourself! To your father. Is it worth it?" she asked.

My father must have noticed my gaunt look for the first time because his facial muscles relaxed and his eyes softened. In a gentle tone, he explained, "You are too young to understand what you're doing. You have to respect the wisdom of the elders, who have seen the world. If you disregard our advice, then you will have to accept the consequences. Your stubbornness will make you *siah-bakht*, will leave you open to misfortunes."

His words had the opposite effect of what he had hoped for. I shrugged my shoulders and sighed. "Can I leave now?"

He then interpreted a passage in the Talmud, "If you mock your traditions and be disrespectful of us, your children will do a hundred times worse to you. Is that what you want? They will pay for your misdeeds with their own terrible kismet."

I shivered. Those words chilled me to the bones. I never forgot them. I never could erase their impact. Throughout my life, whenever my children suffered, his prophecy crossed my mind.

After the lecture, my father ran a few other names by me: a doctor, an engineer, a businessman. "When is a good time for them to meet you?" he asked.

"Whenever," I said. I knew that if I didn't agree to at least meet these men, the family would find more humiliating ways to present me to them. I didn't want to repeat the matchmaking episode when I was told to walk in front of the *khastegar*'s family like a model on a runway. I had fought back then by rejecting my family's set up and protesting to the intended suitor. Now, two summers later, I seemed to have lost the spark to fight back, to oppose my father openly. I ate less after meeting each candidate; the food stuck in my throat and I had to cough it up. After my grandmother's warning about my colorless cheeks, my father watched my eating the way he had counted every mouthful when I was a chubby teenager. Finally one day, when he pushed the food toward me, I lost my temper.

I had become soft-spoken, never disagreeing, and even covered my mouth with the palm of my hand if I laughed to suffocate its sound, to be lady-like. Now I screamed gibberish as I threw plates of food against the walls and the floor. I pulled the tablecloth from underneath the serving dishes and tore it. Bowls of rice and stew flew in the air, spewing red and green sauces on the Persian carpets. I watched myself shout like a madwoman and wondered how I could have all that sound in me. Somehow all the words that I had shoved back inside, all the words that I never uttered for fear of being *verag* and immodest, poured out in one long spasm of incoherent language. My father, uncles, sisters, and brothers watched my outburst silently. My siblings' faces turned pale. My sister cried softly. When I finally wore out my rage, I left the kitchen, crawled into my bed, held myself tightly, and drowned in a deep sleep for the first time since I had returned.

When I woke up, I took the keys to my father's car without his permission. He would have insisted that people gossiped about young women driving by themselves. I didn't want to be jammed in the back of a taxi with three men who weren't afraid to touch. I didn't want to walk down side streets where men cornered women and groped them. In the short time I had been home, I learned quickly that our sleepy city had become increasingly more hostile.

On a busy street, I passed a car that slowed down to let a passenger out. Minutes later, I felt a strong jolt; the same beige Peykan had hit me. I got out and appraised the damage. Other drivers honked, stuck their heads out the car windows and cursed us for causing a traffic jam. Feeling self-conscious and unsure of the next step when the driver didn't come to me, I walked to him, a man in his sixties with stubble and a fatherly demeanor. "Why did you hit me?" I asked amazed.

"You passed me," he said accusingly. In the back of his small car with tinted glass, four women sat wrapped in black *chadors*, two with children sitting on their laps. Although I was in the first generation of Iranian women to be given the right to drive, I had thought it an accepted fact. Now, standing in front of this gentle-looking man, I realized that from his perspective I had demeaned him. By daring to pass him, I had eroded his sense of manhood, embarrassing him in front of his women. This was definitely a changing Iran, going back in time. I returned to the car and drove away, wondering whether there was such a thing as car insurance in Iran and mulling over what I was going to tell my father about denting his beautiful mung bean–colored Rambler.

When I reached my friend Shahnaz's house, she was smoking a cigarette, listening to the Beatles, and cursing the Shah for forcing her to serve in the army. She was on leave from the military for one day, staying with her parents who lived closer to the base. Being a newlywed, she much preferred spending time with her husband who worked at Bandar-Abbas on the Persian Gulf—a much greater distance to travel, especially for an unescorted woman. She argued with her superior officer nonstop, she told me, wishing to be dismissed for insubordination. Shahnaz pressed the butt of her cigarette in the ashtray as if trying to suffocate something more than an inanimate object. "This whole idea of serving in the army is such nonsense. Let her highness, Princess Ashraf," Shahnaz rolled her eyes, "wear army boots instead of her Italian-made shoes. Let her jog around the army compound since she was behind this *great idea* for Iranian women. The officers are all lechers. They want us to jump up and down to watch our quivering breasts." She threw her blond curls over her shoulders, and her blue eyes filled with tears as she lit another Winston.

Shahnaz was my contradictory friend. She wore mini-skirts, didn't shy away from good wine or aged scotch, and danced in the discothèques until early morning hours; yet she was a devoted Moslem. She frequently visited Shah-Cheragh, a religious site in Shiraz, to pray and pay alms, yet her European looks aroused suspicion. When she drank from a waterspout the previous year, an angry mob at the shrine gathered around her, shaking their fists and calling her an infidel, who had defiled water that was used for ablution. She was saved when a family friend spotted her and vouched for her devotion to Islam. Once, Shahnaz made a pilgrimage to the holy city of Ghom and waited in her uncle's car as he ran into a shop to pick up merchandise. In the half an hour he was gone, *molas* in their black caftans, white turbans, and long beards knocked at the car window, *"Sigheh meeshee?"*—asking if she was available for a *sigheh,* a temporary marriage that could last from an hour to a hundred years. Shahnaz laughed as she told me the story, and only at the end did she admit that she had chewed all her nails as she awaited her uncle. Like most of my Moslem friends, Shahnaz and her family venerated Islam even though they made fun of its peculiarities and lived in a very Western style. Shahnaz's father served his guests aged whiskey but washed his mouth with soap to cleanse it from the forbidden drink before praying. Once a year he crawled on his knees to a shrine and gave a portion of his salary to the religious leader of a *maktab,* a religious school, in a show of atonement for straying from Islamic teachings.

Shahnaz's family had always treated me with respect and kindness, and on this day, when I was so distraught from the match-making pressures, both Shahnaz and her mother were surprised that my family's opposition to a man I had chosen was his nationality and not his religion. Three years later, with the arrival of Khomeini in 1979, most Iranian Jews including my family would disperse around the world, but during that long summer, the emphasis was on keeping the family together, close by, and segregated from the larger world around us. I told Shahnaz that even if I had chosen a man from Tehran, the distance would have been unacceptable to the family. Most importantly, had I even chosen someone my own age, anyone not selected by the family, I would have faced severe opposition, for the process was as important as the choice. No woman in the family had ever decided on her own husband. Why should I differ? The women of the family especially questioned my judgment. My progressive Moslem friend, who didn't know of the oppression we had felt as Jews for generations, struggled to understand my family's need to see me bend to the rituals and customs that had embittered their own lives.

Shahnaz was leaving the following day for the boot camp and then to her husband's house for a long weekend. She told me either to hurry home or to go the long way since the movie theater by her house would let out soon. I decided not to take my father's large car through the tiny side streets, thinking that I could beat the crowd. I was beside the movie theater when the doors opened a few minutes earlier than I had expected, and a large crowd of young men poured out. I reached over and locked the doors quickly and tried to keep calm as I inched my way toward the nearby main street.

A young man with stubble jumped in front of the car. "Put it in second gear," he screamed. This was a customary way to make fun of women driving, insinuating that women didn't know how to drive, hoping that the driver would panic and the car would stall, embarrassing her and proving their point. Another man knocked at my window with his hand on his crotch, "No, put it in first gear." The crowd laughed hysterically, surrounding the car and banging on it.

I was strangely stoical. Looking indifferently at their faces for a few minutes, I put the car in first gear and pressed the gas pedal. The men in front of me banged harder on the windows, now cursing and calling me a whore. I accelerated a bit more. The men jumped aside, still pounding on the car, telling me where they were going to put their penises. I calmly made a left turn, grazing a few others, truly not caring, a smile on my face, enjoying the havoc. My revenge. I stopped the car across the street, suddenly aware of the meanness that had penetrated me like a virus. I was becoming them. By breathing the hatred hanging in the air, by sharing the uneasiness surrounding me at the house and on the streets, I was being transformed into a person I didn't know and now didn't like. What if I had seriously hurt one of them? What if I had to face the courts? I shivered. I had to leave Iran soon in order to save myself.

I heard screams and laughter again. Looking back at the theater, I saw an American teenager running away from the men, her pink underwear peeking through her short skirt once in a while, her blond hair blowing behind her. She stuck two fingers in her mouth and whistled for a pick-up truck. When it stopped she jumped over and sat on its flat back, sticking her thumb up to her pursuers in the Iranian middle-finger gesture. The truck driver stuck his head out of the car, waving a colorful kerchief, ululating, "Kiliiliii," as if he were taking home a bride.

A middle-aged man with stubble ran after the truck, screaming, "The lessons of the West, behold the imported abomination defiling our land."

"Western filth," another man yelled. "Look at the sample of ruinous America!"

I shook in fear.

### The Last Days

My flight left without me. The employees of Iran Air were happy to have the extra seat, since there was a large waiting list for flights to New York City, but they wouldn't give me even a partial refund. A few weeks through August, schools in the States had already started. I hadn't signed up for classes. I wasn't admitted through the doors of the newly opened consulate in Shiraz. Although I had taught summer school, I barely had enough money to get on a bus to Tehran, never mind a plane ticket for overseas.

With a strange sense of resignation and emptiness, I lost the desire to talk, to read, or to visit friends. My Jewish friend Fereshteh kept an eye on me and dragged me out of the house to visit some of her American friends. She was the only person who could bring a smile to my face with her funny stories. She told me how her white-haired father showed up in his pajamas at a party at the Organization for Jewish Students, a block away from their home, and insisted that dancing was immoral and everyone should go home. Fereshteh and her sister were mortified as friends watched their father grabbing the women's arms to take them home, his hair uncombed, looking as if he had just left the bed. I wondered why she could laugh at the humiliation and not act bitter. Maybe what I lacked was a sense of humor.

My father arranged for the entire extended family to have an all-day picnic in a garden, hoping that an outing would improve my mood. My male cousins set up a net and played volleyball with gusto. Other men wearing pajama bottoms and dress shirts and ties sat on a Persian carpet under the trees to play backgammon and poker. Morad slapped the ground with his aces and laughed; Jahangeer screamed "double sixes" as he rolled his dice on the backgammon table; two other uncles brought over trays of kabob, cilantro, and radishes on a bed of flat bread. Smelling the food, the players stopped their games, wrapped the meat and the herbs in a piece of flat bread, chewed them greedily, and washed them down with vodka, *"be-salamati, besalamati,* to your health."

Women skewered the meat. Bent over makeshift grills, they frantically fanned the ambers and turned the kabobs. They washed and arranged the vegetables—sweaty, covered with ashes. I sat alone and watched the scene as if it wasn't my life. No one asked me to help. Instead, they pushed food on me. I chewed for a long time before spitting it out. Something was blocking my throat; the food wouldn't go down. Jahangeer offered me a drink. "See how much fun this is? You wouldn't get this kind of closeness among Americans."

I nodded.

My father put a plate of food in front of me and offered me a beer. I took a sip and picked at the bread drenched in the juices of the kabob, my mind too exhausted to come up with a solution for my life. I had contacted the Israeli consulate in Tehran, asking if they could arrange for my *aliyah,* but I hadn't heard from them. The prospect of staying in Iran now certain, I had applied and been accepted to the graduate school at the Pahlavi University in order to avoid being recruited to the army. I saw Morad smiling at me as he wrapped himself another sandwich and my stomach turned. I wondered if Tehran University would give me a scholarship so I wouldn't have to live with the family in Shiraz. I was nauseous. I hadn't heard from Norman and assumed that, tired of the complications, he had let go of me.

Morad's wife sat next to me on the carpet and stared at me for a few minutes, "So, what's all this stuff about America? There is less *shadee* on your face now than before you left. America obviously didn't bring you any happiness, so why are you making everyone miserable because you want to go back?" I couldn't find the words to respond. Thinking that I was rudely ignoring her, she picked up her plate of kabob and stomped away toward the other women.

An aunt brought me a drink and told me that I needed to let go of my stubbornness. "It doesn't befit a woman's dignity," she said. I opened my mouth to tell her how she contributed to my disobedience, to tell her that her words years earlier to my father, that books would ruin my character, took away my only refuge and made the house a more confining prison. I wanted to ask her if she knew how I felt the day I woke up to the smoke coming from the kitchen, my books on fire. My eyes teared, a lump blocked my throat, and I didn't reply. I heard her tell the others that I was too disrespectful to give an answer.

I lost my voice, my language. Sounds wouldn't leave my mouth. Sometimes I forced the words out, but I found the language to be unfamiliar, not communicating my ideas. Or, worst yet, sometimes I didn't understand my own words as I said them.

That night I lay on a platform bed in the yard next to my sisters, brothers, and mother, feeling their rhythmic breathing, feeling the cool desert air, feeling as if I were in the womb of the night. In America, I had forgotten that the skies over Shiraz could be so deeply black, that there were so many stars, so close, so clear, and so breathtakingly beautiful. I outlined the constellations, trying to remember their names, sleep eluding me as I watched a point of light moving in the yard. My father had started smoking again since I had come back. He was now pacing the yard in the darkness. Every time he neared our section, I could hear his soft sobs. Again I thought of myself as cruel and decided I should stay and make the best of it. Maybe all the complications were simply an omen.

Before I could share my decision with him at the breakfast table the following morning, Baba told me, chewing his mustache, that if I insisted on leaving, he would hire the men from the synagogue to read *Tehilim* at our house and he would personally sit *shiva* for me. He would also forbid my sisters and brothers to contact me. Then he put on his hat and left the house.

That was it. I was leaving.

I asked Khanom-bozorg for money, grabbed all the *toman*s I had earned from teaching, and took a taxi downtown. On the way, as we passed the familiar sites, part of me wanted to stop by the ghetto to take another look at the house I grew up in. I longed to go to the bazaar once more, where I first visited clinging to my grandmother's *chador;* a place I later explored with my good friend Shahnaz—bargaining for a sheep-skin coat, eating smothered eggplant and sour yogurt in a converted caravansary, and smoking a waterpipe.

At the post office, scribers sat on low stools on the sidewalk by the long wall and wrote letters for kneeling old women wrapped in *chadors*. Most of them cried as they dictated their words for a loved one, a soldier-son maybe, a husband working in a faraway village, a daughter taken away by her husband to another town. I waited in a long line to send a telegram to Old Dominion University, asking them to send me my transcript. I had been unwise to wear jeans, a blue tie-dyed shirt, and platform shoes, or maybe I just looked different, fairer than most Iranians, too free in my movements, not avoiding eye-contact. I was creating a commotion and finally the clerk behind the desk motioned for me to leave the line and approach him. "What can I do for you?" he asked in English.

Surprised, I spoke to him in Farsi and gave him a piece of paper with the information. He looked disappointed not to practice his English and tried to convince me for my own good, "since you're like my sister," to cut the return address and save money. I told him that it was imperative to keep the address and asked him for the price. I was shocked at the expense of sending a few lines and tried to cut words so I would have enough money for the cab ride back. I could walk, but the thought of making my way back through jam-packed religious neighborhoods and busy shopping areas wasn't pleasant.

The clerk looked at me with curiosity and said, "No worry!" in English. "I fix it."

I paid him and thanked him before leaving. His eyes were still on me when I turned around by the exit doors. Later I would learn that he had cut off the return address.

I waited by the side of the road for a taxi, trying to dodge donkeys with loads of watermelons and kamikaze moped drivers. Not mid-day yet, the temperature had risen rapidly. My sweaty shirt stuck to my back, and I felt light headed and thirsty. The cabs passed me by quickly, not stopping. I wouldn't get into a few that were already filled with men.

A man dressed in a suit and a tie and carrying a briefcase approached me. I inched away from him, not making eye-contact. "I mean no harm," he said in English. "You don't belong here," he added. "Let me help you, please. Where are you going?" he asked.

"The medical school," I told him in English, not trusting him with my address.

He motioned for a taxi with an empty front seat, opened the door for me, and in Farsi gave the driver the address and a stern talk about not putting anyone else next to me and waved.

"Thank you!" I said to him in English, not wanting to ruin his image of me.

I changed my mind about going back to the house and told the taxi driver to drop me off at my uncle's office. Jahangeer was about to go home and invited me to lunch. I happily accepted. On the way, sobbing uncontrollably, I asked him please to help me get out.

"This is so hard for me, you know. I'll be disrespectful to your father by doing it."

"Please! You've been like my older brother. Please help me. I need a sponsor to get a visa."

"Okay," he said finally. "As long as it's between the two of us." Jahangeer was leaving town that week for a long vacation and I feared that my transcript would arrive when he was gone. He gave me a check for a large sum and told me to deposit it in my account if my transcript arrived to prove to the consul that I could support myself independently in the United States. I would have to transfer the money back to his account if I left before he had returned from his trip.

For two weeks, I kept close to the front door or sat outside on the steps, watching for the mailman, trying to intercept him sometimes even before he reached our street. By the end of the second week, I had two letters from American friends who, independent of each other, had sent me copies of my transcript, and I had a telegram from Norman. "You owe me a *mitzvah*. Come back. I love you." All along he believed that I had received my transcript weeks earlier.

Soon I had a student visa but no ticket. I was wondering how to contact Norman for the money. I stopped by the office of Iran Air to make reservations, but all tickets were sold out. I walked around the room that day banging on the wall with my fist, needing to feel the physical pain to dull the greater hurt inside.

At noon, my father came back from work and handed me an envelope with a round-trip ticket to New York City and a check. He took his hat off and motioned for me to sit next to him. "If you need to leave so badly, go!" he said. "But promise me—promise me on my life—that you'll wait a year before you make any decision about getting married. Remember, this is your home. You can always come back."

*Epilogue*

# SEPTEMBER 2001

### Nightmares

I left Iran for the first time on July 4th, 1975, then returned to visit my birthplace for the last time the following summer. Upon my return to the United States in the fall of 1976, I began to suffer from nightmares. I would wake up screaming, soaked in sweat, shivering and shaking uncontrollably. Night after night I dreamt of Iran, of the fate I had escaped.

I was back in Shiraz. The mountains looked taller, closer, looming over me. I couldn't breathe. I stood in the crossroad in front of my parents' house and tried to remember which way led back to America. It was a long journey, I knew.

A man with white stubble stood by his little kiosk. He straightened his curled body. Laughing through his yellow teeth, he pointed his trembling finger at me. "Whore, Jewish whore."

I wanted to ask the jeering old man with yellow teeth if he remembered selling me candy when I was a little girl, when he was not such an old man. I wanted to tell him that I was smacked with a ruler at school because I wrote my homework with the diluted ink he sold me. The letters were faint. I was a cheap Jew, my teacher said. My classmates laughed.

My bare legs were numb. I bent down to massage them, to get the blood flowing, so I could walk, run, escape. My feet were hidden among opium poppies, like those growing in farms beyond our neighborhood. When I was a child, my mother once found me running through the red flowers and wheat stalks in a white dress, laughing, screaming in delight. "Keep away," she scolded, then warned that the pollen would blind me.

*On one of his trips to Iran, my father brought my daughters the costumes of the Ghashghai nomadic tribe outside Shiraz.*

Now in my dream, I covered my eyes for protection. When I opened them again, everything was in black and white.

The old man was still there. "Hee, hee!" He laughed and coughed with a throat filled with phlegm. What was he pointing at? Then I saw them. Those weren't flowers on the ground, just red droplets, the only image in color. I headed toward my friend's house for shelter, wanting to ask if Paree knew where the blood came from, and why it was on my legs and my bare feet.

Her brothers stood on the roof, their zippers open, their penises pointing at me like arrows. "Here! Is this what you are looking for? Here, here." Their laughter traveled from the rooftop and pierced my eardrums.

I backed up and stood in the middle of the crossroad again. From another corner, I saw Shahnaz and Firoozeh coming toward me, wrapped in black *chadors*. "My good friends, my good friends," I cried joyfully as I ran to them, "Save me, save me!" I stretched my arms toward them. "I am lost. Which way are the oceans?"

They spread their arms and their *chadors* flew in the air like the wings of angels in black. They opened their hands and threw stones at me, which changed into daggers as they hit me in the stomach, slowly disappearing into my flesh. The skin closed over the wounds before I could extract them. "We don't know you," they said. "Away, away, filth, filth."

My stomach filled with hurt. The other neighbors joined them—the boy who hung the red swastika in his room facing our house, the teacher who invited my grandmother and me to hear a *mola* cursing the Jews in a ceremonial prayer in her house during the month of Moharam, and the young men down the street who leaped from hidden doorways in side streets to stick their fingers in me. From every door, every window, and every storefront, the young and the old emerged. They darted at me with nails that my body absorbed, my stomach now bursting. "That girl kissed a foreigner, impure, impure," they told one another.

I looked toward the doors of my house to see if I could find a refuge, but my aunts and uncles blocked them, sticks in their hands, my parents' faces hiding behind them. They took turns shaking their fingers at me. "Shame, shame! You've brought us shame."

Or sometimes I dreamt that I was dressed in a white gown, sitting in a chair in our backyard. Musicians played *tonbak* and *setar* over a wooden cover on our key-shaped pond; a belly dancer moved her generous body to the laughter of men drinking *aragh*. I didn't understand how the yard had stretched so deep, so wide, tables set up as far as my eyes could see. My sour orange tree was gone, all the trees cut down to make room for the entire *mahaleh*. I noticed faces that I had never seen before and those I knew, frozen in time—the beggar, the boy with an elongated head, and myself, still a child.

The guests cracked watermelon seeds between their teeth and spit the shells out on the bricked yard and on the flower beds. They saluted each other with their shot glasses, "*Besalamti,* to your health. May the next happy occasion be yours."

My aunts surrounded me, sang *vasoonak*, and threw *noghl* at me.

I looked at the faces from behind a white veil. *This can't be true. I am not going through this. Wake up, wake up.* But it couldn't be a dream—too real to be a dream. I wailed silent cries. *Please no. I don't want to get married. Who is the groom? I have never seen him before. I am already engaged to someone else.*

The guests laughed.

My father was drunk with happiness.

My mother said, *I told you that's the way. I told you there was nothing you could do.*

Or sometimes in my dreams I made it back to the States, losing all family and friends, breaking all bridges behind me, only to find out that the man I had made the sacrifices for, my fiancé Norman, did not recognize me. Every time I was pregnant, these dreams intensified. Norman turned his back on me. I pleaded. *Where can I go, pregnant and unmarried? They'll call me a whore.*

Every time, he turned his back and walked away with an American woman. *I don't care if you are pregnant. Go back home. I'm not marrying an alien.*

My nightmares always seeped into reality for minutes after my eyes were open. Even after I sat up, the horrors still gripped me, and the room, the bed, the man lying next to me looked unfamiliar.

When I finally left Iran in that summer of 1976, I wanted to distance myself from my culture, my society, and even my extended family. Putting continents between us, I vowed never to return, never to miss them, never to think about them, and never to indulge in nostalgia.

The 1979 Islamic Revolution changed all that for me. Now most family members who had never stepped foot out of our southern birthplace of Shiraz, those who never dreamed of leaving, the very ones who laughed and pointed fingers at me as the "odd one" when I decided to leave, have come to the United States. I see them at family gatherings. I hear what they whisper behind me, what they say to my face, and I am even sometimes amused by the irony of my situation.

For me, America had been a naïve utopian dream, and at least for a while a refuge, a deliberate escape from all that was familiar. Many Iranians considered the move a hardship for the sake of a better future for their children, a forced exile into an alien culture, banishment to a country that didn't feel like home, unlike Iran that had been familiar even if hostile.

On 9 September 2001 a large number of my aunts, uncles, and cousins attended a cousin's wedding, just across the river from my Norfolk home, in fact at the same spot where I married my American-born husband, Norman. The bride had been a flower girl at my wedding. Now my three daughters were her bridesmaids. Weddings can be emotional rollercoasters, especially ones with such close ties. My face was wet with tears as my daughters walked toward the *khupah*.

More than anything else, my children's lives affirmed how right I had been to leave Iran. Here they had not personally felt hatred against the Jews; here they didn't know of the fear I had felt, the hostilities I had faced during the Six-Day and the Yom Kippur wars; here they didn't have to worry about their existence being threatened for being a minority or just for being different. As women, they live in a country and an era that give them liberties and choices that I never knew to yearn for. One by one, my daughters turned around and smiled as they passed by me. I wished my mother could be with me to see how her granddaughters had fulfilled her dreams of escape.

As the bride followed, a big smile visible beneath her veil, I viewed the celebration with a double vision both as an unattached spectator and an emotionally involved participant. I was moved by the smiles, the tears, the laughter, the soothing sound of breaking the glass, the familiar ululation, not just by the Iranians but also my husband who had mastered the art at our own wedding. I juxtaposed the past and the present, evaluated the relationships, and marveled at the effect of time. I was joyous beyond words, but at the same time I experienced many of the tremulous moods that had possessed me during the last summer I had spent in Iran.

I have now been in the United States longer than I lived in Iran. The emotional turmoil, the struggle to leave against the will of what felt like the entire community, has become an almost dreamlike memory. But at times, on occasions like this wedding, these rare instances when family comes together again for celebrations, the haze lifts, the memory bites.

The aunt whose garden wedding had mesmerized me as a child was visiting the United States and attended the wedding with her husband. When my aunt tried to leave Iran about twenty years ago, she was arrested along with her husband and son, and imprisoned for attempting to take her military-age child out of the country. Now she and her husband could visit the rest of the children in America only if they left their youngest son as collateral. She cried every time she looked at me. I wasn't the only one thinking of how a close-knit family had been torn apart.

Another aunt was there with her husband, children, and grandchildren, wearing a *shytel*, a wig worn for religious modesty. In Iran she was popular at the weddings because of her loud and clear voice, singing *vasoonak*, Jewish wedding songs. She knew more songs than anyone I knew. She used to clap as she belted the words out, encouraging the other women's participation. At this wedding, she first refused to sing *vasoonak* for the bride because of the restrictions of *kol-isha*—a woman's voice should not be heard in gatherings that include men lest it arouse them. I learned about such Eastern-European Jewish customs only after moving to the United States. When the men cleared the area to give her privacy, my aunt stood very close to the bride and whispered the words.

> The sound of the flute comes from the gates of Shiraz.
> Don't worry any longer the prince-groom;
> It's your fiancée arriving, shy and demure.

Not understanding a word of the Farsi poem in its Shirazi Jewish rhythm, my independent, hybrid cousin brushed her veil aside and smiled bigger.

Uncle Morad and his wife were at the wedding as well. I looked at them in disbelief, my hands shaking, my heart pumping, my mouth dry. His hair gray, lines around his eyes, he still displayed the same sarcastic smile I remembered from twenty-five years ago.

Through writing my book I've learned to confront my past, but this I wasn't ready for. "Go, talk to him," an aunt said.

He had been hateful to my sister even in recent years, telling her that he disliked us both.

A cousin chimed in, "We'll go with you."

My uncle was talking to a few family members when I approached him. He ignored me. I offered my hand, but he stood there for a few minutes as everyone looked on silently. A man I called *dear* uncle for most of my Iranian life, who lived with my family until I left Iran, shook my hand like a stranger.

"*Mazal tov*," I congratulated him on the wedding of his daughter just a few months earlier, an occasion to which no one in my family was invited. "I won't recognize my cousins if I ever run into them on the street," I said.

"Oh, you will," he answered. "There's a family resemblance."

"I don't think so."

I saw his wife quickly withdrawing from the circle. I followed her, called her name, shook her hand, and wished her *mazal tov* too. She pulled her hand away as if she had touched fire. The animosity had reached second and third generations by now, but the touch was strangely calming for me. The demons died. The sediment of the past leisurely settled in time— until the next storm.

Jahangeer was at the wedding with his family, and his daughters bonded with mine as if they had always known each other—as if blood transcended time and distance.

My parents didn't come. The trip from Israel, across continents and an ocean was hard on old bones, uneasy minds. My father lost just about everything he had worked for all his life, the farm, the house, his status, his dignity, and prestige. In his first years in exile, still hoping to return to Iran, he spoke constantly of his apricot trees—little Persian apricots, the kind that simply melted in the mouth. Now with the apricot orchard gone, along with the poultry farm, the house, and the car, he couldn't bear to talk about them. He dreaded humiliating himself in front of us. A man crying. But I could always tell when he missed his orchard. He had known every stone that had to be cleared, every piece of dirt dug out of his well to water the land. Thinking of his apricot trees, his wrinkles deepened. He put his balding head between his two hands, hiding tears.

My two brothers and a sister live in the United States, while our youngest sister Niloufar lives in Israel with our parents. At the wedding, we lined up for a picture to commemorate the rare occasion of being together. We have only four of these pictures of the five siblings shoulder to shoulder, hands laced around each other's waists in the same city, in the same country. My sister Nahid and my brother Farzad speak to Niloufar in Hebrew, but my brother Freydoun and I, who aren't fluent in the language, prefer English. We never communicate in Farsi.

My sister arrived in Israel for the first time in 1979, when she was five years old. Ayatollah Khomeini was on his way to replace the Shah of Iran, and the country bubbled in the heat of an oncoming Revolution. As anarchy ruled, my family members were virtual prisoners at home, frightened to attend school, to shop for food, to visit friends and family. My father alone ventured outside to buy provisions and to find out the news not broadcast on the radio. The entire Jewish community feared mass attacks by young angry crowds, carrying American weapons of the Shah's military. Funeral processions of Moslem "martyrs," those who had died fighting against the Shah's army, passed by our house daily. When my family heard chants of "Allah-O-Akbar, death to America, down with the Shah," they trembled. As any procession went through our neighborhood, men banged on the doors with their fists and a few threw rocks at the windows. "Come out dirty Jews. You are next!" they shouted. The revolutionaries attacked the Bahai section of town one week, mowing down residents with machine guns. The killers promised that the Jews would be next.

Not being a citizen yet, I could not obtain American visas for my family. My father found out about two El-Al planes landing in Mehrabad airport in Tehran to help evacuate the Iranian Jews. My five-year-old sister left the country on my mother's lap, in one of those planes, jammed with frightened and crying Jews. Most of them had never left their cities of birth and had never been on a plane before. They sat in the aisles or two and three to a chair, their luggage abandoned on the tarmac to make room for bodies, and in the darkness, the plane took off without the use of the tower, its own lights off.

A few weeks later, when I visited them in Israel, my mother and I took Niloufar to the preschool. Excited to be with other children, she spoke nonstop until she realized that the words she heard in reply didn't make sense to her. She shrieked and ran back to us. "Don't leave me!" After learning Hebrew, she refused to speak Farsi even to our parents. She wasn't Iranian, she told everyone. For many years, as I lived in the States and she in Israel, my sister and I didn't have a common language. We now communicate in English, a borrowed tongue for both of us.

Relearning it, Niloufar speaks Farsi to our parents with an Israeli accent and Hebrew syntax. The language doesn't carry the cultural experience for Niloufar as it does for our parents, so they constantly misunderstand each other. Speaking in Farsi, they slide by each other, throwing words at one another like stones. Afterward, emotionally exhausted, with no shared words to convey their love for one another, they heal their wounds with hugs.

Niloufar forgot her Farsi when my father went back to Iran to salvage some of his belongings. His passport was confiscated upon arrival, so he became *mamno'ol khorooj*, forbidden to leave the country. For three years he tried to reclaim his passport since he didn't want to leave the country illegally.

For three years, Niloufar didn't have contact with our father. She lived with Maman, who had slid into a deep depression and was paralyzed with uncertainty, indecision, and fear. After all, she had never before been allowed to make decisions on her own. Living with a silent mother, Niloufar turned to her Israeli friends and their parents for love and support. She adopted their European lifestyle, distancing herself from our mother and refusing to speak Farsi.

During those years, either pregnant or tending babies, I didn't have the energy to make the long trip to visit my mother and Niloufar. At the same time, the American embassy in Israel refused to grant them a visa to visit us because they carried Iranian passports at a time when Americans were kept hostage in Iran, and because the American immigration office feared that once they arrived in the United States, they would seek refugee status.

When my father finally received his exit visa, he boarded a plane to the United States. Waiting on the runway, ready to taxi, the plane was turned around. An anonymous phone caller had claimed that his passport was forged. His papers had passed scrutiny a week earlier, but now the inspectors were afraid to verify the passport's authenticity. So, he stayed in Iran for another six months, enduring beatings whenever he dared to go back to various offices to reclaim his passport. At the end, a *mola* asked him to come back with all his money in a cashier's check, took the envelope, and signed for his release. When I picked him up at the airport, he was only a shadow of the forceful man I remembered. Bent over, he followed me with downcast eyes.

The decision to take my mother and siblings away from Iran despite condemnation from the family and my grandmother's pleas for him to stay must have been the most difficult decision my father made in his life. The entire family dissuaded him from leaving. An aunt told my father that these things were "in the hands of God," not man, that he couldn't change his fate by removing himself from the family and the country. Another aunt asked him why Baba thought his family's lives were more precious than the others. How could he be so selfish to act independently of the rest of the family? My grandmother verbally attacked my mother, telling her that it was her fault my father was leaving the family behind and, in her high emotions, her breathing became labored and she fainted.

Khanom-bozorg died shortly after my father had finally made his escape. Baba called Iran to learn that his mother was already on her death bed, asking for him. I had never seen my father so tender, crying softly. He held the telephone receiver lovingly as if holding his mother's hand, whispering his words of comfort and love to Khanom-bozorg in Judi, our forgotten language. I couldn't understand all the words, but then I didn't have to. My father sat on the floor for hours with his head in his hands, moaning. "How could I not be at my mother's side?" he kept asking himself.

My father murmured a retold story, its words vague this time in his grief, but clear to me who had heard it so very many times. One single image of Khanom-bozorg had always overtaken the rest in my father's mind, one that had erased any shortcomings she could have had. One day, Baba, a mere teenager during the post–World War II famine, went home excited, bringing a prized sheet of flat bread he had fought for vigorously at the bakery. Khanom-bozorg told him she had eaten already, and that he should feed the kids, the little starving one first. After the bread was gone, my father went looking for his mother and found her crouched in a closet, gnawing on the tender bark of a tree.

My grandmother had tried to keep the family together, sometimes at any cost, because she feared being alone. The last years I spent in Iran, my father often slept next to her to calm her nightmares, her sudden anxiety attacks that were pronounced in short spasms of lungs trying desperately to pull in air. The sound reverberated throughout the quiet of the sleepy house, like the noise of a cat clawing the walls. It frightened us, kept us awake. One night, trying to rush to her side, my father broke his arm against the bed post. At our grandmother's death, my siblings and I did what we knew best: We kept silent, hid our sorrow, and sensed the past fading away, dying.

At my cousin's outdoor wedding, I couldn't help but remember my Khanom-bozorg; she had been at the same spot for my wedding with her waterpipe and colorful kerchiefs, hesitant at not covering her body with a *chador* in public. Because this was the kind of event she always loved, being surrounded by her children, grandchildren, and great-grandchildren, I couldn't help but think that her spirit hovered over all of us.

We didn't talk about Khanom-bozorg at the wedding. Instead, most aunts and uncles approached me to say, "Your father's place is empty!" I did miss him too. I couldn't remember the last time all of us had been together as a family.

"My mother too," I answered back. "I miss Maman too."

The blunt answer surprised the well-wishers, who quickly replied "Yes, of course!"

In the eyes of the family, Maman's job had been to take care of my grandmother. My siblings and I, and even my father now, recognize that she did her best at a cost to herself. The rest of the family often complained that Maman didn't serve her mother-in-law well. Anyhow, my grandmother was dead now, leaving no need for my mother. She was erased.

Yet I couldn't be bitter. At such a beautiful wedding, under the clear sky, by the waters of the Elizabeth River, among the white lace and laughter, we had all gathered with our own unique stories. What a long journey this had been for us all, filled with biblical-like tales of our wanderings from Iran. Through the deserts of the east, some had struggled across Afghanistan and Pakistan. Through the western mountains some had made their way to Turkey on donkeys behind molesting smugglers. They had been processed in Italy, Austria, Tel Aviv, and New York. They had endured scud attacks in Shiraz, Tehran, and Israel. They had prayed in lonely Iranian jails and Turkish prisons and in sealed rooms in Israel. Many were still trapped in Iran, but others, dazed and unsteady on their feet, had finally come to be cradled in the arms of America. Our last refuge. Our only safe place in the world.

And two days later came September 11.

*My mother leaves myrtle branches at her mother's grave in Israel.*

## A Closure

Writing her autobiography, said Gerta Lerner, took "more nerve than jumping off a cliff into cold water" (*Firewood*, 375). For me, letting my book be published took more daring. I feared hurting people around me, those whom I love, and even some people whom I might not favor. The purpose of writing this book, and publishing it, was simply to tell the truth as I knew it, my truth. I have changed names to preserve the dignity and privacy of many in this work of creative nonfiction.

The writing, though painful, has been cathartic. I have come to appreciate the men and women I have known, to understand how oppression can warp lives, characters, and deeds. Reaching a stage of empathy, I have come to understand myself as well, to forgive and to ask to be forgiven.

After finishing my book, I went to visit my parents in Israel in June 2002, after the "Passover massacre," when the country was numb from frequent acts of violence against its civilians. I needed to see my parents before the book was published, fearing our relationship—one that I had nurtured and tried to mend for many years—might change afterward. For the first time, I visited them as a true adult, not needy, not bitter, not wanting to change them. Now I understood their pain and their boundaries as parents.

I also visited the grave of my maternal grandmother Touran for the first time. No longer angry, I felt humbled by her courage and endurance. My mother and I washed the stone on her grave with care and deep sadness. We lit candles. We put myrtle branches into an urn on the grave. I silently asked for her forgiveness.

# ACKNOWLEDGMENTS

Anita Clair Fellman, Nancy Bazin, Janet Bing, Carolyn Rhodes, Janet Peery, Luisa Igloria, and Sheri Reynolds have been my teachers, friends, and mentors in the Women's Studies and Creative Writing Departments at Old Dominion University. Thank you for putting the pen back in my hand. Thank you, Sheri, for understanding my work, for having the vision to sculpt it, and for your many insights that have guided me with my writing for the past two years.

I would especially like to thank Carolyn Rhodes, my friend and mentor for the past seven years. Thank you, Ernest, too.

My dear friends Annie Laurie and Art Sandler gave me constant encouragement and opened many doors for me. I am grateful.

I am deeply indebted to The Hadassah International Research Institute on Jewish Women, its founding director, Shulamit Reinharz, and its senior research director, Susan Kahn. They have empowered Jewish women around the world.

I would like to thank my editors, Phyllis Deutsch and Mary Crittendon.

For their constructive comments and encouragement, I thank Marjorie Agosin, Helen Epstein, Joseph Skibell, Marita Golden, Edward Jacobs, and Madison Smartt Bell.

Thank you, Gina Nahai, for paving the road for Iranian Jewish women writers.

Finally, I am indebted to my siblings Nahid, Freydoun, Farzad, and Niloufar. They have enriched my memories by sharing their own stories. And thank you, Steve, Alisa, and Suzy.

# GLOSSARY

*aftabeh:* water jug
*agha:* sir, Mr., also a common name for father
*ameh:* paternal aunt
*aragh:* an alcoholic drink
*aroosak:* a little bride, a doll
*baba:* father
*bamieh:* confectionary
*bandandaz:* a woman who removes body hair
*baseh:* enough
*biaboon:* desert
*bolbol:* nightingale
*brakha:* prayer
*brit-milah:* the circumcision ritual
*chador:* a full body covering
*choobak:* a shrub whose bark was used as soap
*daee:* maternal uncle
*dard:* pain
*dard-e-del:* talking of the ache in one's heart
*dayan:* judge, spiritual leader
*del:* heart
*farangee:* foreigner
*gele-zard:* yellow clay, soaked and used as hair conditioner
*gha'edeh:* a woman's period
*ghaltak:* a cylindrical stone for packing earthen roofs
*ghalyan:* waterpipe, hookah
*ghalyoon:* waterpipe in the dialect of Shiraz
*gherti:* a show off
*ghorbat:* being away from home
*goh:* excrement
*halwa:* sweets
*hamam:* bath, public baths

*hamami:* a bath keeper

*hejab:* veil, modesty

*hejleh:* wedding canopy

*jaan:* dear

*javeed:* long live

*jihad:* holy war

*Judi:* Judeo-Persian, a language spoken only among Jews of Shiraz

*khaleh:* maternal aunt

*Khan:* a leader; Mr.

*khanom:* lady, Mrs.

*khanom-bozorg:* a great lady, a title we used for my grandmother

*khastegar:* a suitor

*khastegaree:* marriage proposal

*khatam:* inlaid wood and ivory

*khodaye bozorg:* the Great God

*khoshgel:* beautiful

*kiddush:* prayer over wine

*kilim:* a pileless, woven tapestry rug

*kippa:* prayer cup

*kiseh:* a square glove used as a washcloth

*konar:* pulverized leaves used to wash hair

*koofteh:* large meatballs made with rice, herbs, and chopped beef

*mahaleh:* a place, also a ghetto

*maman:* mother

*manghal:* brazier

*mashalah:* what wonders God has fashioned, or may you be preserved from the evil eye

*matalak:* dirty phrases

*mava:* mother in Judi

*mikvah:* a ritual bath

*mola:* a religious leader, Jewish or Moslem

*moshaverat:* gathering of elders to make a decision

*naan:* bread

*najeeb:* chaste

*najes:* dirty, often refers to more than physical uncleanness

*pa-do-ak:* "running legs," boys who run errands

*rafigh-baz:* the game of having friends

*sabzee:* greens, herbs

*shadee:* happiness

*shalomalekhem (shalom alekhem):* may peace be with you

*shamee:* potato and chopped meat pancakes

*sharbat:* a fruit drink

*shekhitah:* ritual slaughtering

*shema:* refers to the Jewish people's proclamation of their belief in a single God

*shiva:* the seven-day mourning period

*shokhet:* a kosher butcher

*simkha:* a happy event

*sofreh:* a cloth that is often spread on the floor underneath the food

*taarof:* the custom of exchanging polite words and niceties

*taher:* pure

*tamei:* impure

*tanoor:* clay oven

*Tehilim:* Psalms of comfort

*toman:* Iranian currency

*tsedakah:* charity

*vasoonak:* a collection of wedding poetry often sung by Jewish women of Shiraz

*verag:* one who talks too much

*veragi:* talking too much

*zaben-deraz:* one with a long tongue, one who talks back

*zaifeh:* the weak one (female)

*zarbol-masal:* Persian proverbs

*ziarat:* pilgrimage